THE
HARVEY
GIRLS

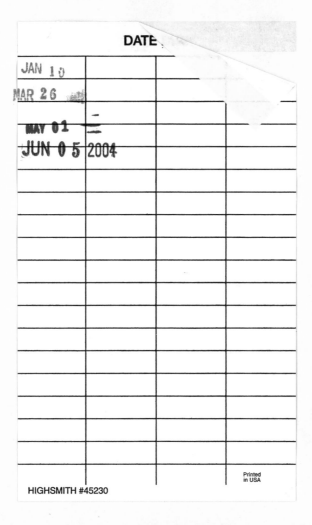

DATE			
JAN 1 9			
MAR 2 6			
MAY 01			
JUN 0 5	2004		
			Printed in USA

Unknown and Della Cameron Carter,
Barstow Harvey Girls before World War I.
(Credit: Lundgren Collection, Mojave River Valley Museum)

THE
HARVEY GIRLS

WOMEN WHO OPENED THE WEST

LESLEY POLING-KEMPES

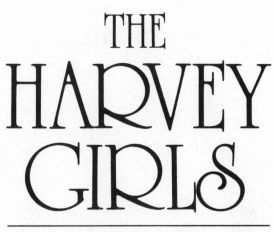

PARAGON HOUSE

NEW YORK

For Jim:
husband, best friend, and fellow traveler.

First paperback edition, 1991

Published in the United States by

Paragon House
90 Fifth Avenue
New York, NY 10011

Copyright © 1989 by Paragon House

Interior Design and Map by Virginia Norey

Library of Congress Cataloging-in-Publication Data

Poling-Kempes, Lesley.
The Harvey girls / Lesley Poling-Kempes.
p. cm.
Bibliography: p.
ISBN 1-55778-461-2
1. Southwest, New—History—1848– 2. Southwest, New—Social conditions. 3. Waitresses—Southwest, New—History. 4. Women—Southwest, New—History. 5. Tourist trade—Southwest, New—History. 6. Fred Harvey Company—History. I. Title.
F786.P84   1989   89-3400 CIP
979—dc19

Manufactured in the United States of America
The paper used in this publication meets the minimum requirements of American National Standard for Information Sciences—Permanence of Paper for Printed Library Materials, ANSI Z39.48-1984.
10 9 8 7 6 5 4 3 2 1

ACKNOWLEDGMENTS

I WOULD LIKE TO THANK the following individuals for their help in obtaining information and photographs: Susan Metcalf, William Burk, formerly of the Public Relations Department, Atchison, Topeka & Santa Fe Railway, Chicago; Robert E. Gehrt, Public Relations Department, Santa Fe Southern Pacific Corporation, Chicago; Lynn Guy, former archivist, Panhandle-Plains Historical Museum, Canyon, Texas; Robert Dauner, Curator of Photography, the Albuquerque Museum, Albuquerque; Dawn Letson, archivist, DeGolyer Library, Southern Methodist University, Dallas; Nancy Robertson, Raton Historical Society, Raton, New Mexico; Margaret Hays, former mayor, Gainesville, Texas; Daggett Harvey, Jr., Chicago; Mr. and Mrs. Vernon McNally and friends, Waynoka, Oklahoma; Bessie Suffield, Florence Historical Society, Florence, Kansas; and Barbara Peirce, Hutchinson Community College, Hutchinson, Kansas.

Additional information and pertinent materials were obtained from: the Kansas State Historical Society, Topeka; the Mojave River Valley Museum

Association, Barstow; the Arthur Johnson Memorial Library, Raton, New Mexico; the Citizens Committee for Historic Preservation, Las Vegas, New Mexico; the Layland Museum, Cleburne, Texas; the Mohave County Historical Society, Kingman, Arizona; Santa Fe Railway offices in Chicago, and Amarillo, Texas; Special Collections, the University of Arizona, Tucson; the Heard Museum, Phoenix; the Hayden Library Special Collections, Arizona State University, Tempe; the New Mexico State Records and Archives, Santa Fe.

I extend warmest thanks to my brother, Charles Poling, who edited, typed, and gave needed commentary on early drafts of the manuscript; to Vera Norwood, professor of American Studies, University of New Mexico, Albuquerque, for her thoughts and suggestions; and to David and Ann Poling, my parents, for their continued support and encouragement.

The Money for Women Fund, Florida, supported the completion of this project with a generous grant. The extended family of Ghost Ranch shared their office supplies and good humor, and seemed to have no end to their patience towards me and my endless trips past their desks. And my own secluded office, the rambling old adobe that is home for my family, and the time to work on this book is due, in part, to the generosity of John and Frances Hernandez, landlords extraordinaire.

Public Media Arts, Inc., Santa Fe, New Mexico, especially Gary DeWalt, producers of the film, *Fred Harvey and the American West,* gave friendly assistance in the obtainment of many valuable photographs.

I thank the dozens of individuals who gave me their time, their memories, even their treasured family photographs. I regret that everyone connected to this project cannot be mentioned; my gratitude to all of you is measureless.

CONTENTS

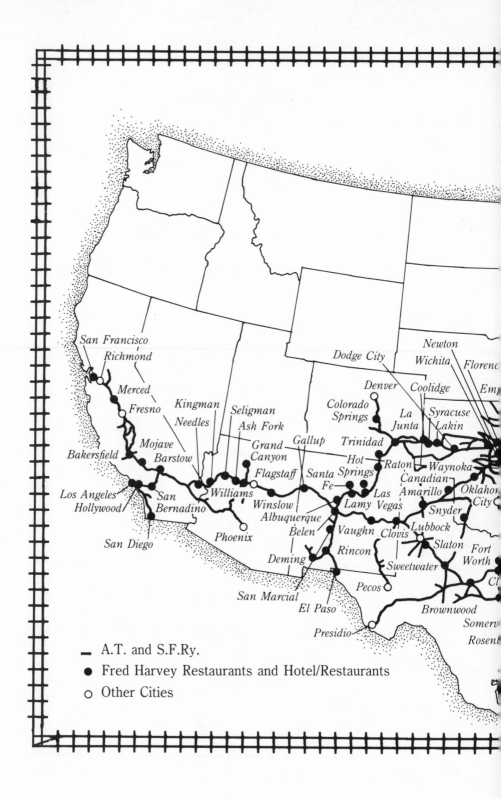

San Francisco
Richmond

Merced
Fresno

Kingman
Needles

Seligman
Ash Fork

Mojave
Barstow

Bakersfield

Grand
Canyon

Gallup

Flagstaff

Los Angeles
Hollywood

San
Bernadino

Williams

Santa
Fe

Winslow
Albuquerque

San Diego

Phoenix

Belen

San Marcial

Deming

El Paso

Presidio

Newton
Dodge City
Wichita
Florenc

Denver
Coolidge
Emp
Colorado
Springs
La
Junta
Syracuse
Lakin

Trinidad

Hot
Springs
Raton
Waynoka
Canadian
Las
Lamy Vegas
Amarillo
Oklahom
City

Vaughn
Clovis
Snyder
Lubbock

Rincon
Slaton
Fort
Worth

Sweetwater

Pecos
Cl

Brownwood
Somerv
Rosent

— A.T. and S.F.Ry.
● Fred Harvey Restaurants and Hotel/Restaurants
○ Other Cities

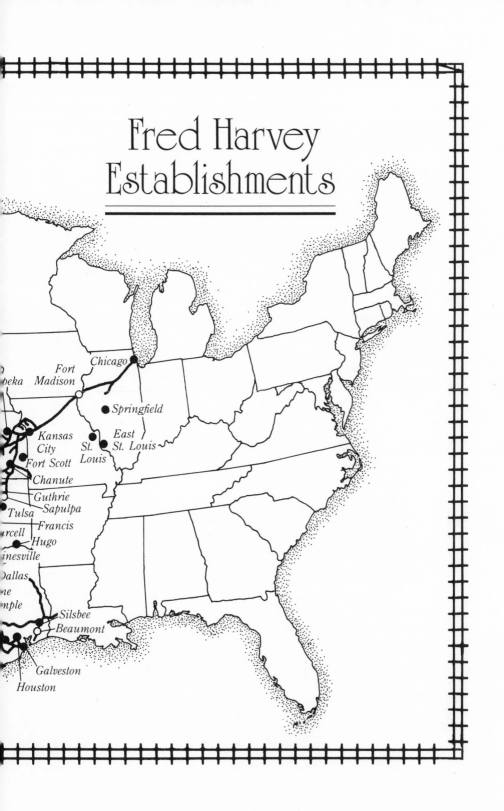

Fred Harvey
Establishments

Chicago

Fort
Madison

peka

Springfield

Kansas
City

East
St. Louis

St.
Louis

Fort Scott

Chanute

Guthrie

Sapulpa

Tulsa

Francis

rcell

Hugo

inesville

Dallas

ne

mple

Silsbee

Beaumont

Galveston

Houston

INTRODUCTION

TALKING WITH WOMEN who were Harvey Girls in the early part of this century confirmed two suppositions: one, they were women who wanted to know life beyond their immediate family sphere; and two, they were interested in experiencing for themselves the unknowns of the Southwest. They wanted to be part of the adventure taking place along the railroads of the West. Most of these women needed to work; many used the need to work as an excuse to leave home. It may not have been a conscious motivation, but the women who went to work with Fred Harvey wanted to explore their own potentials, test their individual characters, and expand their knowledge of themselves and the world they were part of through the experience.

In a conversation with a southwestern newspaperman about the Harvey Girls, it was brought to my attention that "they were, after all, only waitresses." I wanted to dispute his insinuation that they were unworthy of closer study, but at the time was not certain why. They were only waitresses. They served a four-course meal in under thirty minutes—perhaps an impressive feat among restauranteurs, but not really worthy of historical recognition. They were not paid so well as to be considered better off than most other people in their communities. As a group, they did little or nothing actively to advance women's rights. They weren't highly educated, and there are no towns or buildings or roads named for them in a region where virtually every mountain, path, and community is named in honor of some early citizen.

The Harvey Girls were waitresses. They were also single women between the ages of eighteen and thirty who answered newspaper and magazine advertisements in the East and Midwest to go out into the southwestern territory to work for Fred Harvey and his hotel/restaurant chain along the Santa Fe Railway. Some one hundred thousand Harvey Girls came west between 1883 and the late 1950s, when the Harvey system declined as the railroads lost ground to the airlines. Of those one hundred thousand, approximately half returned home after their Harvey contracts were completed; but an equal number remained in the Southwest, many marrying and settling on ranches and farms, in mining communities and railroad towns.

"If there is a moral to the history of the westward movement," wrote E. D. Branch, "it is this: the transcendent importance of small things and of unimportant people."[1] The Harvey Girls were a group of unimportant people—women who came west to work, to marry, who became absorbed into the vast lands of the Southwest. The new social history focuses on the affairs of ordinary people, and seeks to unearth the lives and details of those whose names are not known, but whose contributions are worthy of attention.[2] In examining their lives, we examine the origins of our own.

"The Harvey Girls" summons up for many the image of Judy Garland, who starred in an MGM movie of the same name in the 1940s. Although there was nothing offensive or overtly misrepresentative about the movie, it perpetuated the general public's unrealistic image of the Harvey Girls. The film, like much fiction found in popular magazines of the twenties, thirties, and forties, made the Harvey Girl out to be a kind of mythical figure, rather than an active contributor in the American West. This sort of attention may have endeared the Harvey Girls to readers and moviegoers, but it did little to tell their story accurately or locate their place in the greater history of women in the West. The nostalgic stories about pretty uniformed heroines, which became the only historic renderings of the

Harvey Girls, ignore the controversy that often surrounded them: the suspicion in many communities that they were really prostitutes in disguise, or that they were not acceptable, not "nice girls," simply because they were waitresses. Many Harvey Girls carried the burden of these social labels throughout their working lives.

The story of the Harvey Girls is unique in American history. The Lowell factory girls of Massachusetts shared certain aspects of their work and social background with the Harvey Girls, and are briefly studied and compared with them later in this book. But their history has neither the geographical scope nor the diversity of individual background found in the stories of the women who worked for Fred Harvey throughout the Southwest.

The story of the Harvey Girls is a story of women, but more importantly it is a story about women and the western railroad. There were few women working along any American railroad in the late nineteenth century, or even well into the twentieth. But the Harvey Girls could only have appeared in the West, where there was a new country in search of a new identity, where great distances spanned only by the railroad made working at the Harvey Houses a complete way of life. The West had communities whose only history was that of the railroad. Harvey Girls and Harvey employees, along with Santa Fe railroadmen, were often the founding fathers, and mothers, of entire towns.

The Harvey Girls contended with the social stigmas attached to all single working women in early twentieth century America. Eastern attitudes found their way west as surely as eastern dreams. Women who worked were socially inferior and morally suspect. But the West had elbow room and Fred Harvey made use of it in establishing his own idea of the working woman. His employees were never to be called waitresses: they were Harvey Girls. They were expected to act like Harvey Girls twenty-four hours a day. They were told where to live, what time to go to bed, whom to date, even what to wear down to the last detail of makeup and jewelry. And although the majority of these young women were most certainly not out to attract attention as advocates of women's rights, the Harvey Girls demonstrated a dedication to their jobs, and an independence in their lives, that would later become common among young women involved in the pursuit of their chosen profession. It was all done under the protective and fatherly arm of the Fred Harvey system, but it was a system that for its time was fair to women and one that honored hard work and loyalty with security and benefits.

Fred Harvey, himself an English immigrant, was to be called "civilizer" of the American West again and again by historians and journalists of his time. This title reflects the attitude of the era: Indian and Hispanic culture, already well rooted and flourishing in the Southwest, was not "civilized." Harvey and the railroad brought Anglo-American culture west, civilizing the territories of New Mexico, Arizona, Colorado, Texas, and California with American language, food, dress, money, and values. And the Harvey Girls embodied this notion within their ranks: only white women were hired as Harvey waitresses. European immigrant women were acceptable, but there were never black Harvey Girls, and only a very small number of Hispanic and Indian women ever served in Harvey Girl uniforms. Harvey Houses were islands of American culture, linked to the "homeland" by the Santa Fe rails.

In the chapters that follow, the Harvey Girls are revealed through their own words, through their own memories of the Harvey system and the people that made the Harvey standard into an imposing and impressive business. This book is based on interviews and letters gathered from seventy-seven individuals in nine states. The emphasis has been necessarily placed upon Harvey Girls who worked from the early twentieth century through the twenties, thirties, and forties. Harvey girls who worked earlier are not living. Those who worked after World War II were not part of the most successful era of Harvey and the Santa Fe. The years from the early part of this century to the late 1930s were the golden years of the Harvey Girls. Women who worked for Harvey after this time were members of a system that was diminishing in importance as the trains that served the Harvey Houses became less traveled with the advent of air and automobile traffic in the West.

This book does not attempt to analyze the Harvey Girls as a social or economic force, nor does it systematically study Harvey employment practices, company prejudices, or corporate attitudes. Had this been my intention I would have been sadly disappointed, as there are no Harvey personnel records available for historians to ponder. There is no "official" data other than what I have gathered myself through interviews and letters, and derived from the few collections of historical, and usually romanticized, writings about the Harvey Girls.

The majority of women and men interviewed were retired, many for twenty years or more. Some of them were active; some were bedridden and spoke of their past—forty, fifty, even sixty years ago—as the best years of their lives. Often this meant remembering the transition from childhood to young adulthood, from life on a rural farm to life in a thriving urban community; for some it was even the beginning of life beyond poverty and struggle, a life where the promises of the American dream began to take form, and the land of opportunity became something tangible beneath their feet. Because the railroad that once put their communities on the map no longer operates passenger service to most of the Southwest, I had to drive hundreds of miles into the great nowheres of America to reach former Harvey Girls, head waitresses, busboys, managers, chefs and cooks, Santa Fe engineers and telegraphers. Their nostalgia for a past that was centered around the great transcontinental trains often became my own as I was taken to visit empty Harvey Houses and deserted or half-used depots in towns like Waynoka, Oklahoma; Newton, Kansas; Kingman, Arizona; and Gainesville, Texas. Retired Harvey employees, like their partners, the Santa Fe railroadmen, continue to follow daily train schedules and listen for the whistles of engineers, as ingrained in their memories as the passing of the seasons.

Even after Fred Harvey died in 1901, his employees went on saying, "I work for Fred Harvey," as if he were alive and still actively running the system. Harvey the person may have passed away, but the concept among Harvey employees of a family of people working for one man continued for fifty years. Harvey Girls, chefs, managers, bellboys, and bakers love to talk about their years with the Harvey Houses. With only a handful of exceptions, they answered inquiries about the details of their lives and work enthusiastically and openly. Those who did not—former Harvey Girls I learned of through their friends, or to whom I spoke directly but who declined to be interviewed for this book—often refused because of a fear of being "discovered": their working woman's background was still perceived as a threat to their often hard-earned social status. Several had married very prominent men, and even the passage of half a century could not erase in their minds the stigma that was attached to a woman who had worked as a waitress.

But these were the rare exceptions. Harvey Girls and their colleagues eagerly discussed all aspects of their work. And they worked hard. They put in ten-hour days and six- and seven-day weeks. Their work in Harvey restaurants and hotels was physical and demanding, as serving the public (especially the travel-weary public) always is. But the comradery within the system provided a major source of support and energy to all who worked at the Harvey Houses. Harvey employees, even today, though they are retired and scattered throughout the Southwest and the rest of the United States, form a family unit rare in American business.

Oral historians and other collectors and investigators of recent history must separate the real from the almost real and tell the true picture from the embellished memory. Nostalgia for lost youth, as Julie Roy Jeffrey found, often colors the memory.[3] Most former Harvey Girls remembered the good times, the satisfying and happy times of their work. And when reading the reminiscences of the Harvey Girls, it is important to remember that they lived and worked in a time and a society that did not always applaud their choice to "go west" as single women, even when made out of economic necessity. They did not live in a time that admired spunk and independence in working women, despite the American West and its promises of freedom and space. That promise, historians are beginning to realize, was reserved for its male immigrants.

The myth of the West was largely a male dream—an adventure of danger, risk, excitement, and high stakes. Neither women nor Indians counted.[4]

We have learned that both women and Indians did count; the extent of their contributions is still being uncovered. It is only recently, in a society interested in its women's history, that women like the Harvey Girls have been hailed as contributors to the American story. Only a few decades ago, the women in this book would have told their life stories to a stranger reluctantly, questioning the premise behind so many inquiries into their daily lives. Their pride and enthusiasm for the work they did, the role they played along the Santa Fe Railway, has only now found an appreciative audience.

One would like to believe that all the Harvey Girls were adventurers—spirited single women with a vision of excitement and freedom luring them west on their own. But most were prompted by economic necessity and the knowledge that the West had an abundance of single men. Even so, these women took a considerable risk by stepping on board a train in Chicago or St. Louis or Kansas City, rattling across deserts and mountains and prairies to end up on a platform in some southwestern town where cowboys and miners and farmers eked out a living. Places like Raton, New Mexico and Williams, Arizona had only a handful of female residents— schoolteachers, missionaries, and cooks, and a few prostitutes and dance-hall girls. But women were still scarce, the Southwest was still rough and isolated, and the Harvey Girls joined the ranks of American trailblazers when they set down their bags and settled into these early railroad communities.

The Harvey Girls were just waitresses. Their counterparts were just cowboys; just miners with nothing to call their own but a mule and a pick; just trappers without families or homes; farmers fighting the elements to grow a few acres of wheat; stagedrivers and stockmen, prospectors and cattle ranchers, railroadmen following the rails. Just ordinary folks, some educated and well-to-do, others poor but hopeful, and all seeking life in a young land.

Following the Santa Fe Railway and Fred Harvey across the Southwest means following the wagon ruts of the old Santa Fe Trail. The history of the Santa Fe Railway is infused with the history of the great trail that was its predecessor. And all three—the old trail, the railroad, and the Harvey Houses—are linked by a shared ulterior motive: to bring west the trade and culture of the white man—and eventually white woman.

The years which saw Fred Harvey and the railroad at their combined greatest also witnessed the transformation of the Southwest from a largely unknown desert and mountain wilderness to a popular region of small, thriving cities, a region that became a mecca for American and foreign tourism. The Southwest became less the rugged frontier than the exotic backyard of America in the early decades of the twentieth century. The Santa Fe Railway and Fred Harvey, and the thousands of women known as Harvey Girls, accelerated a change in eastern and midwestern attitudes toward the areas known today as the states of Kansas, Oklahoma, Colorado, Texas, New Mexico, Arizona, and California.

The history of the Santa Fe Trail and the Santa Fe Railway have been aptly chronicled, but the phenomenon of Fred Harvey has only recently found its way into the history of American business. Here is the story of the Harvey Girls: the history of the Southwest would be incomplete without them.

THE
HARVEY
GIRLS

CHAPTER 1

The Old Santa Fe Trail

T HE STORY OF THE OLD SANTA FE TRAIL . . . *is a most thrilling one . . . When the famous highway was established across the great plains as a line of communication to the shores of the blue Pacific, the only method of travel was by the slow freight caravan drawn by patient oxen, or the lumbering stage coach with its complement of four or six mules. There was ever to be faced an attack by those devils of the desert, the Cheyennes, Comanches, and Kiowas. Along its route the remains of men, animals, and the wrecks of camps and wagons, told a story of suffering, robbery, and outrage more impressive than any language. Now the tourist or business man makes the journey in palace cars, and there is nothing to remind him of the danger or desolation of Border days.*
W.F. Cody, "Buffalo Bill"[1]

When Fred Harvey and the Santa Fe Railway first took their partnership west in the 1870s and 1880s, they often followed the path blazed by the old Santa Fe Trail. The flavor established by Harvey and the railroaders owes much to the historic old trail that preceeded them. The early years of the railroad were often difficult, but they were easy in comparison to the opening of the Santa Fe Trail forty years before.

Unlike the other two trails to the West, the Santa Fe was primarily a trade route. The Oregon Trail was the major route to California and served emigrants, settlers, and gold seekers. The Mormon Trail was pioneered by the group whose name it bears and whose city—Salt Lake City—it established. Although the Santa Fe Trail never boasted as many travelers, it is the oldest of the three and possibly the most colorful in legend and culture. Its course was carved out by the American Indians, Spanish *conquistadores*, French trappers, and American traders, and was frequented by the great herds of buffalo that once roamed the Great Plains.

The Santa Fe Trail began in what became Independence, Missouri, and ended in remote Spanish-Indian Santa Fe. There were eight hundred miles of poorly-marked, often treacherous ground between: the flat, monotonous plains of Kansas, the dry, waterless desert of Indian territory, and the seemingly uncrossable mountains of the Rockies through what is now southern Colorado and northern New Mexico. A crossing of the Santa Fe Trail from either direction was not an easy undertaking. But the rewards in trade and precious metals, and eventually in territorial acquisition for the United States, made the obstacles worth overcoming.

The Santa Fe Trail was probably first used by Francisco de Coronado and his men in 1540 on their famous trip through the Southwest in search of the Seven Cities of Gold. By the early 1800s, when Americans first traveled along the Trail, the town of Santa Fe was an isolated village of mud and adobe houses owned by Spain and connected to the greater world only through its neighbor to the south, Mexico. In 1804, a merchant from Kaskaskia, Illinois, William Morrison, sent Baptiste La Lande, a French Creole, to Santa Fe with pack animals loaded with goods. La Lande reached Santa Fe and fell in love with its Old Spanish social customs, simple lifestyle, friendly men, and exotic women. Instead of returning with Morrison's fortune, La Lande settled in Santa Fe where he spent the remainder of his life in comfort and luxury.

La Lande was followed by James Purcell (called Pursley in Lieutenant

Zebulon M. Pike's account), a carpenter from Kentucky. Purcell was not headed for Santa Fe, but planned to trade on the Great Plains. His convoy's plans changed when their horses were stolen by Indians. Purcell and his men walked the prairie until they were found by another trading party headed up the Missouri River. Purcell became a well-known trader among the Indians in the mountains of Colorado, and was asked to represent them to the Mexican governor in Santa Fe. In 1805, Purcell arrived in Santa Fe and asked the governor to allow the Indians to remain in Colorado territory. Like La Lande, Purcell was smitten by the hospitality and charm of the Spanish hamlet, and stayed to become another of its adopted residents.

One of the most familiar explorers of the Spanish Territories is Lieutenant Zebulon Pike, for whom the famous peak was named. Pike was twenty-seven when he set out from St. Louis in 1806. Although he followed the Santa Fe Trail a considerable distance, he veered north to the mountains at the Purgatoire River instead of south to the Spanish frontier. After near disaster in the winter mountains of Colorado, Pike found the Rio Grande in January of 1807 and built a fort. One of Pike's party was Dr. John Robinson, sent by Morrison to find La Lande. Pike sent Robinson to Santa Fe in the guise of a bounty hunter, though he was really seeking firsthand information about the Spanish military for the United States government.

The Spanish were not ignorant of Pike's ulterior motive, and sent a hundred of their men to Pike's fort on the Rio Grande. The Spanards were not hostile, but they took Pike back with them to Santa Fe. Pike traveled in safety and comfort, and witnessed places and events no ordinary American could have seen in New Mexico at the turn of the nineteenth century.

Although Pike was not immediately impressed with Santa Fe, the area gradually charmed him. After a trip south with his Spanish escort to Chihuahua through the Rio Grande valley, Pike was sent home via the Texas border to St. Louis.

Although Pike's mission to the Southwest may have been predominantly military, and he gathered most of his information in order to help the United States in its eventual infiltration of Spanish territories, Pike's account of his year in the Southwest also inspired hundreds of traders and explorers to take their chances on the Santa Fe Trail.

The Spanish, who had been good-natured and tolerant of Pike, La Lande, and Purcell, were however not about to give up their dominance of New Mexico trade to Americans who wanted to flood the market with their goods. By 1809, American traders on the Santa Fe Trail were arrested by Spanish soldiers and thrown into jail without trial with lengthy and often indeterminate sentences. Despite the possibilities of imprisonment, the loss of their goods, and Indian attacks, American traders kept plodding with their pack horses and mules out to the attractive markets of Santa Fe.

Two events changed the Santa Fe Trail and the trade struggling to develop over it: in 1812, Captain William Becknell, a courageous and enterprising pioneer businessman, took the first wagon train over a route previously crossed only by men and pack animals. The Santa Fe Trail was still a grueling eight hundred miles long, but after Becknell's successful journey with wagons, larger loads could be hauled at one time. This made the effort far more worthwhile and a bit more comfortable for American traders.

The second major change affecting the trail came in 1821 when Mexican revolutionaries took Mexico City and ended Spanish rule in Mexico and the Southwest. American traders received the news of Mexican independence from Spain with excited and eager ears: markets once dominated and regulated by Spanish laws were suddenly anxious to receive Yankee goods.

In 1825, in response to the burgeoning interest in the Southwest, the U.S. government surveyed two routes of the Santa Fe Trail: from Independence southwest through Kansas, across the Arkansas River, and straight across to the Colorado mountains and south to Santa Fe; and through Kansas, turning southwest across the desert via the Cimmarron cutoff, through what is now the Oklahoma Panhandle to northeastern New Mexico. The Santa Fe Trail offered travelers a choice between the difficulties of mountain crossing via the Raton Pass in northern New Mexico, or the open desert from what is now Dodge City to the Cimarron River of northeastern New Mexico. The former route had the tribulations of severe grades and terrible surface conditions (a wagon could cross one mile over Raton Pass on a good day), while the latter offered a passable, flat surface but no water and often a deadly amount of sun.

The Santa Fe Trail was never a proper road. Its route became a dusty, often muddy path of wagon ruts, of people, wagons, horses, cattle, and oxen moving west between designated landmarks. There were no towns between Independence and Santa Fe; there were no ranches or farms. Eventually there were forts and outposts, but even these struggled to hold their own against the indigenous Indians and the extremes of southwestern weather.

In the 1830s and 1840s, activity on the Santa Fe Trail escalated. Wagon trains, oxcarts, and mules laden with American textiles and wares all made the slow journey west. The exchange between Santa Fe– and Independence-based traders quickly grew from a small frontier enterprise to big business: in 1822, some 70 traders took $15,000 worth of American goods to Santa Fe; only eleven years later, 350 men hauled $350,000 of American trade over the Santa Fe Trail. It cost a merchant $10 per hundred pounds to ship freight to Santa Fe; an average wagon earned between $500 and $600 a trip.[2]

Although a willing trade partner, the Mexican government exercised stiff tariffs on all goods from the United States. Under the administration of Governor Manuel Armijo, every wagonload of merchandise brought into Santa Fe, no matter its worth, paid $500 to the Mexican government. There was also a tax on precious metals headed east from Santa Fe.

If the regulations of the Mexican government combined with the difficulties of crossing the trail did not thwart the efforts of the new Santa Fe traders, the activities of the Utes, Arapahoes, Comanches, and Pawnees could. The Indians of the Great Plains watched their hunting grounds invaded and abused by the newcomers from the white world. The enormous herds of buffalo that had always sustained the Indian suddenly faced extermination by white men who hunted them for sport instead of necessity. Buffaloes were easy to kill and although many travelers on the western trails used buffalo meat for food and their chips for fuel, more hunted for sport. It is not surprising that the Indians along the trail were seen as unholy terrors by any and all who came from the east. Although the actual number of deaths from Indian raids on Santa Fe wagon trains were few in comparison to the numbers crossing the trail, when the Indians did attack a caravan they were ruthless and violent, making the "Indian problem" of the Southwest a substantial concern for western pioneers.

It is difficult to know what non-Spanish or non-Indian women thought about the Santa Fe Trail and the Southwest in the early 1800s because there were no white women in the territory. There were diaries kept by pioneer women on the overland trails to Oregon, Utah, California, and the Great Plains. But the Santa Fe Trail was a route for traders, not a trail used by families or men with their wives. It was dangerous and difficult and there was little promise of a new life in the Mexican territory at the other end.

Perhaps the first white woman to see Santa Fe was Susan Shelby

Magoffin. Magoffin was the wife of a successful trader, Samuel Magoffin, who with his brother, James, became well known in the Southwest and Mexico in the mid-1800s. Not only was Susan Magoffin a keen observer of the details of the trail and of Spanish and Indian life in the Southwest, but she was also an avid diarist. The diary of her journey to Santa Fe from Independence in 1846 and her accounts of overland travel, people, and customs has become a valuable historical resource.

Magoffin was eighteen when she began her journey over the Santa Fe Trail. Her husband's caravan was large and Magoffin traveled in what were considered privileged circumstances: she had a private carriage, a small library, a tent house that was erected at each campsite, a maid, her own driver, and two servants. Even so, it was a hard journey for the new bride across the prairie, through the desert, and over the mountains into New Mexico. Her journey did not end in Santa Fe: it continued down through Chihuahua and finally to Matamoras, Mexico. The fifteen-month trip took its toll on Magoffin. She died in 1855 in Kentucky after several years of ill-health precipitated by a bout with yellow fever in Mexico.

Although hardly typical of women traveling west on the overland trails in the mid-1800s, Magoffin did share the same fears and daily hardships of the journey with her less privileged sisters: she walked miles beside her carriage when the trail was too rough for riding and often slept in a tent whose floor was a sea of mud and sloshing water during a prairie downpour. Magoffin suffered various maladies and illnesses on the trail, went without food when dry firewood could not be found, and watched helplessly as animals and drivers tried to negotiate impossible ground at all hours of the day and night. Although the Magoffin wagon train had no trouble with Indians, it did see signs of Indian hunters and bands, and Susan spent her share of hours worrying about what might surprise them over the next hill.

Magoffin wrote a vivid and detailed description of the caravan's crossing of Raton Pass. "We have been rather unfortunate today," she noted on Friday, the 14th of August, 1846, as the wagons began negotiating the mountains,

> *a wagon was turned over this morning, and the bed so broken as to cause a delay of some hours to repair it sufficiently to travel on. "The Raton" is not the best place to keep such articles new;*

*almost every fifty or hundred yards there are large stones, or steep
little hillocks, just the things to bounce a wagon's wheels up . . .
   And as for myself, I have been walking till I am covered with
dust till instead of being black any longer, I am brown changing
back to white again.*

The following day Magoffin wrote:

*Worse and worse the road! They are even taking the mules from
the carriages . . . and half a dozen men by bodily exertions are
pulling them down the hills. And it takes a dozen men to steady
a wagon with all its wheels locked—and for one who is some
distance off to hear the crash it makes over the stones is truly
alarming . . . We came to camp about half an hour after dusk,
having accomplished the great travel of* six or eight hundred
yards during the day. [Emphasis Magoffin's.][3]

Magoffin reached Santa Fe on August 30, 1846. She was probably the
first "American lady" to enter the city, and certainly she was the first one
to traverse the Santa Fe Trail. General Kearny had declared New Mexico
a possession of the United States twelve days earlier, but Magoffin noted
that the "habits, religion &c. of the people" were as yet unmolested.
Magoffin met Kearny and with her husband entertained him on one of his
later visits to Santa Fe.

Although American relations with Mexico were friendly, the influx of so
many Americans into Mexican territory was bound to create tension. Mexico controlled the regions known today as Texas, New Mexico, Arizona,
Nevada, California, and parts of Colorado and Wyoming. American settlers
were arriving by the dozens each day and most of them assumed it was
only a matter of time before the United States acquired their new homeland. The desire for American independence from Mexico arose first in
Texas.

By 1830, twenty thousand Americans were living in the Texas province.
The Mexicans understood the threat they posed, and promptly put a halt
to further American immigration. Six years later, the Texans under Mexican rule adopted their own constitution and declared themselves indepen-

dent. The battles that ensued are legendary, particularly the battle at the Alamo in San Antonio. Texas won its independence and was annexed by the United States in 1845. Thus began the American foothold in the Mexican territories of the Southwest.

The United States declared war on Mexico in 1846 and sent troops into New Mexico and as far as California. In terms of actual battles, the Mexican-American War hardly deserved the name. Mexico surrendered California in 1847. The following year, Mexico signed the treaty that ended the war, and the western and southern boundaries of the United States now enclosed an additional half million square miles of frontier served by the Santa Fe Trail.

Shortly after the acquisition of New Mexico by the United States, the "Indian problem" along the Santa Fe Trail escalated. The Utes, often accompanied by the Apaches, declared unofficial war on the white newcomers. Bands of Cheyenne, Kiowa, and Comanche Indians descended upon overland caravans to kill and plunder. The bloodshed and skirmishes along the Santa Fe Trail lasted from the late 1840s well into the 1860s. In 1847, after a massacre of passengers on a stagecoach bound for Santa Fe, and the kidnapping of several female passengers, the United States government called into service several notable western pioneers, beginning its official efforts to solve the "Indian problem."

Kit Carson and Richens "Uncle Dick" Wottoon (or Wootton) were among many southwesterners who volunteered their services as scouts and guides. Before Carson was a government scout, he was a revered rifleman and pioneer, known and respected by the Indians of the plains. Carson was one of the first white men to intimately know the life of the American Indian, and was a frequent visitor at the camps and lodges of the Comanches, Utes, Arapahoes, and Sioux.

Richens Wottoon is not widely known today, but in his time his stature was equal to that of Carson among the Indians and early traders of the Santa Fe Trail. Called Uncle Dick by Americans who could not pronounce his first name, Wottoon later played an important role in the history of the Santa Fe Railroad.

After thirty years of scouting and guiding in what is now southern Colorado and northern New Mexico, Wottoon settled down on top of the mountains near Raton Pass. Wottoon figured, and rightly so, that a good income could be had by anyone who could make the Raton Pass into a toll road easily passable by wagon. In the 1860s, horses could navigate the high mountain road, but wagons still struggled to move safely, if at all, over the narrow, rock-infested pass. After securing the right to repair and widen the road from the government, Wottoon felled great pine trees, moved immense boulders and cut into the steep ledges of the high mountains. Wottoon opened his toll road, inn, and supply store in 1865 and settled into a house on the pass to live out his life. His plans changed only with the arrival of the Atchison, Topeka and Santa Fe Railway thirteen years later.

The ten-year escalation in western immigration during the 1840s and 1850s created the need for better communication and transportation between Missouri and Santa Fe. The overland stagecoach was introduced in 1850. It was an enormous improvement over the ox-pulled wagon, but was still not a luxurious or even comfortable way to travel west. The stage carried nine people packed into its small interior and on its outer bench. It crossed 80 miles of trail a day, and during the two weeks it took to reach the Holy City of Santa Fe, there was little sleep (one had to nap upright in one's seat) and always the very real fear of Indian attack. Inclement weather could strand the stage anywhere along the trail: snow, rain, and hail storms were frequent in the Southwest. The final fear was that of a stampede: early stage stories include numerous accounts of passengers leaping from a coach to safety or injury on the desert floor.

Later, forts were established and soldiers accompanied the stage. Eventually, stage stations were built at intervals along the trail where horses and drivers were changed. Overland coach travelers could find a meal at these stops, but it was strictly utilitarian fare.

When it came time for the Santa Fe Railway to forge its way west from Kansas in the late 1860s, trade with Santa Fe was a secure and profitable venture. The volume of trade along the Santa Fe Trail had grown steadily in the years before the railroad. By 1860, 9,000 men with 6,000 mules, 28,000 oxen and more than 3,000 wagons crossed the trail. Six years later, between 5,000 and 6,000 wagons used the trail to Santa Fe.

When the railroad laid its first rails into Kansas, headed for New Mexico, Colorado, and the Pacific coastline, the era of the wild, uncharted West was rapidly coming to an end. But the builders of the Atchison, Topeka and Santa Fe Railway, like those who secured the Santa Fe Trail before them, would struggle through hardships of weather, topography, finances, and politics. The rails of the Santa Fe Railway eventually covered much of the old Santa Fe Trail and made the territory once so overwhelming and dangerous into the main artery west for settlers, sightseers, and coachseat adventurers. The Santa Fe Trail became the stuff of legends as its route west was covered with stakes, gravel, and railroad ties, and its deep ruts dissolved back into the dirt and dust.

CHAPTER · 2

The Atchison, Topeka, and Santa Fe Railway

T HE ATCHISON, TOPEKA AND SANTA FE RAILWAY began as the dream of one man, Cyrus K. Holliday. In the early 1850s, Holliday was a young lawyer living in Meadville, Pennsylvania. He was approached by the promoters of the Pittsburgh and Erie Railroad to write up their charter. An avid believer in the future of railroads, Holliday asked for stock instead of cash for his legal services. A little more than a year later, the twenty-eight-year-old Holliday had $20,000 in his bank account, and a plan to begin his own railroad somewhere "out west."

In 1854, Holliday headed west, temporarily leaving his wife, Mary, who was six months pregnant. Holliday's sights were set on Kansas where he planned, at the very least, to begin his own law firm; at the most, he hoped to begin a railroad. In either event, he planned to send for Mary as soon as he was settled. After traveling by train and boat throughout the Midwest, he took a stagecoach to Lawrence, Kansas. Although Holliday first lived in a pole-and-brush hut with a dirt floor, he liked Kansas and wrote Mary that it would become their home.

But before Holliday saw his wife and child, he distinguished himself in the young Kansas Territory. Kansas was still frontier country waiting to be settled and developed. Holliday saw the need for a new community and took it upon himself to found and promote the town of Topeka within months of his arrival. Holliday was Topeka's first town president, presiding over early town meetings standing on a sack of flour. He soon became a member of the territorial legislature, where he worked fervidly to insure the future of Kansas as a free state.

The Civil War stalled the arrival of Holliday's wife and daughter to his new home. He became a colonel in command of the Second Kansas Regiment, and was later promoted to brigadier-general, leading Kansas's abolitionists against invading pro-slavery Missourians. After the Kansas border was secured in June of 1856, Holliday returned home to visit his family in Pennsylvania. He returned to Topeka, alone, later that same year.

Although the conflict continued (and Holliday remained a participant in various capacities) his mind turned again to railroad building. Hundreds of northerners and southerners were heading west, leaving their battles behind for the challenges and opportunities of an uncharted, uncluttered frontier. Holliday was convinced that a railroad from Atchison, Kansas, to Santa Fe would be not only profitable but valuable to Kansas and the entire United States. In 1859, when it seemed that Topeka could be greatly enhanced with the aid of a railroad, Holliday turned his enthusiastic, tireless energy to the building of railroads in Kansas.

Several railroads were struggling to form in Kansas, and many envisioned Santa Fe as the final destination. Anyone with a little imagination could see the potential for trade and emigration along the first railroad to cross the Southwest. Holliday was like many of his contemporaries who dreamed of starting railroads—but he knew how to put his ideas onto paper and his thoughts into action.

Drawing on his previous experience with the Pittsburgh and Erie Railroad, Holliday wrote the charter for the Atchison and Topeka Railroad Company in only two days in a hotel room in Lawrence, Kansas. With a board of directors that included some of the most influential men in the territory, the charter stipulated that the railroad would travel west in the direction of Santa Fe, and south to the Gulf of Mexico. It was a big dream, a railroad that would connect so much unsettled and for the most part still unknown territory, a dream that made Holliday the object of jokes and much public ridicule. But the railroad that was said to begin nowhere and go nowhere was legally incorporated a month later, in February 1859. Thus began the journey of Holliday and the Santa Fe through the Southwest.

It was an opportune time: gold had been discovered in Colorado in 1858; Texas cattle empires were looking for rail connections to the east, and Kansas's new settlers had few roads and no waterways by which to send or receive goods. A Kansas railroad would answer all of these needs. But even so, it was several years before the Santa Fe began constructing its line westward. First and foremost, Holliday and his board needed financial help in the form of a land grant along the proposed railroad line. A push for such legislation began in 1860, but the Civil War stalled progress until 1863. Upon passage of the land grant by President Lincoln in March, the Atchison and Topeka was given ten years to reach the Colorado state line. At the time, this seemed to be a reasonable deadline: later it loomed as a near impossibility.

For the next few years Holliday and the Santa Fe (the name was changed to the Atchison, Topeka and Santa Fe in 1863—even the founding fathers saw the promotional possibilities in the romantic name of Santa Fe) took three steps forward and two back as bond issues were organized in Kansas counties, stocks were sold back east, and the politics of railroading and the development of a new state ran their course. Although money was nearly always a problem for the young Santa Fe, its leadership was not. Holliday and the board of directors all believed fiercely in their railroad's importance. Holliday himself canvassed door to door for support, and others on the board spent months on the East Coast finding financiers for their railroad.

Initially, eastern financiers weren't as convinced as the board of directors that a railroad into nowhere was viable. The West was an unknown entity, financially and otherwise. But Holliday and his team held firm to their dream and continued to press for local support as well as national backing. In 1868, after the town of Topeka and Shawnee County together gave subsidies of $250,000 to the Santa Fe, construction began.

The completion of the first seven miles of Santa Fe rails southwest from Topeka in 1868 occasioned a long-awaited celebration. Holliday and the Santa Fe organized an excursion train and steamed one hundred passengers at fifteen miles per hour to a company-sponsored picnic at the end of the new line in Wakarusa. There was food, drink, and many speeches, the most notable of which was made by Holliday himself. Holliday predicted the seven-mile-long railroad would one day reach Chicago, Santa Fe, Galveston, San Francisco, and Mexico. Even to the supportive and enthusiastic crowd listening from picnic blankets that April afternoon, the good Colonel Holliday seemed to be boasting about impossibilities. Reporters at the beer-and-soda-biscuit lunch quoted one Major Tom Anderson: "The Damn old fool! You're taking in too much territory, H! (sic) . . . Oh, Lord, give us a rest!"[1]

During the next decade, virtually every mile of track laid by the Santa Fe was the result of another round of hard fundraising. The Santa Fe's western progress was not easy and was often slowed by financial or natural obstacles. The men who made up the Santa Fe crews worked hard, long hours in the middle of the Kansas prairie. There was little assistance from machinery of any sort. Mile after mile, picks, shovels, and men's muscles moved soil, rocks, and hills. Horses and mules pulled scrapers and breaking plows through the buffalo sod, with farm boys and war veterans following behind them. Santa Fe track gangs in Kansas were often composed of Irish, German, and Swedish immigrants, midwesterners, Confederate and Yankee veterans, and young men seeking a way west. As the railroad reached farther into the west, men were hired from the surrounding territory— miners in the mining country of Colorado and New Mexico, Mexicans in New Mexico or up from Mexico, Indians from nearby tribes in Arizona, and eventually Chinese laborers in the mountains of southern California.

Towns formed along the railroad only as it arrived, making for some of the roughest types of communities known to man. There were few comforts for the crews, but the Santa Fe paid its men well and they in turn put money into Kansas's new economy. The slogan went "It's work all day for damn sure pay on the Atchison, Topeka and Santa Fe!"[2]

In the early years, there was no telegraph line along the Santa Fe. Two passenger trains ran during the day, and freight was hauled at night. This system functioned until traffic became too heavy for the single-track railroad, and a wire was run pole to pole from Topeka to the end of the track in 1869.

In 1870, Emporia was founded and a rail connection with the Texas cattle trade was established. This provided the young railroad with its first sub-

Cyrus K. Holliday,
founder of the Atchison,
Topeka and Santa Fe Railway.
(Credit: Santa Fe Railway)

The "end of the tracks" in 1872 was three miles east of Hutchinson, Kansas. The original caption for this photograph taken by the founder of Hutchinson, C.C. Hutchinson, states: "The extreme poverty of the road at that time is shown by the material used in building the track. For ties, any kind of material was used which would aid in supporting the rails, and 26 foot iron rails were fastened to these ties with old fish plates." (Credit: Santa Fe Railway)

Front Street, Dodge City, Kansas, 1873. The Santa Fe tracks and depot are to the right. The second building from the left is the United States Post Office. (Credit: Santa Fe Railway)

Two hundred thousand buffalo hides passed through Dodge City during the height of the buffalo slaughter on the Great Plains, 1874. (Credit: The Kansas State Historical Society)

The California Limited crosses the Canyon Diablo Bridge in Arizona. No date. (Credit: Santa Fe Railway)

stantial source of revenue: hauling highly prized beef cattle east. Emporia thrived in a rowdy, bawdy, frontier way until a year later when Newton usurped its colorful position at the end of the trail and became the primary cattle shipping center. Dodge City would later claim the title from Newton as the Santa Fe pushed its rails west.

Holliday and the Santa Fe directors were scrapping for the money needed to continue, especially in lieu of the quickly approaching 1873 deadline for reaching Colorado. Three hundred and thirty miles of track had to be laid in less than one year to connect Newton with Colorado. Through dogged persistance the railroad kept finding the necessary money, the track crews kept breaking ground and laying rails, and by the fall of 1872, the Santa Fe had reached Dodge City.

The track gangs met their greatest challenge in the country west of Newton. Dodge City and its surroundings were the wild frontier in 1872. Other than the track gangs, the only humans found on that dry, flat land were buffalo hunters, cowboys, Indians, and the gamblers and prostitutes who followed the rails west. The men on the gangs slept in the prairie grass, or in tents and shacks, living on a diet of buffalo steaks when the herds were close by, and beans, pork, and dried fruit when they were not. Weekends were made for one thing only: diversion in the nearest community—usually a tent or shanty town where prostitution, liquor, and gambling operations were the only commodities.

The closer to Colorado the gangs and the tracks came, the more trouble they encountered with ruffians and desperados. Robbery became increasingly common as supply trains ran deeper into the western frontier, and farther from the laws of Kansas. Soon all Santa Fe engineers, conductors, and train crews were well armed and prepared for a fight as train robbers and roving gangs led by infamous outlaws flourished. Even passenger and cattle trains headed east were held up. There was much bloodshed in these encounters and neither soldiers nor county and federal law officials could keep up with the problem. The Santa Fe was alone on the Kansas frontier and it soon learned it had to provide its own law enforcement in order to move westward.

Indians were never a problem for the Santa Fe track gangs, although they were known to sneak into a camp at night and steal tools or livestock. Some accounts claim they were superstitious about the steel rails cutting through their hunting grounds, refusing to cross the tracks or walk under telegraph wires. Hence the paths of local tribes crossed under the tracks wherever the railroad built bridges.[3]

The surveyors who preceded the crews had more to fear, as there were still hostile tribes watching for small bands of white men for whom it would be easy to make trouble. The Santa Fe surveyors traveled with rifles and six-shooters, and in western Kansas they were escorted by fifteen soldiers. The days of the old Santa Fe Trail didn't seem so long ago to the men working for the young Santa Fe Railway.

The 1873 deadline was approaching. As hard as the crews worked, they were still slowed by frozen prairie sod in winter and stifling heat in summer. The board of directors certainly had reason to feel desperate when an entire shipload of rails was lost in the Atlantic. But the track continued west. The crews were laying track at the unbelievable rate of one full mile a day in the fall of 1872. By December 1872, there were only fourteen miles between the end of the Santa Fe's line and the Colorado border. Through snow and ice storms, the men laid the rails over the state line on December 22, having laid 271 miles of track in 222 days.[4] Just as the celebration was beginning, federal surveyors informed the crew they were actually four miles short of their legally binding destination. What few sober men could be found were sent back out on the line to finish the job.

The management of the Santa Fe was so delighted with their victory that they ordered the gangs to push on to Granada, a small settlement a few miles farther west. The first big hurdle for the Santa Fe had been crossed. The obstacles to follow would be no less daunting.

The Santa Fe Railway's desire to reach the Pacific Ocean and provide transcontinental service became the stuff that wars are made of in the 1870s and 1880s. The Santa Fe had to overcome not only the same difficulties of uncharted territory, violent weather, and frontier lawlessness as the great trail before it; it also had to contend with rivalries and power struggles with other western railroads, both legal and otherwise. The Santa Fe was not an innocent bystander in these western railroad wars; it was often the aggressor and almost always the winner.

To those living in treeless Kansas, the great forests of Colorado were enough of a reason to lay track west. But Colorado offered even more: the mineral wealth of the territory was just becoming known, and the Rockies were already being billed as the "Switzerland of America." The Santa Fe decided to build into Colorado to share in its promise.

In 1875, the Santa Fe found enough support to resume building and pushed its tracks toward Pueblo from Granada, planning to reach into Leadville silver country within the year. The railroad reached La Junta in December 1875, and Pueblo in February 1876.

Unlike the empty, unsettled plains of Kansas, Pueblo already boasted a railroad with similar plans to the Santa Fe's. The Santa Fe, Denver and Rio Grande was a narrow gauge railroad, but it had plans as large as the Santa Fe's for Leadville and the mining regions of Colorado. It also had its eyes on Santa Fe. To heighten the tension between the two railroads, there was only one way into New Mexico from southern Colorado: Raton Pass. There was also only one way to the mining country in the west: through the Royal Gorge of the Arkansas River.

Fortunately for the Santa Fe, the DRG was not moving quickly either to the west or the south. Unfortunately for the DRG, the Santa Fe hired William Barstow Strong as its general manager in 1877. Strong, and the young Santa Fe engineer he worked with, A. A. Robinson, were the kind of individuals who make—and change—history.

Strong was everything his name implied. He steered the Santa Fe, first as its manager and later as its tenth president, with unerring hands to its ultimate goal: the Pacific. The Santa Fe operated 786 miles of track when Strong joined the railroad as its general manager; when he retired as president in 1889, the railroad covered more than 7,000 miles. Always a supporter of early Harvey House expansion, Strong also directed the Santa Fe to build reading rooms and clubhouses, and a hospital association for Santa Fe employees.

Albert Alonzo Robinson was a first-class engineer who thought quickly and clearly in moments of duress, of which he experienced many in his years with the Santa Fe. Robinson, like all the engineers and surveyors who preceded the railroads in their westward drive, was among the last of the great American trailblazers. A Vermonter like Strong, Robinson was all of twenty-seven years old when he joined the Santa Fe in 1871. Over the next twenty-two years, he oversaw the construction of more than five thousand miles of Santa Fe track, and was privy to some of the most colorful, dramatic, and historically important events of the young railroad. With his right-hand man, Ray Morley, Robinson rode horseback and buckboard over old trails and along many new ones, seeking the best rail route into the frontier.

Strong did not hesitate in his decision about Raton Pass: if the Santa Fe wanted New Mexico and a route to California, it would have to take Raton Pass right out from under the Denver and Rio Grande. The DRG had surveyed the pass in 1876 but had failed to file a plat and profile for its railroad, believing there was no rival in the vicinity to dispute its rights. This assumption cost the DRG passage into New Mexico.

In the fall of 1877, Robinson quietly and discreetly sent Ray Morley to "tend sheep" in the mountains surrounding Raton Pass. The DRG survey-ors were also working on the slopes of the same mountains, but they did not realize the campfire they saw at night among the pine trees was illuminating the notebook of a Santa Fe suveyor dressed in shepherd's clothes.

In the winter of 1878, with the DRG's own grading crews waiting com-fortably and ignorantly in nearby Pueblo, Strong sent Robinson to survey the eight-thousand-foot pass. With Morley and his notes to guide him, Robinson quickly accomplished his task despite difficult winter conditions.

Upon receiving Robinson's reports, Santa Fe president Thomas Nicker-son instructed Strong to proceed with construction over the Raton. The first war with the DRG began in late February when Strong sent Robinson to begin grading in the pass. Railroad lore claims that the chief engineer of the DRG, J. A. McMurtrie, a friend of Robinson's, was on the same southbound train to El Moro as Robinson and Morley, who were en route to the pass. There are two versions of the story: one claims that McMurtrie saw Robinson but did not believe the Santa Fe could pull together a crew in time to beat his own gang up the mountain the following morning; McMurtrie is supposed to have alerted his men that they would head for the pass at dawn and then retired for the night in a hotel in El Moro. The second version claims that Morley spotted McMurtrie and alerted Robin-son, the two men hiding in another car, their faces buried in their coats, until McMurtrie climbed off the train at El Moro.

According to both accounts, Robinson and Morley forfeited their rest and opted instead to ride all night on horseback to Uncle Dick Wottoon's house on the pass. With Wottoon's help, Robinson secured a group of men to begin work in the dark at 5:00 A.M. At 5:30, McMurtrie and his rested crew arrived at Raton Pass only to find the Santa Fe's men claiming the only route to northern New Mexico. The Santa Fe's legal basis for possession was the right established by prior construction. The DRG crew looked for another route over the mountains, but soon gave up. The Santa Fe had won the first round.

The DRG was thus cut off from the south at El Moro. The small railroad desperately needed the westward Leadville connection to survive. But the Santa Fe wanted to control access to the mineral wealth to the west. The second war began in late 1877 when the Santa Fe made known its desire to lay track through the Royal Gorge near Canon City, the exact route chosen and surveyed, but not filed, by the DRG.

In early 1878, the two railroads began spying on one another, the Santa Fe using codes (which the DRG easily broke) to send messages over the DRG-owned telegraph lines. Each railroad waited for the other to begin the race through the canyon. Like two generals gathering their armies, Robinson and McMurtrie armed their men with picks and shovels for battle at the Royal Gorge.

To slow the Santa Fe's efforts, the DRG began refusing telegraphed messages between Strong and Santa Fe crews. Robinson, who was still working on Raton Pass, sent Morley north to wait and watch for any movement by the DRG for the gorge. At the same time, Strong gathered a work crew in El Moro and asked for a train to Canon City. His request was refused. The DRG knew what the Santa Fe was up to and Strong was not going to be allowed to take his men to the gorge via their tracks.

It was April 1878. Neither Robinson nor Strong could reach the gorge with their men and the DRG was obviously about to launch its own attempt. Morley was waiting in La Junta; Robinson was able to reach him by telegraph and instructed him to head for the gorge. Morley took a trainful of men to Pueblo but he, too, was refused further passage west over DRG tracks.

Alone this time, Morley again postponed sleep for the Santa Fe and rode all night to cover the forty-three miles between Pueblo and Canon City. Accounts of this nightly dash have been greatly exaggerated—some even claim the horse dropped dead from exhaustion—but suffice it to say Morley rode at a good clip through difficult Colorado mountain terrain. Morley could supposedly hear the whistle of the DRG train, bound for the gorge, in the distance. In what was becoming true Santa Fe Railway style, Morley reached Canon City in time to pull together a work crew of local Santa

Fe–supporting citizens. With shovels, picks, and a few Colt .44s, Morley's gang beat the DRG's to the gorge.

This time the DRG did not walk away in defeat. The latecomers began work in another section of the gorge, and for the next few days both camps secured their positions with additional men, arms, and fortress-like structures. The war between the two railroads then began in earnest. Daily skirmishes plagued the track gangs in and around the gorge with rocks, bullets, and curses in between serving for ammunition.

Quick-drawing gunmen were hired by both sides. The Santa Fe went to Kansas and paid Bat Masterson to commandeer one hundred armed men. But nearby Pueblo's gambling facilities—including one gambling house reputed to be among the largest in the country—made it difficult to keep the Santa Fe guard on duty in the canyon.

Both crews attempted to lay track, but sabotage was frequent and there was much harassment and shooting between the two forts. Bridges were burned, dynamite destroyed rival track, tools were stolen in night raids, and survey stakes were pulled out and erroneously reset. Each side lured its opponent's workers away with offers of more money, causing much traffic between the two camps. It was no way to build a railroad, especially through one of the deepest (about two thousand feet from rim to river) and narrowest (only thirty feet at one point) gorges in the west.

Lawyers for both railroads fought the matter out in federal court, and finally a judge ordered both sides to withdraw from the disputed area until rights could be determined. Tensions were eased until August 23, when the first substantial decision was handed down: both railroads could continue work through the canyon. The armies that had been disbanded over the summer were recalled and the frustrated DRG appealed the decision.

On April 21, 1879, after months of scuffle in the gorge and almost complete financial collapse of the narrow gauge railroad, the Supreme Court issued its decision: the DRG had prior right to the canyon. Both companies could continue to build, but the DRG had right of way.

Another year of friction ensued between the two railroads, with hostilities continuing to gain momentum both in and out of court. In February of 1880, the war came to an end in an out-of-court agreement. In exchange for the abandonment by the DRG of its plans to reach Santa Fe, the ATSF relinquished all rights from Canon City to Leadville. The Santa Fe was paid for its track and agreed not to invade DRG territory, including the stretch from Leadville to Denver. The war ended. The Santa Fe reverted to Colonel Holliday's original plan: a route through the territory of New Mexico and then on to the Pacific.

Expansion into New Mexico was never as colorful or eventful as Colorado, but the Santa Fe collided with another rival railroad when it looked for a route out of New Mexico towards California.

New Mexico and Arizona in the late 1870s were largely uncharted territories. Robinson, Morley, and two other Santa Fe surveyors, Henry Holbrook and Lewis Kingman (whose contributions are remembered in towns of the same names in Arizona), became New Mexico mapmakers before they became railroad surveyors, riding through river valleys and across flat-topped mesas with few known trails or landmarks to follow. This was a wild, untouched frontier that would soon be transformed forever by the arrival of the Santa Fe Railroad.

The foremost adversary New Mexico offered the Santa Fe was the terrain and grade of Raton Pass. While the railroad war raged in the Royal Gorge, Santa Fe crews built up, over, and eventually through the mountains of Raton. Before a tunnel could be completed, the Raton switchback with its eight-thousand-foot summit, 6-percent grades, and sixteen-degree curves took building materials from one side of the pass to the other. A special engine was purchased by the Santa Fe to pull trains over this switchback. Baldwin Locomotive Works built for the Santa Fe what was then the most powerful engine known to man. It was named the "Uncle Dick" for Wottoon, whose road had helped pave the way for the Santa Fe. At the end of 1879, the track reached Willow Springs, soon renamed Raton, and several months later the tunnel opened, superseding the difficult switchback.

During the last year of the Santa Fe's war with the Denver and Rio Grande, Robinson had surveyed southwest through Glorietta Pass and along the Rio Grande to Albuquerque. Because of its size, and the difficult mountains that nearly surrounded it, Robinson and his superiors could not justify the main line reaching Santa Fe itself. To the terrible disappointment of the citizens of the small city, the tracks would be laid seven miles east. Lamy, New Mexico, the new railroad town built outside of Santa Fe, was reached in February 1880.

Albuquerque, San Marcial, and Rincon, New Mexico, were reached the same year. From Rincon the Santa Fe branched south to El Paso, Texas, and west to Deming, New Mexico, where a link with the Southern Pacific Railroad would give the Santa Fe its connection to the Pacific Ocean. In March of 1881, the Santa Fe could boast a direct route from Kansas City to the coast of California. But it was not the landmark accomplishment the board of directors, its new president William Barstow Strong, and Colonel Holliday had hoped for.

The Southern Pacific Railroad, although willing to make track agreements with the Santa Fe, had no intention of making the Santa Fe's transcontinental dream come true. The Southern Pacific, with its partner the Missouri Pacific, enjoyed a railroad monopoly in southern California. The rates it established for Santa Fe freight were exorbitant and soon after the agreement was reached, the Santa Fe abandoned its plans to ship via Southern Pacific rails to California.

Under Collis P. Huntington, the Southern Pacific had a prosperous and firm hold on California railroad trade. They had the skill, the finances, and the motive to engage in war with the smaller Santa Fe. In an effort to outsmart the Southern Pacific, the Santa Fe built to Guaymas, Mexico, and what it hoped would prove to be a lucrative trade port. It wasn't, and the railroad never made any money from this line. But it did force the Southern Pacific to lease its track from Deming to Benson, Arizona to the Santa Fe, which threatened to build parallel track. In 1882, when the Guaymas route was completed, the Santa Fe was the longest railroad in the world under one management.

In 1878, Robinson and Morley surveyed both the thirty-second and thirty-fifth parallels as possible routes to California. Although they recommended the southern route through Tucson because of its mineral possibilities and seemingly easier terrain, Strong and Nickerson opted for a route through northern Arizona along the thirty-fifth parallel. What was first viewed as an enormous handicap to the Santa Fe's trade potential—the Grand Canyon and its complete blocking of any traffic possibilities from the north—was to become one of the railroad's most important assets. But neither Strong nor Nickerson foresaw the Canyon's future as one of the greatest scenic attractions in the world: the ultimately profitable decision to build along the northern route was simply the result of good luck.

In 1866, the Atlantic and Pacific railroad had obtained the right to build along the thirty-fifth parallel from Albuquerque to California. The St. Louis and San Francisco ("Frisco") Railroad, owner of a majority of AP stock, entered into an agreement with the Santa Fe whereby jointly they would build west across Arizona along the AP right of way. This partnership worked relatively well, aside from some friction due to construction difficulties.

Road grading and rail laying in Arizona in the 1880s was even more difficult than in Kansas ten years before. The desert soil was hard and rocky, and unpredictable arroyos and washes often made a straight road impossible. The track gangs were composed of Anglos, Mexicans, Irish immigrants, and even Apache, Navajo, and Mojave Indians. There were few people to be found and almost as little water. Santa Fe men were rationed one pint a day while working across one of the hottest deserts of the American West.

Western movement was halted for six months while a bridge was built over Canyon Diablo, twenty-six miles west of Winslow, Arizona. The iron bridge was 560 feet long and reached 222 feet above the canyon at a cost of $250,000 and thousands of difficult man-hours.

While the Santa Fe was pushing west to California, it was also building branches off its main line into Kansas, Colorado, and New Mexico territory. Emigrant trains brought hundreds west with their carpetbags and canvas bundles. Young couples with small children, grandparents, missionaries, businessmen, and adventurous people of all ages and nationalities climbed aboard the Santa Fe trains in Kansas City, bound for the end of the line or places in between. The train cars were crude, with wooden seats that were pulled together at night to form beds, and one large community stove for cooking at the end of the car. Firewood was gathered at each stop and food was cooked, and sometimes hunted, as the train chugged west.[5]

By August of 1883, Santa Fe rails crossed the Colorado River to Needles, California, where they again connected with the Southern Pacific. Huntington had decided to build a branch line to Needles from the Southern Pacific's main line at Mojave. The Southern Pacific connected with the Atlantic and Pacific, and although another transcontinental link was formed, it was useless to the frustrated Santa Fe. Huntington sent freight over the Southern Pacific's El Paso route or via the northern route through Utah, ignoring the Santa Fe altogether.

Fortunately for the Santa Fe, the Southern Pacific found itself in moder-

ate financial trouble in 1883. Huntington had to sell certain bonds pur-
chased in its attempt to direct the future of the Frisco's, and the Santa Fe's,
California lines. At the same time, Huntington agreed to sell the Needles-
Mojave line.

The Santa Fe had begun construction from San Diego, a city overlooked
and neglected by the Southern Pacific and several other California railroads. The citizens of San Diego were easily roused to support the Santa
Fe's efforts to build its own transcontinental link using their port and land.
Wealthy and influential businessmen from San Diego courted the Santa Fe
for several years with generous land offers and other support. In 1880, the
California Southern Railroad Company, a subsidiary of the Santa Fe, was
incorporated. The chosen route placed the railroad once again on the old
Santa Fe Trail—north to San Bernardino, over Cajon Pass through the San
Bernardino and San Gabriel mountains, and then north and east to link up
with the Santa Fe's main line.

Equipment for the California Southern was brought around Cape Horn
to San Diego harbor. Construction proceeded effortlessly to Colton, California, where the tracks had to cross the Southern Pacific's main line in
order to reach San Bernardino. The Southern Pacific refused to grant
passage over its tracks. Huntington then offered to buy out the California
Southern, but the railroad refused. He then turned to local law officials,
convincing the sheriff at Colton that seizure of the California Southern's
crossing was legally necessary to protect the rights of the Southern Pacific
Railroad.

Another war began. Ignoring local law enforcers, CS men seized the
disputed crossing by force. CS lawyers received a court order allowing the
railroad to continue its work over the SP tracks, but the SP ignored the
order. SP men retorted with brute force, placing three locomotives as a
barrier across the tracks. The fracas ended with a court order served to
the Southern Pacific Railroad offices in San Francisco. The California
Southern reached San Bernardino in September of 1882 without further
mishap.

In 1883, the Santa Fe bought out the California Southern. Only eighty-
one miles of track needed to be completed for the Santa Fe to accomplish
its ultimate goal: a main line all its own from Kansas City to the Pacific.
The land to be crossed was between Barstow and San Bernardino and it
was among the most difficult terrain in the state of California. Cajon Pass

was the only possible route through the San Bernardino and San Gabriel mountain ranges. The pass was a long, slow climb of one thousand feet through the Mojave Desert from the south. The top was 3,823 feet above sea level and was covered with thick juniper and piñon trees. The railroad hired twenty-two Chinese track gangs for this section of the line. Construction over Cajon Pass was not nearly as difficult as that over the Raton had been, but it was a tough challenge of engineering skill and manpower all the same.

Cajon Pass was completed in 1885. The importance of the opening of this part of the Santa Fe, and its transcontinental link to San Diego harbor, was reduced by the decision of the Santa Fe to lease Southern Pacific track into Los Angeles, and by its acquisition in 1887 of the Los Angeles and San Gabriel Valley Railroad. Los Angeles, much to the disappointment of San Diego, gave Santa Fe the west coast market it had always wanted and the major, competitive transcontinental link it had dreamed of from the beginning. On May 31, 1887, the first transcontinental Santa Fe train arrived in Los Angeles. The rate war Huntington and the Southern Pacific had connived to avoid officially began.

Los Angeles underwent massive economic growth and a population boom. The Los Angeles area changed from a sparsely settled farming and ranching region to a small, bustling city. The low shipping rates brought about by the presence of the Santa Fe enabled the region's agricultural community to ship east for a fraction of what the Southern Pacific had previously charged. The Santa Fe charged ten dollars to Missouri; the Southern Pacific cut its ticket to five. For a day one offer permitted a passenger to cross the country from Los Angeles to Kansas City for one dollar.[6]

With these low rates came an influx of farmers and businessmen curious to see the warm, rich-soiled land of milk and honey for themselves. Most of these overland-train emigrants stayed. With the new low fares, the average midwestern family man could afford to travel to California, look over and purchase land, return home, sell out, and move his family west permanently. In 1887 alone, twenty-five new communities formed along a thirty-six-mile stretch of track between San Bernardo and Los Angeles.[7]

In 1886, Strong announced that another subsidiary of the Santa Fe, the Southern Kansas Railroad, would build southwest from Kiowa, Kansas, across Indian Territory (Oklahoma) to Panhandle City, Texas. The Santa

Fe wanted a larger share of the Texas cattle and agricultural trade. Time was of the essence once again, as another local railroad, the Fort Worth and Denver City, was building northwest across Texas for Colorado. Santa Fe track gangs built quickly to Canadian, Texas, and reached Panhandle City in January, 1888.

There was one major destination the Santa Fe had yet to reach: the Gulf of Mexico. In the mid-1880s, Strong sent surveyors into Texas seeking the best way south to the Gulf. Galveston, located on the gulf near Houston, had suffered years of trade problems promoted by Houston businessmen and the railroad that served them, the Houston and Texas Central Railway. After an 1867 yellow fever epidemic in Galveston, Houston claimed Galveston goods were unsafe. For years, Houston initiated yellow fever scares in Galveston and forced embargoes between the two cities. As a result, Galveston was cut off from trade with either Houston or the rest of the country. It needed its own railroad to survive.

In 1873, the Gulf, Colorado and Santa Fe Railway (no relation to the ATSF) was chartered. By 1882, the GCSF reached Dallas. The success of this railroad, with its direct route between the Gulf and the Dallas–Fort Worth area, made it an obvious candidate for acquisition by one of the larger railroads in the Southwest, most notably the Southern Pacific. Although Huntington decided not to try and buy the GCSF, his ally, Jay Gould, and the Missouri Pacific sought a Texas traffic pool agreement. When the GCSF demanded terms not compatible with the Missouri Pacific and Southern Pacific's trade monopoly in Texas, a rate war began that harmed the stability of the small GCSF.

In the spring of 1884, when the Santa Fe sent surveyors into Texas seeking the best route to Dallas through Indian Territory, it began quiet and friendly negotiations with the GCSF. After two years, the Santa Fe acquired the GCSF for what many viewed as an exorbitant price. But Strong predicted that the Santa Fe's route from Kansas City to the Gulf of Mexico would end Gould's and Huntington's hold on Texas trade. He was right.

By 1886, the Santa Fe needed only one line to ensure its future independence: a direct route from Kansas City to Chicago. There were several other railroads chartered through this region and the Santa Fe did business with the Chicago, Rock Island and Pacific Railroad, and the Chicago, Burlington and Quincy. But Strong argued that the Santa Fe needed its own track and ordered a survey in 1883. Local traffic would be nonexistent with so many railroads already serving the area between Kansas City and Chicago. Therefore, the Santa Fe would be able to offer a straight track with the fastest rail service between the two cities. In late 1886, Strong chartered the Chicago, Santa Fe and California Railway Company. In 1887, the CSFC began building east from Kansas City, and bought the Chicago and St. Louis Railway, "two streaks of rust" running 154 miles south from Chicago.[8]

One year later, the first through train from Chicago to Kansas City ran over 350 miles of new track, 100 miles of rebuilt track, and five new bridges, all the workmanship of Chief Engineer Robinson. Robinson had been working without the help of his old friend, Ray Morley, who had died at his campsite on the Sonoran Desert in Chihuahua, Mexico, in 1884. Morley was working with his survey team on the last lap of the Sonora Railway. Apparently, Morley was asked to show his gold-mounted Winchester, a present to Morley from William Barstow Strong for his efforts, heroic and otherwise, at the Royal Gorge. Morley pulled the gun out from under his gear muzzle first, and was killed when the gun accidently went off. Near the Santa Fe tracks in Las Vegas, New Mexico, a monument was erected to Ray Morley.

When Strong resigned as president of the Santa Fe in 1889, Santa Fe employees hoped the forty-five-year-old Albert Robinson would be his successor. But Robinson never became president. He worked as the Santa Fe's chief engineer out of his office in Topeka for several more years before leaving to take over the construction, and eventually the management, of the Mexican Central railroad. When Robinson left the Santa Fe in 1893, he left it the longest rail system in the world.

Cyrus K. Holliday died in 1900. He lived to see every mile (and then some) of his dream brought to reality. The railroad that once lived only in his imagination and in his letters home to his wife, that would cross the Rockies to the Pacific Ocean, touch the Gulf of Mexico, and link Indian territory, buffalo prairie, and roadless, open desert to the Midwest, was now the means by which generations of people would cross America east to west and west to east.

A new era in railroading was beginning: the Santa Fe gained access to Dearborn Station in Chicago and was soon the single most important passenger line departing for the west. Trains up to six hundred feet in length ran daily between Kansas City and Chicago, offering luxurious Pullman cars decorated in the tradition of Louis XV, coaches trimmed with mahogany and velveteen, antique oak paneling and electric lights. Other railroads could offer the same luxuries and passenger service throughout the United States, but only the Santa Fe included "meals by Fred Harvey." This seemingly small asset, combined with the length and the unique territory of the Santa Fe, would soon make it one of the great railroads of the world.

CHAPTER · 3

Fred Harvey and the Santa Fe Railway

ALL RAILROADS, L. L. WATERS SAID, were served by Western Union, the Pullman Company, and the Railway Express. But the Santa Fe had a fourth ally—Fred Harvey.[1] Both the railroad and Harvey have been hailed as "civilizers." The Iron Horse is an obvious candidate, but what about Fred Harvey?

> There was little about Harvey to suggest a Roman proconsul bringing the enlightened authority of the Empire to the farthest reaches of Gaul or Asia Minor. . . . And yet on a scale and to a degree of perfection that has become part of the folklore of the trans-Mississippi West, Harvey imposed a rule of culinary benevolence over a region larger than any Roman province and richer than any single British dominion save Indian.[2]

The character of the Fred Harvey Houses, the dining and lunch rooms, small hotels and elegant resorts, that coexisted with the Atchison, Topeka and Santa Fe Railway in the Southwest for over seventy years, directly reflected the personality and character of Fred Harvey, the Englishman who began it all in the 1870s. His story and the story of the Santa Fe Railway are closely intertwined, because the success of one was directly supplemented by the success of the other. As with many great business partnerships (the term is used loosely, as the Santa Fe and Fred Harvey were never legal partners), one partner—the Santa Fe—has received more lasting and farther-reaching fame. But the railroad might not have become so great, so fast, had Fred Harvey not walked into its offices in 1876.

Before Fred Harvey found the Santa Fe, there was no real effort made to alleviate the certain gastronomical discomfort experienced wherever and whenever a meal was sought en route to the West. Meal stops were often at a town that consisted of one shack, called the depot, and a water tank. Railroad towns were often called "hell on wheels"—buildings and railroad facilities slapped up when the first crews arrived, usually taken down and moved along as needed. They were rough towns that survived only because of the railroad, and if they became real communities, they did so slowly. They were hardly the place a genteel man and woman wanted to spend the night, or even eat a meal.

This situation was not unique to the Santa Fe. All western railroads in the early days shared this void in their customer services. The completion of the transcontinental railroad in 1869 ended an era of isolation for the West; but this is not to say that travel west was now easy or comfortable. Eastern trains had dining and Pullman cars, and with good-sized cities between most destinations, a traveler could choose to stop over for rest and refreshment, according to his means. But out west, where the railroad crossed hundreds of miles of open country, mountains with snow far into summer, endless deserts and wild prairies, the few communities where the train stopped were little more than boom towns, mining camps, cattle holding-pens, or government outposts.

There were virtually no clean hotels—their place was taken by shacks or public rooms with cots. The food was usually served by a bartender or saloonkeeper. In the middle of nowhere, without adequate manpower, food supplies, or motivation, home cooking meant making do. There is no shortage of firsthand descriptions of these early railroad eateries. It seems that most travelers to the West developed a sense of humor towards their predicament, as well as an iron stomach:

The tea tasted as though it was made from the leaves of the
sagebrush. The biscuit was made without soda, but with plenty of
alkali, harmonizing with the great quantity of alkali dust we had
already swallowed.[3]

Meat was greasy and was usually fried, beans were canned, bacon rancid, and coffee was fresh once a week. Pie, if found, was of the dried-fruit-and-crust variety, biscuits were known as "sinkers," and eggs were shipped "fresh" from back East, preserved in lime.[4] A "chicken stew of prairie dogs" was not uncommon, and "the chops were generally as tough as hanks of whipcord and the knives as blunt as a bricklayer's trowel."[5] If the food didn't frighten a traveler, the atmosphere of a train dining stop could, complete with "dangerous looking miners in big boots and revolvers," and "tables dirty and waiters not only dirty but saucy."[6]

The final insult to a traveler's stomach was the twenty minutes allowed for eating and relaxing at each stop. It seems that at many of these early fast-food joints, the railroad crew and the cook may have been in cahoots, with the food coming too late or the train leaving too early to make it possible for a customer to eat the food he, in the unclear frame of mind brought on by starvation, had ordered and paid for. The restaurant management and the railroad men split the reward for this ingenious timetable, and probably doubled their profits by re-serving the untouched meal hours later to the next hungry train victim.

The non-fasting train passenger, burdened by a normal appetite three times a day, was a prisoner in the frontier West. His only alternatives were to drink himself into oblivion at each stop—good liquor was not hard to come by and often the most comfortable facilities were to be found at the local saloon—or carry food along in box-lunches and hope his supply didn't give out before the end of the line. Some trains did offer on-board food-stuffs sold by a "butcher boy," but educated travelers brought along cheese, bread, and fruit from home. However, on the average summer day in Kansas, jolting at twenty miles an hour across the humid, dusty prairie, in a train where people were scarcely more comfortable than cattle in a freight car, those little boxes of homemade goodies could undergo a sudden change of character; if the smell became unappetizing as heat filled the train, the taste of those lunches grew even worse:

*Many years ago when you went for a trip on the cars, somebody
at home kindly put up a fried chicken in a shoe-box for you. It
was accompanied by a healthy piece of cheese and a varied
assortment of hard-boiled eggs and some cake. When everybody in
the car got out their lunch baskets with the paper cover and the
red-bordered napkins, it was an interesting sight. . . .
The bouquet from those lunches hung around the car all day,
and the flies wired ahead for their friends to meet them at each
station.* [7]

There was just no getting around it: food and the first western railroads
were not compatible. The Great American West was not supposed to be
comfortable. Romantic and beautiful, yes, but comfortable, no.

On February 26, 1876, the Santa Fe laid the completing track to Pueblo,
Colorado. The company decided to promote a sightseeing excursion to
Colorado, with a special round-trip fare from Topeka. The trip was to take
a day and a half each way; the only meal offered by the railroad would be
at Newton, about halfway out. Other meals, the promotional material
stated, were to be packed and carried on by each passenger. It would be
a long trip, but early Kansans and other western enthusiasts (including
members of the Kansas legislature) were not easily intimidated. Four
hundred and forty-six adventurous souls—eighty-three of whom were
women—climbed on board the excursion train bound for Pueblo on March
5, 1876.

The two trains carrying the group met heavy snow outside of Hutchinson, slowing the progress of the trains to a crawl. Further on, there was
an unplanned layover, where hotel accomodations proved insufficient for
even half the passengers. One Kansas town's entire food supplies were
quickly bought and devoured by travelers who had not planned for any
change in the train's schedule, and had long since run out of personal
provisions. The next day, the snowplow ahead of the trains ran into a cow,
causing another long delay. The only food to be found on the Kansas prairie
consisted of provisions found at a station agent's residence. The trains
finally arrived in Pueblo twenty-four hours late, where homes in the town
were opened to aid the half-starved, exhausted excursionists. [8]

After the Pueblo excursion, it took the Santa Fe only a few months to begin to turn customer services around. And this improvement set a new standard for passenger railroading in America.

Frederick Henry Harvey was born in London in 1835. At the age of fifteen, Harvey emigrated to the United States. He landed in New York City, where his first job was as a two-dollar-a-week busboy at the Smith and McNeill Cafe. It was not a very rewarding job, financially or otherwise, but it provided an appropriate beginning for the English-Scottish immigrant who would one day build a food empire known throughout the world.

Harvey was probably a keen observer of the cafe business, and after several years of "apprenticeship" he left New York with dreams of establishing his own restaurant. After reaching New Orleans in 1856, he contracted yellow fever. The illness stalled his plans but did not alter them, and by 1857, at the age of twenty-two, Harvey opened his own cafe in St. Louis.

In 1859 he married a seventeen-year-old Bohemian named Barbara Sarah Mattas, whom he affectionately called his "Sally." With a partner, Harvey ran a thriving and successful restaurant and was enjoying prosperity when the Civil War began. The struggle between the states became a struggle for small businesses to survive, and Harvey was soon deeply in debt. Business was already bleak when Harvey's partner disappeared one night with what little money the concern had, and Harvey himself was stricken with typhoid.

Harvey recovered his health, however, and returned to the restaurant business once again, working in St. Louis as a pantryman in someone else's cafe. The war ended, and Harvey turned his eyes and hopes west, where opportunity was rumored to abound.

After working at odd jobs around packet boats, Harvey was hired to work as a mail clerk for the Hannibal and St. Joseph (popularly known as the Horrible and Slow Jolts) Railroad in 1862. Under William A. Davis, postmaster of St. Joseph, Missouri, Harvey distinguished himself when he became one of two clerks to sort mail while in transit on the train. Davis's "traveling post office" was immensely successful and the "Railway Mail Service" was born.

The Hannibal and St. Joseph was soon absorbed by the Chicago, Burlington and Quincy Railroad. Harvey remained as an employee of the larger railroad and by 1876, after years of hard work and slow promotion, became its general western freight agent.

The Harvey family now included four children, and resided in Leavenworth, Kansas. Had Harvey's job been of the behind-the-desk variety, "Harvey food" and "Harvey Houses" historically might only have referred to Sally Harvey's home cooking (which was excellent) and to the various family homes occupied by Harvey offspring. But as a railroad employee, Harvey was on the road, via the rails, throughout the Midwest, for much of his workweek. Unsanitary lodging, poorly prepared food, and the risk of illness from one or both, made Harvey's time away from home an ordeal of discomfort. He lost two children to scarlet fever (leaving the four mentioned above), and with his own health scarred from typhoid and yellow fever he was not tolerant of what seemed to be a widely accepted standard of inadequate and even sordid traveler's services. With his knowledge of the restaurant business and his professional experience on the midwestern railroads, Harvey believed he might be the person to introduce good food and clean service to the traveling public.

In 1875, just before his promotion to freight agent, Harvey optimistically began a second business partnership. With Jeff Rice he opened two cafes on the Kansas Pacific Railroad, one in Wallace, Kansas, and the second in Hugo, Colorado. With a growing family to support, Harvey had to maintain his full time position at the CB&Q, as well as taking part time work as an newspaper advertisements solicitor for *The Leavenworth Conservative.* Harvey could only guide the operations of the two railroad cafes from a distance. It was soon evident that the food and service standards Harvey demanded for his cafes were not important to Rice. The Harvey standard would make Fred Harvey famous and very wealthy, but its future value was lost on Harvey's partner. The restaurants did very well—as did Harvey as a solicitor (he reportedly pulled in more than $12,000 for the *Conservative* in one year)—but the operational dissention between Harvey and Rice led to the dissolving of their business within the year.

The restaurant and sideline soliciting work left Harvey with money in the bank. He was now even more certain of the need for quality railroad services, and of his own ability to provide superior food to passengers. Harvey devised a system of restaurants linked by the railroad and took his proposal to his longtime employer, the Burlington Railroad. Officials of that railroad were not impressed with Harvey's experience or his business ideas, nor did they believe food was worthy of extensive financial consideration by a railroad company. The Burlington executives told Harvey to go to the young Atchison, Topeka and Santa Fe Railway, because they "would try anything."[9]

The Santa Fe would not have tried *anything,* but it was ready to try something to alleviate the shortage of decent food threatening the success of the railroad. After being turned down by his own railroad, Harvey contacted Charles F. Morse, a friend and also the superintendent of the Santa Fe Railroad. Morse, like Harvey, traveled the railroads and had plenty of firsthand experience with the famed hash-slingers of the West. Harvey was a distinguished-looking Englishman with good business sense who seemed worthy of a chance at solving a problem no one else even addressed. Morse took Harvey's ideas to Santa Fe president Nickerson who, like Morse, was immediately interested.

With Nickerson's blessing, Morse and Harvey launched what was to become one of the most successful and influential business partnerships in the early American West. There was no formal contract, only a gentlemen's agreement sealed with a gentlemen's handshake. The details of this oral agreement have not survived, but the gist was that Harvey would provide equipment and management and the Santa Fe would give Harvey the small depot restaurant in Topeka and would transport whatever he needed, free of charge, on its trains. The profit, if one was to be had, would be Harvey's.

This informal arrangement was followed by the first formal contract between Harvey and the Santa Fe on January 1, 1878. However, this written contract only covered the operation of the dining room at Florence, Kansas. It ran for a term of five years, and it said that the Santa Fe agreed to stop its mainline passenger trains for two meals per day at the Florence dining room, and that in the event dining cars were placed on the line, the railroad would take over the Harvey House and pay Harvey a price agreed upon at the time of the contract. The contract was renewed and supplemented at various times, but the second formal contract between Harvey and the railroad did not come about until May 1, 1889. This contract gave Harvey the exclusive right, with some minor reservations, to manage and operate the eating houses, lunchstands, and hotel facilities which the Harvey company then owned, leased, or was to lease at any time in the future upon any of the Santa Fe's railroads west of the Missouri River. Coal, ice, and water were to be provided by the railroad; supplies and Harvey employees were to be hauled free. Profits from the operations were to go to Fred Harvey.

Guy Potter, a friend of Harvey's from Leavenworth, was hired to manage the original Topeka lunch counter under Harvey's strictest supervision. In a small room above the old Santa Fe depot, Harvey and Potter turned a third-rate traveler's eatery into a first-class dining facility. They scrubbed floors, polished silverware, ordered new linen, and completely changed the menu. Within a few weeks of its opening, the Harvey lunchroom in Topeka, although a flight of stairs above the street, was doing a capacity business. Train passengers, Santa Fe crewmen, businessmen from Topeka's small downtown district, and even families came into Harvey's new lunchroom to enjoy the food and efficient, spic-and-span atmosphere.

The quick success of Harvey's lunchroom caused local newspaper writers to speculate as to when Harvey would lower his standards. Instead, Harvey sought better recipes and fresher food sources. The daily traffic jam at the lunch counter in the depot threatened to impede westward progress on the Santa Fe:

> *For a few months it looked as though civilization were going to stop short in her onward march at the capital of Kansas, and that the westward course of empire . . . would end at the same spot. Travelers positively declined to go further once they had eaten with Fred Harvey. Traffic backed up, and it became necessary for the Santa Fe to open similar houses at other points along its right of way in order that the West might not be settled in just one spot.[10]*

Morse and the Santa Fe encouraged Harvey to open more restaurants on their line. As the Santa Fe's men built westward, so did Harvey's. Harvey quit his job with the Burlington, and operated his expanding business out of a small office at the Hannibal and St. Joseph Railroad depot. Soon there were Harvey lunchrooms, dining rooms, and hotels in Newton, Hutchinson, Dodge City; in La Junta and Trinidad, Colorado; and then in

Santa Fe crew, 1887, laying 350 miles of new track between Chicago and Kansas City.
(Credit: Santa Fe Railway)

Fred Harvey. "Some day a book will be devoted to detailed description of the Harvey system, its hotel, dining room, and the extraordinary features of a management which allows a traveller to dine on brook trout in the middle of the desert, and on the rarest fruits in vast reaches of country where nothing is raised but cactus and sage brush.

The Castañeda at Las Vegas, a great building of dark red brick in the mission style, the Alvarado at Albuquerque, fronted by long collonades and well proportioned arches; the Cardeñas at Trinidad; the Fray Marcos at Williams; the Escalante at Ash Fork; the El Garces at Needles—all these, and many others are, in their many departments, worthy of the study of the artist, the epicure, the student of Indian life, and of many men in the United States who lay claim to the title "hotel manager." "Fred Harvey was the Napoleon of hotel managers." Albuquerque Morning Journal, July 29, 1911.
(Credit: Kansas State Historical Society)

Before Harvey and the Santa Fe organized a hotel and restaurant business along the line, layovers due to weather or train trouble caused difficulties to train passengers and local residents alike.
(Credit: The Collection of Gary Britton, circa 1900)

Topeka A.T. and S.F. frame depot, 1880.
(Credit: Kansas State Historical Society)

Copy: advertisement.

Albuquerque and small towns west across Arizona, eventually reaching into California.

In 1886, the Santa Fe began its march to the Gulf of Mexico through Indian Territory (Oklahoma), and Texas high-plains cattle country. Harvey opened houses in Guthrie and Purcell, Oklahoma, and in the Texas Panhandle on the banks of the Canadian River. The same principles used in Topeka were applied to all other Harvey Houses. The Santa Fe provided coal, ice, water, and other provisions free of charge, and all Harvey employees were given free passage on the line.

By the late 1880s, Santa Fe passengers could find a Harvey House every hundred miles along the entire line. The first structures were of frame construction, under the same roof as the Santa Fe's depot and offices. In the more remote parts of New Mexico and Arizona, Harvey Houses were even found in boxcars, but Harvey made no excuses for these houses: they were to look the same inside as any other house. The food was to be fresh and gourmet, the linen clean, the silver polished and gleaming.

Harvey's good taste and immaculate manners influenced young communities along the Santa Fe. With the entire railroad at his disposal, Harvey could import items of convenience and even luxury to places no one could previously afford to bring them:

> *Where the name Fred Harvey appears, the traveling public expects much. It may be on the desert of Arizona, a hundred miles from water, but if it is a Fred Harvey place, you get filtered spring water, ice, fresh fruit and every other good thing you can find at the same season in the best places in New York City or Chicago. How the miracle occurs, you do not know—it is a Fred Harvey concern—that is enough.* [11]

"Meals by Fred Harvey" became the slogan of the Santa Fe Railway. The Santa Fe made enough of a profit through increased ticket sales on its line to subsidize Harvey's restaurants and hotels, which usually operated at a loss. But Harvey preferred—in fact demanded—that his establishments lose money. It assured him that his standard was being maintained:

> *Harvey made no secret of the fact that he was giving more in food and service than he was taking in in currency. At one depot hotel there had been a steady loss of $1,000 a month until an ambitious manager came along and, with an eye to gaining the good graces of his employer, cut portions and corners until the loss had been pared to a mere $500. Outraged, Harvey fired him at once, and started looking around for a manager who would promise to lose the original sum.*[12]

The customer-drawing power of Fred Harvey justified the Santa Fe's half of the partnership:

> *Has it ever occurred to you how much Fred Harvey meals are worth to us as an advertising feature? Probably at no other time is the public so critical of their food service or cuisine as when traveling. There may be several reasons for this, among them the tedium of the journey and the inability of the average traveler to fully occupy his time. . . .*
>
> *Fred Harvey has become a byword for all that is good in the way of railway meals, be it dining room or dining car, and consequently our little slogan, 'Fred Harvey Meals all the Way' has a world of meaning to it.*[13]

At last, someone had challenged the assumption that western train travel and personal comfort were incompatible, and won. Harvey and the Santa Fe had forged the way; the standard was set. Although improvements in services on all western railroads quickly followed, the Harvey system was always a step ahead of its contemporaries, and nearly impossible to match.

Acting as his own supervisor, Harvey visited each and every one of his Harvey Houses on a regular, and usually unannounced, basis. In a manner that would be imitated by Harvey inspectors until the middle of the twentieth century, Harvey's location inspections were not just of house accounts and food orders (he kept a close eye on these as well), but were of the hands-on variety: he dusted his handkerchief across countertops, windowsills, and pantry boards; he examined plates for chips (if he found one, the plate was placed in the trash); he could overturn a poorly set table, or dismiss a waitress with a poor attitude:

Some Harvey inspections reminded me of the army. The
superintendent didn't just glance in the kitchen, greet the chef,
and inquire after his health. He looked the place over as if he
suspected a murder had been committed and the search was for
clues. If he found a pitcher of orange juice in the refrigerator, you
would think they were about to serve the guests arsenic. Orange
juice was to be squeezed out as needed so it would be fresh.
Storing it in the refrigerator for use later was an intolerable
attempt to get out of a little work.[14]

Harvey was a strict and awe-inspiring boss, but his uncompromising
values, good pay, and fair promotions for employees who "kept up the
standard" won him a loyal and respectful family of managers, chefs, and
Harvey Girls:

Fred Harvey's desire was always to place the comfort and pleasure
of his patrons first. One day a guest complained to Mr. Harvey
that a certain manager had not dealt with him fairly. Of course,
Mr. Harvey called the manager's attention to the matter. The
manager replied that the guest was a regular crank. Whereupon
the manager was informed that he was hired to please just that
kind of people [sic].[15]

The staff at all Harvey Houses, whether in a bustling city like Topeka,
or in the middle of nowhere in Ashfork, Arizona, was large. A typical house
(with a lunchroom, a dining room, and without extensive hotel facilities)
would include, in order of importance, a manager, a chef, a head waitress,
between fifteen and thirty Harvey Girls, a baker, a butcher, several assistant cooks and pantry girls, a housemaid, and busboys. The entire house
operated under the authority of superintendents from Harvey's offices in
Kansas City and Chicago, who visited each establishment on a regular
basis.

In the chapters that follow, the women and men who comprised the staff
at Harvey Houses throughout the Southwest are portrayed in detail. Although Harvey was considered a fair and honest employer, who rewarded
his employees with promotions and with vacations and railroad passes, the

prospects for upward mobility within the system were different for its male and female employees.

For Harvey Girls promotion was usually fairly given and even guaranteed if an employee worked steadily for a number of years. Harvey Girls worked their way up through a house, wearing badges with numbers indicative of their position among the waitresses. A Harvey Girl could eventually become a head waitress, which afforded better pay, a different and often distinctive uniform, and a single room in the women's dormitory. If a woman remained in the system long enough, and worked hard enough to attract attention from the head offices and various Harvey higher-ups, she could even become a manager. Women managers were rare but they were treated equally in terms of job description and pay.

However, for other Harvey House female employees—maids, and kitchen help—there was little or no prospect of promotion into the ranks of the Harvey Girls. Promotion for male Harvey employees was more extensive: any male employee—busboy, bellhop, dishwasher—could conceivably work his way out of the kitchen and into the main dining room as maître 'd, behind the newsstand as manager, even into the house manager's quarters.

Lacking the certainty that would have been afforded by Harvey employee records, it can still be assumed that Harvey hired only white women—though this included European and Mediterranean women—as Harvey Girls. With a handful of exceptions during World War II, when Hispanic and Indian women were hired as troop train waitresses, Harvey Girls were always white. Black, Hispanic, and Indian women were never recruited as waitresses. Minority workers, both male and female, dominated the kitchens of Harvey Houses from Kansas to California. But Harvey placed only white women in Harvey Girl uniforms and in direct contact with the traveling public, with black and other minority women working as maids, dishwashers, and pantry girls.

Harvey was considered by contemporaries to be an honorable, even progressive, employer in terms of his treatment of women; but his employee practices were in fact discriminatory towards minority women, and maintained the status quo in American business with respect to the position of blacks, Hispanics, and Indians. The majority of Harvey's minority workers, both male and female, occupied the bottom of the system's scale in pay and responsibility. The Harvey organization did offer some mobility to

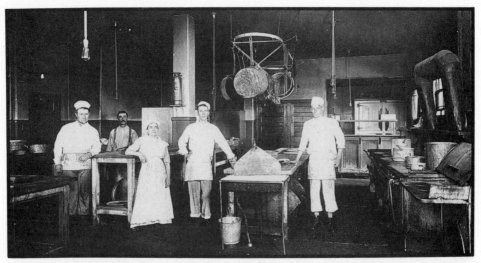

Every Harvey House kitchen crew, like this group in Syracuse, Kansas, 1915, was always ready for a spot inspection of countertops, cupboards, pots, pans, food, even kitchen walls and floors. Harvey superintendents regularly disembarked trains unannounced for a "tour" of a house's standards. (Credit: Olive Loomis, husband far right)

Dining room, Syracuse, Kansas, 1909. A conductor circulated the cars on a Santa Fe train speeding towards a meal stop at a Harvey House, asking if a passenger preferred the more expensive dining room meal, or the a la carte service of the lunchroom. These totals were wired ahead from the next telegraph stop, enabling the Harvey Girls, chefs, busboys, and House staff to prepare for the arrival of the train. Tables were set, the food was prepared, coffee was hot and ready; the dining room was ready to leap into exact and efficient service as the train rolled into the depot. (Credit: Margaret Becker Crist)

"The manager of a Fred Harvey Eating House must be in accord with the Fred Harvey system. He must be intelligent, quiet, alert, courteous. Everything about the place must reflect decency, order, thrift, cleanliness, good cheer, system." Elbert Hubbard, Leavenworth Times, 1905. The manager, D. Adams, stands to the right, his wife, the house bookkeeper, on the stairs behind him; 1915, Syracuse, Kansas. (Credit: Olive Loomis)

"The girls at a Fred Harvey place never look dowdy, frowsy, tired, slipshod or overworked. They are expecting you—clean collars, clean aprons, hands and faces washed, nails manicured— there they are, bright fresh healthy and expectant." Elbert Hubbard, Leavenworth Times, 1905. (Credit: Margaret Becker Crist, far right)

its male minority employees (see Chapter 6). But the majority of the Harvey upper echelon (with the exception of European chefs specially sought out and hired by Harvey), both male and female, were white Americans.

Although most Harvey employees spoke of surprise visits by superintendents as frightening and intimidating, they were often very good friends with the Harvey management. People liked working in a Harvey House. The pay ranged from fair to very good, depending on position, and benefits included room and board, railroad passes, and a place in the Harvey extended family. This meant job security, because a Harvey Girl or long-time employee would be moved to another house in the event of a closure; often requests for a particular location were honored. Thus, a modest income could go a long way.

Serving at least two, and more often three, meal trains a day meant coping with a highly concentrated rush hour several times in a twelve-hour period. Trains had a maximum stopping time of thirty minutes, but if the Harvey employees were in a frenzied rush, it was kept from the passengers. They knew that in a Harvey House, the meal they ordered would be served and enjoyed with plenty of time before the "all aboard" sounded.

Harvey cooks and waitresses were given an advance warning by telegraph of the numbers of people who would be in the lunchroom and dining room. When the train pulled in to the depot, a gong sounded and passengers were ushered into the Harvey House, where the staff and food were ready and waiting. In the dining room, prices were higher and men were required to wear jackets. If they did not have one, the house would provide one. (The "coat rule" was often the cause of controversy, especially in small, frontier towns where it was viewed with disdain by local cowboys. The rule was challenged legally in 1921 in Oklahoma, and ruled discriminatory. But the decision was appealed and in 1924 was set aside by the Supreme Court of Oklahoma.)

With the aid of the railroad's ice cars, Harvey brought fresh whitefish from the Great Lakes to the deserts of Arizona and New Mexico; California cantaloupes, fresh and cold, to the humid prairie of Kansas; sage-fed quail to the mining towns of Colorado; and Texas beef to southern California. Sea turtles and sea celery from the Gulf of Mexico were standard fare at the Montezuma Hotel in Las Vegas, New Mexico. Good water was brought in to many communities to ensure that Harvey's special blend of coffee would not be spoiled by alkali. And dairy products, including ice cream, were supplied by Harvey's own dairies located at Newton, Kansas; Del Rio, Arizona; La Junta, Colorado; Las Vegas, New Mexico; and Temple, Texas.

A Harvey House menu in the 1880s might include bluepoint oysters on the half shell, English pea soup au gratin, roast sirloin of beef au jus, pork with apple sauce, salmi of duck, queen olives, New York ice cream, bananas, grapes, oranges, Edam and Roquefort cheese, French coffee, and homemade pie. (Harvey House pies were always sliced into four servings, not the traditional six.) The price for a meal was seventy-five cents. A passenger was guaranteed a satisfied, if somewhat enlarged, belly, insuring a measure of gastronomic safety should the train run into delay somewhere on the frontier.

The food along the line was coordinated so that if a passenger had chicken in Needles, he had steak or fish in Barstow. The menus rotated every four days, and Harvey chefs exchanged recipes, all authorized by Fred Harvey.

The Harvey Girls joined Fred Harvey's empire along the Santa Fe in 1883. The first waitresses were hired in Raton, New Mexico, when Harvey fired all of his waiters because of poor service. According to Tom Gable, interviewed by Erna Fergusson in the 1930s, the waiters were blacks who had become involved in a midnight brawl, and were "carved beyond all usefulness, and the manager was distracted. Fred Harvey had no use for distraction in managers, so he fired that worthy along with his entire force."[16] Mr. Gable became manager the same day, and suggested to Harvey that women might be employed because they were less likely "to get likkered up and go on tears. . . . Those waitresses were the first respectable women the cowboys had ever seen—that is, outside of their own wives and mothers. Those roughnecks learned manners."[17]

Harvey's new waitresses were so popular in the community and among railroad passengers and employees that he decided to replace all the waiters on the line. Harvey advertised in midwestern and eastern newspapers and women's magazines for "young women 18 to 30 years of age, of good character, attractive and intelligent," to go west to work.[18]

Skeptics said the kind of woman Harvey wanted would not work for him.

The world of railroad men, frontier towns, and cattle empires with saloons, prostitutes, and general lawlessness was no place for a single young lady to venture without a father and several brothers to protect her virtue. But Harvey had no intention of letting the Wild West ruin a good idea; it had not stopped him before, and it would not stop him in 1883.

Harvey set about recruiting women to waitress the same way he had set about locating the finest food, furniture, chefs, and managers. Harvey set his sights on the best, and followed his own perfectionist methods to obtain it. After advertising in newspapers and magazines all over the country, Harvey set up an employment office in Chicago to review all applications and interview applicants. The formal application procedure was to be no empty pretense: Harvey wanted women who were well educated (in the 1880s, this meant having completed high school, or at least the eighth grade), and exhibited good manners, clear speech, and neatness in appearance. Vulgarity of any kind would not be tolerated. Upon acceptance, a young woman usually had only twenty-four hours to say her goodbyes at home before she began rigorous training. When a Harvey Girls signed her contract for twelve, nine, or six months, she agreed to learn the Harvey system, follow instructions to the letter, obey employee rules, accept whatever location she was assigned to for work, and abstain from marriage for the duration of her initial contract. Some women did break the marriage rule, but they forfeited their pay and railroad pass if they did so. Contracts in the early years were usually twelve months in length; later they were more often for nine or six months.

The women who answered his ads did so for many and varied reasons—economic considerations were the most prevalent, but adventure, a change of scene, and life in a new territory were also factors in young women's decisions to join Harvey in the West. In the chapters that follow, the details behind their choices to become Harvey waitresses and the reactions of their families and friends, are described at length.

With the regimentation of an army boot camp, Harvey initiated the Harvey Girls into service along the railroad. Harvey had no shortage of applicants—thousands of women applied and were accepted every year from 1883 until the 1950s. There were great variations and many exceptions to Harvey's rules over the years, but the women who were Harvey Girls were consistently good workers who charmed and impressed passengers on the Santa Fe for three quarters of a century:

Many children and grandchildren of former Harvey Girls boast
about their mother or grandmother being a true pioneer, and
coming west with the Harvey Houses. It carries a great deal more
prestige than coming west in a covered wagon. Anybody could ride
in a covered wagon, but only a lady could become a Harvey
Girl. [19]

Fred Harvey's mystique was fully developed upon his death on February 9, 1901. After suffering for more than fifteen years with intestinal cancer, Harvey died in Leavenworth, Kansas, where he and Sarah had raised their five children. His entire family was present when he died. Harvey had sought medical help in London and in California but even surgery with the world's most eminent surgeons proved useless. Writing of Harvey's death, *The Leavenworth Times* of February 10, 1901, declared that "during the prolonged illness of his last years he has had a struggle with pain of unusual intensity. Death comes as a rest and relief from suffering."

Fred Harvey was respected and well-liked in both business and civic circles. The *Times* article remembered that Harvey "was always ready to help every institution that was for the good of this community." Harvey was known for his "geniality, good nature, and integrity," and had "hosts of friends . . . both in Leavenworth and all over the country." Harvey's obituary recalled that the most pleasing part of Harvey's life "and the one which Mr. Harvey more highly valued than any other was the fact that during his lifetime he had the full confidence and highest esteem of these men with whom he had been associated," (op. cit.) citing among others, Santa Fe presidents William Barstow Strong and E. P. Ripley.

Business relations between the Santa Fe and Fred Harvey had been formalized back in May of 1889, when President Strong and Harvey signed a written contract giving Harvey first choice of all hotel/restaurant sites on the railroad's owned or leased lines. By the late 1890s, when Fred Harvey's sons Ford and Byron assumed leadership of their father's now enormous hotel and dining room chain, the Santa Fe Railway was fully cognizant of Harvey's role in their line's popularity in the West.

Fortunately for the railroad and for Harvey Houses, of which there were fifteen hotels, forty-seven lunch and dining rooms, and thirty dining cars on the new breed of deluxe trains, the Limiteds, the Harvey successors were as able, ambitious, and respectful of the Harvey "standard" and

"Keeping up the standard" in Emporia, Kansas, this Harvey Girl always wore a starched, spotless uniform. Uniforms were usually owned by the Harvey Girls themselves, but were laundered and even ironed at Newton. Harvey replaced the uniforms when they began to show wear, and a woman was given a refund for her uniforms when she left employment as a Harvey Girl, the amount determined by the condition of the uniforms. *(Credit: University of Arizona Special Collections)*

Byron Harvey (right) is shown in a favorite family portrait. Seated with him below the painting of Fred Harvey are his father, Byron S. Harvey, Sr., and his son Byron III.
(Credit: Hospitality Magazine)

Harvey Girls on train, circa 1917.
(Credit: Joanne Stinelichner George)

methods of operation as their father. In 1906, the trustees of the Harvey estate organized Fred Harvey, a closed corporation chartered in New Jersey. This corporation entered into another formal contract with the Santa Fe and the two continued their business partnership until December of 1968.

Over the next sixty years, there was always a Harvey man in charge of the Harvey business. Son Byron led the organization for half a century. Fred Harvey's three grandsons, Stewart, Daggett, and Byron, Jr., also took leading roles in the Harvey corporation in the 1940s. The Harvey men did not rest on their famous ancestor's reputation, but brought with them a variety of acquired skills and degrees: Byron, Jr., majored in philosophy at Stanford University and then worked as a stock clerk in the basement of Chicago's Carson, Pirie Scott & Company before joining the Harvey empire. Stewart Harvey attended Yale but left school to work in the Palmer House kitchen before leaving to work his way to vice president of his grandfather's corporation. Daggett Harvey, also a Yale man, worked at jobs around the Grand Canyon, earned a law degree, and later became Harvey vice president in charge of legal matters.

A fourth grandson, Frederick H. Harvey, served as vice president in the 1930s, but was killed at the age of forty when his plane crashed into the Allegheny mountains. Before his death, Frederick Harvey attended Harvard, joined the Army Signal Corps where he served as captain, and later became a director of Transcontinental and Western Air, where he was a veteran pilot.

The "Sage of Emporia," the renowned William Allen White, was a loyal customer of Fred Harvey, and made no attempt to hide his partiality to him and the Santa Fe. A frequent passenger on U. S. railroads, White often testified that the Santa Fe had the best food to be found in American train travel. Fred Harvey may have died, but his influence continued for many decades:

The table service of the Santa Fe route is furnished by the Fred Harvey system. It is the best in America. The Harvey system is in a class by itself. The service is better, quicker, cheaper, cleaner, more intelligent. And intelligence is the secret of good cooking as well as any other of the fine arts. And the head of the Harvey system has now and has had from the beginning, intelligence and

*nerve. That combination, by the way, is the essence of luck. Many
people, indeed most people, are smart enough—Fred Harvey . . .
was a great man because he dared to force his theories of good
service into reality.[20]*

Eleven years after Fred Harvey's death, there were more than sixty-five
eating houses on the Santa Fe and Frisco railroads, a dozen large hotels
and sixty dining cars in the Harvey system. They employed about five
thousand people, half of whom were women. In 1930, one writer claimed
that Harvey served fifteen million meals a year—the equivalent of provid-
ing a town of fourteen thousand people with three meals a day for one
year.[21]

*Mr. Harvey's genius for administration is displayed in an
efficiency system which is unrivaled in all business enterprises of
America. It ranges from the more prosaic details of a microscopic
system of auditing, to the rifling of the markets of the world for
the materials which go upon his table. His architectural artistry is
evidenced by the beauty and the refinements of the buildings
which are scattered from Kansas City to the Pacific.[22]*

In the late 1940s, the Harvey system operated approximately fifty restaurants, a dozen major hotels, one hundred newsstands, and several dozen
retail shops, and supervised the service on over one hundred Santa Fe
dining cars. Meals by Fred Harvey were even found on several airlines.
Harvey superintendents and disguised officials no longer yanked the table-
cloth off a poorly set table, but they did continue their mentor's habit of
unannounced visits to various Harvey Houses, and would still fire a manager for cutting corners on quality and customer service. One diligent
manager of a late 1940s Harvey House said "when I want more business,
I serve roast beef that is twice as thick as a boy's hand and half as broad
as his chest. That brings them in."[23] This quote would have made Fred
Harvey, whose legendary last words are reputed to have been, "Don't cut
the ham too thin," smile.

Other restaurateurs called the Harvey method of operation in the mid-
twentieth century "economic suicide," echoing Harvey competitors of the
late 1800s who had questioned Harvey's insistance to operate at a loss.

Union Station newsstand, gift shop; Harvey operations at union stations in Cleveland, Kansas City, St. Louis, Chicago and Los Angeles included barbershops, several newsstands, a liquor shop, private dining room, a restaurant, coffee shop, cafeteria, haberdashery, candy and fruit stand, miniature department store, a cocktail lounge and soda fountain. Harvey was among the first to market its own name-brand "designer" goods—Fred Harvey hats, shirts, shaving cream, candy, playing cards, even Harvey Special Blend Scotch Whiskey. In 1948, Harvey packaged its own select coffee for public sale; the blend was already famous among Sante Fe travelers, and Harvey sold 7,000 pounds in the first two weeks.
(Credit: University of Arizona Special Collection)

The Chicago Union Station, ca. 1915, like that at Kansas City, was an imposing structure to a young farm girl called in for an interview at the Harvey offices located inside. Two women employment agents, one each at Chicago and Kansas City, interviewed and hired nearly all Harvey Girls. Many Harvey Girls were hired on the spot: Harvey's staff knew a potential Harvey Girl when they saw one.
(Credit: University of Arizona Special Collections)

Chicago Union Station Fred Harvey Coffee Shop. (Credit: University of Arizona Special Collections)

Portable trackside newsstand.
(Credit: University of Arizona Special Collections)

Little changed in the Harvey "standard" from the day it was established to the day it was absorbed into modern history.

Both the Santa Fe and Fred Harvey were visionaries; both initiated and served a new age in American transportation and public exploration and mobility. The scope of their partnership reflected the beginning of a time when mass transportation would influence and expand all avenues of human endeavor, male and female.

CHAPTER · 4

The Harvey Girls

T HERE HAS BEEN A GREAT DEAL of historical and sociological discussion about women's lives in, and attitudes about, the western frontier. Women in the mid-1800s have been described both as weary, forlorn frontier wives, and as sturdy helpmates and civilizers in the American West.[1] Although the position of women in western communities is somewhat disputed—were they liberated or passive participants? happy or disappointed settlers?— their role on the trail during the move out west is generally agreed to have been one of great strength in the face of numerous emotional and physical unknowns. Women may have worked side by side with their husbands, fathers, and brothers en route west, but this did not necessarily mean they adopted new attitudes and behavior once they were settled into their new western homes. Some historians, in fact, believe they returned to their former sphere of house and family with a new zest and appreciation of the status quo: "They had never been told to look for adventure, excitement, freedom. . . . The essential things, for them, were relationships with other people, and cultural, social, and religious activities."[2]

Though the American West may have given men the opportunity to redefine themselves, to develop a new character unique to the new region, historians of women are gathering evidence that the West did not necessarily offer the same chance for re-evaluation of the eastern status quo for its women emigrants.[3] After months of struggle and hard work on the trail west, encountering situations and emotions never before known or even heard of, women often settled into their new environments intent on reconstructing their former lives:

Their behavior and their attitude toward their family, their attempts to replicate female culture suggest that their new environment, although it changed what they did, had only a limited impact on their views.[4]

While men "drank, gambled, speculated, made deals, invested, lost and won"[5] in the spirit of a new country, with room for personal exploration and risk taking, many women set about rebuilding and transplanting traditional views of the "woman's sphere" in their new communities. Liberation may have been a side effect, rather than a motivating force or premeditated goal, for women in the new society of the American West.

But there were aspects of the West attractive to women for quite traditional reasons, especially in the late 1800s. The prospect of finding a husband was very good; in 1870, a census listed 172,000 women to 385,000 men from the Mississippi River to the Pacific Ocean.[6] Sending single schoolteachers out west became a form of social action in the late nineteenth century. Single teachers were thought to be "on the road to honorable independence and extensive usefulness" and were not to worry about overstepping the boundaries of a woman's place.[7] Because women so outnumbered men in New England, many social activists advocated opening the "door of emigration to young women who are wanted as teachers, and for every other appropriate as well as domestic employment in the remote west," because those single women were "leading anxious and useless lives in New England."[8] Catharine E. Beecher, sister of Harriet, wrote a book about the need for women to go west to civilize and Christianize, entitled *The Duty of American Women to Their Country*, urging, "Go West, Young Woman." Beecher's plea caught the attention of many people, including one newspaper editor who wrote:

> *To supply the bachelors of the west with wives, to furnish the pining maidens of the east with husbands, and to better equalize the present disposition of the sexes on these two sections of our country, has been one of the difficulties of our age. . . .*[9]

The East was hardly out to liberate young women with its pleas for them to go west, work, and marry, but inadvertently, this may have been the result for many women. Female schoolteachers were not given equal pay, but they did have opportunities for advancement, and were often prominent in western communities, involved in public life and leadership to a degree rare in the East. Women in the West usually sought work that was within the limits of the female sphere of family and home, such as teaching and working as cooks and laundresses. But ranching and homesteading were also considered acceptable for a woman, because they were connected to home and family life.[10] Hotel and restaurant work were within the home sphere—both were necessary to a town's early survival and growth, when so many men and women were without their own homes—and so women who started hotels and opened dining facilities were community builders.

Extreme stereotypes have been perpetuated in popular literature about women in the West in the 1800s. There were the hardened prostitutes and dance hall queens of the cattle and railroad towns, the "soiled doves" of the West, many of whom became wealthy and prosperous citizens, earning a place in the community through their material means. There were the pistol-carrying "bad girls," ruffians with little to distinguish them from their male counterparts save their names or female physiques buried beneath the boot and chaps worn by all good outlaws.

But the less notorious western women were the successful, single and married women ranchers and homesteaders, teachers, missionaries, hotelkeepers, shopowners, even newspaper publishers and mining company supervisors. By 1850, most western states legally allowed women to homestead land. In 1886, it has been estimated that one-third of the land in the Dakotas was under ownership of women. During the land rushes into the

Indian territory of Oklahoma in the 1890s, there was one all-female "sooner company," so-called because it managed to enter and establish its claims ahead of the scheduled runs into Cherokee and Arapaho lands. Another company of twenty-two women established a claim of 480 acres in the Cherokee Strip. Both groups were successful in the development of their farms.[11]

On western ranches, women were usually found in the home, raising children, cooking, keeping the domestic life of the ranch operating. But women were often found working alongside their husbands during ranch roundups, branding, and fence mending. And widows of ranchers often took over their former spouse's business, becoming as knowledgeable and competent at herd and land management as their husbands were.[12]

Women doctors found wider acceptance in the West: under Brigham Young, Mormon women in Utah were encouraged to pursue medicine as early as 1873. Michigan, Oregon, and Kansas had all established coeducational medical schools by 1893. "Everywhere in the West, by the end of the nineteenth century, women were entering new professions and businesses and were finding new roles outside the recognized scope of woman's place."[13]

Historians may argue whether these opportunities in the business and personal spheres changed the way women thought of themselves, but they generally agree that the society of the West gave the women freer rein in business ventures, more involvement in community life, and the opportunity for economic advancement. We know that many women did not openly or consciously challenge their roles, or overtly question their way of thinking about themselves, yet the popular literature of the period often claimed, true or not, that the West offered influence and power to women who ventured into it.[14] There seemed to be a collision of signals and values: a chance for women to expand their roles in the new West, along with an equally strong expectation that they would maintain the status quo.

Was it easier, or even better, to be a working single woman in the West than elsewhere? It probably was. Because so many women came west to work, it became common and accepted for single women to work and live away from home. A working single woman was a familiar and even necessary part of early western communities. The single woman in the West may have ultimately wanted the same things as her eastern sister—marriage and security—but while working and living on her own, she was not risking her good reputation and choice of respectable suitors. People in the West stretched their ideas of acceptable behavior; they had to because their own lives demanded it. The West was new and so were many of the nuances of its society.

What might appear today to be strict and unnecessarily stifling rules imposed on the Harvey Girls were really necessary guidelines that assured the public that these single women, hundreds of miles from home, were upstanding and respectable citizens. And the women themselves were thus promised that their status as ladies would be protected by their employer.

These were not idle concerns in the 1880s and 1890s. The early Harvey Girls had several serious stigmas to overcome in their work. First, as already discussed, single women living on their own, away from the protective eye of a mother and father, were socially suspicious in many parts of the country. Single, wage-earning women at the turn of the century were often labeled "adrift." Society's moralists were concerned about the welfare of these young women who comprised 16 percent of the female work force in large eastern cities.[15] These women usually worked in factories and lived in boarding or rooming houses, with few close relationships and only subsistence-level incomes. The fear among moralists was that the impoverished circumstances of these women, combined with distance from home and parental guidance, would lead them into prostitution.

Secondly, all working women were viewed as occupying the very bottom of the American female social scale, and waitressing itself was among the lowest professions a woman could choose. The Harvey Girls, unknowingly in most cases, challenged these public attitudes, possibly changing the opinion of many a staunch conservative who met pleasant, attractive, intelligent Harvey Girls from one end of the Santa Fe line to the other. Still, it was not easy. The social and economic climate surrounding the Harvey Girls was not for the weak at heart. The saying went, "No ladies west of Dodge City; no women west of Albuquerque."[16] What could be an adventure for a spirited woman might be a nightmare for her meeker sister.

To middle-class women of the 1800s, wage earning itself was a social and economic transgression.[17] Work, with the exception of teaching and nursing, was avoided by all "nice girls." Even a young, lower-class woman terminated her job as soon as she married. The social climate was so overwhelmingly disapproving of married women working that it was not until 1910 that even 10 percent of the female work force was married.[18] The full-time homemaker in the late nineteenth century was the epitome of the successful woman. Women who were not of the upper classes worked in marginal, underpaid jobs until they married, when they hoped to be fortunate enough to work as homemakers.[19]

By the turn of the century there were clear lines drawn between the work appropriate to "proper" white middle-class women on one hand, and black, poor, and immigrant women on the other.[20] The "best" jobs for women were in teaching and nursing, both attainable only to those with a good education, and hence out of reach for lower-class women. If a middle- or upper-class woman wanted to work, she would nurse or teach to maintain her social position. The next best jobs were found in offices and department stores. At the bottom of the female work scale was factory work, domestic service, and waitressing. There were strict social boundaries drawn between these jobs, with black and immigrant women usually occupying the bottom, and middle-class WASPS the top.

Even at the bottom of the wage-earning ladder there were many prejudices about certain jobs. Domestic service, with its "advantages" of better pay and a healthier work environment, was shunned by many lower-class women who favored more "prestigious" factory and industrial work: a servant was a servant. Factory work was considered respectable employment among wage-earning women, but a maid was an underling, her apron "the badge of the servant." A factory girl was independent and enjoyed a high enough social standing to be "received in good circles."[21] Even the possibilities of consumption, pneumonia, and industrial accidents while working long hours in poorly lit, badly ventilated sweatshops did not outweigh the stigma attached to the demoralizing and socially inferior position of domestic servant. This stigma applied directly to serving food to the public. Waitressing was considered inferior even to domestic work.

Waitressing in the East was a degrading occupation. Waitresses were considered to be coarse and hard, too free in their manners and speech. A waitress usually earned more than either a domestic servant or a factory girl, but the social disgrace of the job was more than money could compensate for. In 1920, a reporter named Frances Donovan donned a waitress's uniform and began working in restaurants in order to study waitresses. Shocked at first by her co-workers' sexual lives, and the easy manner in which they related their experiences in unbecoming and off-color language, Donovan eventually came to admire and respect these hardworking, socially snubbed women.[22]

In the West, to the aforementioned beliefs regarding waitressing were added several peculiar to the region: the high male-female ratio in western communities, coupled with the abundance of music and dance halls where some meals and many drinks were sold by "pretty waitress girls" who were reputed to double as prostitutes, heightened the public's suspicion towards all waitresses. (In fact, a survey of California prostitutes in 1888 revealed this to be an erroneous assumption: only 2 of the 471 women questioned claimed previous work experience as a waitress.)[23] Public eateries abounded in new western towns where transient residents were often a majority. Saloons, eateries, lunchrooms, boardinghouses, restaurants—all blurred together in the western frontier, and standards for waiters and waitresses were hard to come by. The informality found in these crowded establishments often encouraged waiters and waitresses to take social liberties, such as joining in a patron's conversation or offering an opinion when one was most certainly not sought. Among the socially sophisticated, western waiters and waitresses were considered even coarser than their counterparts back east.

With so much against him, how did Fred Harvey find, hire, and manage to keep so many "nice" women in his restaurants as Harvey Girls? Harvey either ignored the universal understanding that waitressing was at the bottom of the scale and could not possibly be treated as a "good job," or he believed from the outset that his Harvey Girls would be so much more than waitresses that the usual labels would not apply. He changed the ideals, or lack thereof, associated with waitressing just as he had changed those associated with railroad food and service. Perhaps it was his English background and subsequent assumptions regarding passenger services, but Harvey cared little for other people's opinions and attitudes. His way— the vaunted "Harvey standard" that would one day bring to the traveler's mind immaculate facilities, gourmet food, and unvarying, sophisticated service—was the only way, period. And it would overcome all obstacles, real, implied, historic, social, and otherwise.

Harvey made serving food in the West into a profession and joining the staff of a Harvey House into a way of life. And because Harvey really believed in the value of his restaurants and hotels, so did his employees.

The women who were Harvey Girls still contended with social prejudice and bias, but considering the time in which they lived, and the work they did, they were treated quite well. The fact that most of their customers were transcontinental passengers on the Santa Fe, and were often wealthy and worldly, gave the Harvey Girls a better class of clientele than a waitress in a New York cafe. The entire atmosphere of their lives was regulated, ordered, and clean. Among working women in America, Harvey put them in a class by themselves.

The signing of a six- or nine-month contract with the Harvey company in Kansas City or Chicago meant agreeing to comply with a highly organized and strictly observed set of rules and regulations, which included a promise not to marry during the contracted time. Harvey Girls accepted mandatory residence in a Harvey House dormitory, usually upstairs in the house itself and often in beautiful and well-kept rooms. The women lived two to a room, with a house mother or matron acting as a chaperone. A strict curfew was enforced at all houses and was the same for a woman whether she was eighteen or forty years of age. Special permission could be obtained from the house manager to stay out later, but the doors were locked at curfew. Many a Harvey Girl tells of being locked out and persuading the night cook to let her in the back door, or climbing up a tree to a friend's window. Men were forbidden in the women's dorm, although there was usually a parlor where men and women could meet.

The appearance of the Harvey Girls mirrored the appearance of the Harvey Houses: clean, businesslike, and efficient, with little or no personal variation from person to person or place to place. Their uniform, hair, and makeup codes were outlined in detail by Fred Harvey. Harvey must have been acutely aware of the opportunity for public criticism of single women away from home, and so he dressed the Harvey Girls in outfits befitting a nun: plain, starched, black-and-white skirts, bibs, and aprons; and high-collared shirts, with black shoes, black stockings, and hairnets. The uniform was first introduced in 1883 and changed little over the next fifty years. Skirts, even in the 1920s when styles shortened, were precisely eight inches from the floor. Harvey Girls wore no jewelry and could not chew gum or wear any makeup. "I heard stories about the early years," Harvey Girl Violet Bosetti Grundman remembers, "about how the management would take a damp cloth and run it over a girl's face to make sure she had absolutely no makeup on!"

In many Harvey Houses, the girls at the lunch counter wore all-black uniforms, while those in the dining room wore all white; in other years, it was exactly opposite. But the Harvey Girls always wore black and white, the only exceptions coming in the 1920s when the waitresses at the Grand Canyon hotels at La Posada, La Fonda, and the Alvarado wore full Mexican-style skirts and blouses for special occasions. And for the weekend of the annual Rough Riders Reunion in Las Vegas, New Mexico, Castañeda Harvey Girls were outfitted in denim cowboy skirts and vests.

If a woman spilled on a uniform, she immediately changed into a clean one no matter how small the stain. Each Harvey Girl had several sets of uniforms, sometimes owned by the house, other times owned by the women themselves. Harvey Girls did not launder their own uniforms. For many years, all house laundry, including the uniforms of the staff, was sent to Newton, Kansas, or Needles, California, by train. The women did, however, spend long hours starching and ironing each uniform they wore.

Harvey Girls worked six- and seven-day weeks, usually twelve hours a day, often in split shifts around meal trains. When they were not serving customers, they polished (and polished and polished) the house silverware, kept their stations spotless, and prepared for the next meal rush. Harvey's system left little free time for any of its employees, male or female. Reflecting on their long days of constant duty, Harvey Girls often protested the old accusation that they were troublemakers ("wild" single women) in communities along the railroad: "We didn't have *time* to do all the bad things people claimed we were doing!" Like a domineering and watchful father, Harvey kept his Harvey Girls occupied "keeping up the standard" within his Harvey Houses. Harvey Girls were rarely, if ever, seen sitting together after the rush enjoying a cup of Harvey's famous coffee. Harvey Girls were not to be seen sitting *at all.* Keeping one's station "up to the standard" was not to be taken lightly by a waitress. It meant putting away everything that had been used, and leaving tables, chairs, countertops, salt and pepper shakers, coffee urns, *everything* spotless and gleaming. One Harvey Girl remembers a manager sending her upstairs to fetch another girl who had not left her station completely shining. She found the young woman soaking in a hot bath, exhausted after a fourteen-hour day. She told the manager but he instructed her to get the young woman out of the tub and downstairs, in uniform, immediately. There was no excuse for work left unfinished, and there were no exceptions to this rule in any house.

Most Harvey Girls could and did save money, even in the depression years when pay dropped from $50 a month in the 1920s to $30 in the 1930s. From the 1880s until the decline of the Harvey system in the 1940s, the wages of the Harvey Girls compared favorably with those of their contemporaries, skilled and unskilled, male and female. In the late 1800s, when a Harvey Girl was making approximately $17.50 a month plus tips, room, board, laundry and travel expenses ($210.00 annually, excluding tips), waiters in California averaged $48 a month, with meals but not room, and waitresses averaged exactly half that—$24 a month.[24] A male farm laborer of the same era averaged $11.70 a month plus board. A skilled laborer in manufacturing, again male, made an average of $54.24 a month, $650 a year, with no room or board added to his annual compensation. A woman employed as a public-school teacher earned $256 in the 1880s and 1890s, often with housing provided by small-town school boards.

From the turn of the century until the First World War, the Harvey Girls made approximately $25 a month plus tips, room, board, and travel. Many women banked most of their $300 annual pay, or sent it home to their families. In Denver, under union scales adopted in 1900, waiters were paid $12 a week plus meals, and waitresses $10 a week plus meals for the same seven-day workweek of eleven-hour days.[25] Domestic workers of the early 1900s earned an average of $240 a year, with liven-in maids or servants adding room and board to this annual income. At that time, a male or female worker in manufacturing averaged $487, and by 1910, $651, a year.[26]

Until the 1940s and the beginning of the Second World War, the Harvey Girls were undoubtedly at the top of their profession's pay and personal treatment scale. Along with an implied promise from Harvey that her job was secure as long as she obeyed house rules, the tips earned at the large Harvey Houses—especially the resort hotels in Arizona and New Mexico—could double a woman's income. A Harvey Girl was also entitled to a leave of absence at the end of a six- or nine-month contract. Not only did this include job security after the vacation, but a ticket home and a meal pass en route.

Opal Sells Hill remembers being told in the 1920s, during her first year of work in Amarillo, that four years of employment with Harvey would earn her an expenses-paid vacation to California. Opal worked for four years and was treated to her trip to the West Coast, a guest at the Harvey dining rooms en route, and at Harvey Hotels wherever she stopped overnight or visited for a few days.

The only exceptions to the rail pass privilege existed in small-town Harvey Houses, where managers themselves often hired local women as Harvey Girls: in that case a railroad pass was not part of the arrangement.

The service routines were exact and religiously performed. When the train pulled into the depot, a bellboy or busboy rang a loud gong on the station platform, showing passengers where the lunch and dining rooms were located, as well as signaling Harvey employees to jump into action. The Harvey Girls stood silently at their assigned stations in the lunch or dining areas while passengers walked in and were seated. The first course consisted of fruit or salad, and was either waiting at each person's place, or was served immediately. A woman asked each person in the dining room what he or she cared to drink. The waitress then arranged the cup by each customer at a precise position that told the next waitress, who was pouring the drinks, what each person had ordered.[27] (The cup code did not include alcoholic beverages, which were served in cocktail lounges in many Harvey Houses and, in later years, in some Harvey restaurants. Except for the prohibition years, Fred Harvey served, and sold under its own label, a Scotch distilled by Ainslie & Heilbron in Glasgow, Scotland. Fred Harvey himself chose the distillery in 1896, and for many, many years, it was only through Harvey that this blend of Scotch whiskey could be purchased in the United States.)

Although the Harvey organization was famous for its tolerance and special care given to the "difficult customer," Harvey Houses were equally famous for their intolerance of variations in the rules:

One snowy, blustery day a friend and I arrived at a Harvey House, and the Southwest offers no more grateful refuge after a hard trip. Aching with cold and weariness, we longed for tea in front of the roaring fire in the lobby. But no, tea could not be served there, though seven employees stood about, doing nothing, and were ready to fetch it. The manager said he had no discretion; no authority nearer than Kansas City could grant our plea for tea taken cozily by the fire. So we perched, perforce, on tall stools in the lunchroom and drank our tea like nice children. The

*Harvey System, on such occasions, is like nothing so much as a
good old German nurse, starched and firm.*[28]

Fred Harvey needed a steady, reliable work force willing to be sent to
and moved about in the often remote regions of the American West. He
saw how to get that work force from the best source available, single
women, by giving them what they needed: security, income, a place to live
where they were not alone, and ample opportunities to meet prospective
husbands through daily contact with passengers and employees of the
Santa Fe Railway. In return, the Harvey Girls made the Harvey system
work.

If some Harvey Girls in retrospect appeared to be liberated (remaining
single long after most women their age or working for years after marriage), they were probably the exceptions and usually not aware of their
"liberation." And though Harvey allowed women to climb up into the ranks
of managers, the system's success lay to a large degree in its ability to use
women in roles in which they felt comfortable—as motherly, sisterly helpers—while giving them fair pay, promotion, and a sense of responsibility
and partnership in the success of a respected business. Harvey Girls knew
they made Harvey Houses what they were: the finest eating establishments in the West, even in the United States. They were proud of their
jobs, their skills, their professionalism. Fred Harvey gave thousands of
working women from lower-income families the opportunity to feel good
about themselves, whether single or married. Independence, self-esteem,
travel to interesting places, were all by-products of the system. The primary product was decent jobs for women in the American West.

The move west in the late 1800s and early 1900s was, for men, a chance
to break with the past, look at the world beyond the family porch, and begin
a new life. Fred Harvey gave young women a similar opportunity. Under
his paternal arm of authority and professional, yet extensive, concern, a
young woman could move about easily and safely, assured of a job, a place
to live, and people to care about her. She could often choose where she
wanted to work, knowing that if she did not like a location, she could leave
in six months without losing her job. A woman could take her time selecting
a spouse, knowing there would be no shortage of possible suitors, even
as she neared and passed the age of thirty. A sociologist could not have

invented a better method by which the West could become inhabited by so many young women anxious to take part in the building of a new region.

The phenomenon of the Harvey Girls may be unique in the settling and development of the West, but in the history of labor they are reminiscent of a group of working women found in New England in the early 1800s. The similarities of experience and opportunity between the Harvey Girls and the female mill workers of Lowell, Massachusetts, in the 1820s and 1830s are worthy of comparison. The Harvey Girls mirror the Lowell factory women both in the unusual social and cultural opportunities their employment afforded them, and in the extent of the structure and discipline imposed upon them by their employer.

The Lowell factory workers were young, single women from New England's rural communities hired to work as millhands in the textile factories of Lowell and other neighboring industrial centers. Single women found decent work, adequate income, and a supportive community of female workers at the Lowell mills. Part of an extensive corporation of textile mills owned by a group called Boston Associates, the Lowell factory system of operation was designed to make Massachusetts's mills the finest in the world.

The boarding house system introduced by Francis Cabot Lowell in 1821 was specifically designed to make New England's female mill workers a step above their American and European counterparts. Like Fred Harvey half a century later, the Lowell corporate fathers saw that good business came from a dependable, disciplined work force. And to attract that work force—in both cases, hundreds of single, unmarried women—the employer had to guarantee the safekeeping of young daughters away from home. Boston Associates sought to create a labor force "that would be a shining example of those ultimate Yankee ideals: profit and virtue, doing good and doing well."[29]

Paternalistic rules and regulations regarding work and leisure time insured respectability in Lowell, Massachusettes, just as they did at Harvey Houses throughout the Southwest a half century later. Curfews, dress codes, and a highly structured work and social environment served both to alleviate the doubts of fathers back home, and to enlarge corporate profits through the smooth functioning of the mills.

Lowell workers signed a year's contract, promising to give two-week notice should circumstances force early departure. However, many young women left without giving the proper notice, only to return and find themselves quickly rehired. As in the Harvey system, a trained worker was an asset. Active recruitment was unnecessary, as factory women often returned from a trip home with a younger sister. When one millhand married, she was often replaced by a younger sibling anxious to keep the Lowell paycheck within the family.

The female employees at Lowell and its related factories lived in boarding houses owned by the mills. The dormitories were mandatory for single women and were partially subsidized by the mill. The house mother was often a widow with a family who enforced dress and social codes, and maintained the rules of the house. The young women ate all their meals together, spent leisure time in common rooms, and were required to attend church. Any deviation from the rules of the house was punishable by dismissal and even company blacklisting.

Lowell women worked eleven- to thirteen-hour days, often in poorly lit rooms with inadequate ventilation. But their own stories, often published in *The Lowell Offering,* a widely acclaimed literary magazine that published the poems and stories of female mill workers, reflect their satisfaction with their situation. Although the work the Lowell factory women performed varied greatly from that of the Harvey Girls, the value of their work experience in the shaping of their lives is nearly identical: the mills of New England in the 1820s and 1830s, like the Harvey Houses of the late 1800s and early 1900s, offered many single women from rural backgrounds entry into a new world of cultural and economic opportunity, and allowed many to break definitively with their rural past.[30]

Like the Harvey Girls, Lowell workers became part of a community of women, a sisterhood of workers living away from home. And as the Harvey Girls also demonstrate in the stories that follow, Lowell women achieved an economic and social independence that set them apart: they became the upwardly mobile women of their generation, marrying later than their peers back home, and often controlling substantial bank accounts of their own. The Lowell workers usually traveled only a few miles from their rural homes to begin work, while the Harvey Girls traversed several hundred miles to a job in the Harvey system. But the consequences of their enlistment were the same: a new independence from parental authority, a vision of life and self that was centered upon personal choice, and social and cultural mobility.

It is not known if Fred Harvey was cognizant of the Lowell factory system. But his vision of how best to keep a large business running smoothly and efficiently through the recruitment and supervision of young, single women was strikingly similar to the approach of the Lowell planners to the milling of cotton in the early 1800s.

The names and stories of the very early Harvey Girls have survived only in small sketches and references found in histories of the Santa Fe Railway or of individual towns and communities along it. It is difficult to know what the Harvey Girls before the 1900s were really like—what they thought of their work in the Southwest, how they were treated by railroad men and travelers, if their work as waitresses was considered "special" for their times or just like all waitressing jobs everywhere.

Oral histories collected from women who were Harvey Girls after 1918 or so begin to reveal collective attitudes, thoughts, and experiences. Where possible in the following pages, the story is told by women who were Harvey Girls, and by people who worked with them in Harvey Houses and for the Santa Fe Railway. Through these personal reminiscences, common aspects of shared experiences of the Southwest, the railroad, and the Harvey Houses emerge. The personal stories placed together offer a fascinating portrait of the entire Harvey Girl era.

The story of one Raton Harvey Girl, circa 1885, has survived in the memory of her daughter-in-law. Although the experience of Minnie O'Neal, as told by Helen Gillespie, contains events probably not widely shared by other Harvey Girls of her era, her Kansas background, her year at a Harvey House, and her life as a New Mexico rancher's wife were similar to many Harvey Girls before the turn of the century.

Minnie O'Neal lived at home with her family in Leavenworth, Kansas, and was reputed to be very beautiful. Her father worked for the railroad. When Minnie turned eighteen, she was approached by a close family friend, Will Gable, to join the Harvey Girls. Gable was a Harvey supervisor, and although he was a trusted friend, Minnie's mother forbade her to leave home and work for him. After a year of unsuccessful recruitment, Gable found the O'Neals had changed their minds: they were separating and probably faced financial strains that made it necessary for Minnie to work. He was asked to find Minnie a job, and in 1885 he took her with him on the train to Raton, New Mexico, where she was to work as a Harvey Girl.

Although the Santa Fe Railway had reached Raton only six years earlier, Minnie found a thriving railroad community of some four hundred people. Raton was a railroad division point in those days, and Harvey had opened a Harvey House in a small, red, two-story frame structure next to the depot in 1882. To Minnie O'Neal's twenty-year-old eyes, the frontier town with its clapboard stores, saloons, and houses, surrounded by hundreds of square miles of mountain and high country meadowland, inhabited by railroad boomers, drifting miners, and cowboys following the cattle trails, was the real outback of America. If not for the little Harvey House, a woman like Minnie O'Neal would quite simply never have come to such a part of America.

Minnie's life, like that of all Harvey employees, revolved completely around the Harvey House. She lived in the dormitory provided for the girls and worked long days, her schedule centered around the arrival and departure of Santa Fe trains. The House served many railroadmen, who had special meal rates at all Harvey Houses, and also served local cowboys and ranchers, and local businessmen. The Raton Harvey House had one very distinguished patron—Senator Stephen W. Dorsey. Dorsey was a Republican from Arkansas who left the Senate, and Arkansas, after being accused of leading the Star Route Mail Fraud plot. Planning to become a cattle baron, Dorsey came with his wife Laura to New Mexico and built a thirty-five room mansion of stone on the northeastern plains forty miles southeast of Raton.

No doubt the senator had prestigious visitors at various times during the year, but even so, the eastern plains of New Mexico are a huge and empty place. The senator and his wife made frequent trips to Raton, where they could find a good meal and overnight lodgings in the Harvey House, a civilized establishment in New Mexico in the 1880s. Minnie O'Neal often served the Dorseys, and Mrs. Dorsey developed an interest in the young woman from Kansas. She must have seen the potential for a personal maid and helper in Minnie, who already knew the finer points of serving and accomodating the public. Minnie was offered a job at the Dorsey mansion within the year. She accepted and moved out of the Harvey House onto the Dorsey ranch in 1886.

It was inevitable that Harvey Girls in places like Raton met and fell in love with either cowboys or railroadmen. Minnie, although working as Mrs. Dorsey's personal maid, met and fell in love with Dorsey's ranch foreman, who Minnie had probably seen working around the house and barns, rounding up the cattle, and meeting with the senator in the evenings. Minnie was at work hardly a year at the Dorsey's when George Washington Gillespie asked her to marry him. She accepted and returned home to Kansas where they were married in 1887. The couple returned to New Mexico and took up claims in the mountains near Raton where they built their own house and ranch. On this remote homestead Minnie gave birth to six sons. One of her boys was named Will Gable Gillespie, but young Will died on his tenth Christmas when, out shooting and chasing rabbits with his older brothers, he fell on a gun and shot himself.

Most Harvey Girls of the 1880s and 1890s weren't wooed away to jobs in houses that boasted the elegance and distinction of the Dorsey Mansion (now a historic landmark), but they were in daily contact with America's distinguished travelers via the Santa Fe. And like Minnie, many never returned home, but raised families with husbands who had also left homes in the Midwest or East to begin something of their own out west. How could these young men have stayed if they had not found suitable partners together with whom the isolation and difficulties of a new frontier could be overcome and made into familiar territory?

Although many different kinds of women became Harvey Girls, as is demonstrated in the following pages, Minnie O'Neal, the Kansas small-town girl of lower-middle-class background, attractive, respected, with a future that would assuredly include marriage and a good home life, was a familiar type in turn-of-the-century Harvey Houses.

A study interested in portraying the Harvey Girls must begin with the women of rural, midwestern America. There were Harvey Girls from the East Coast, Harvey Girls from urban centers like Chicago, St. Louis, and Milwaukee; there were Harvey Girls from Europe and the British Isles— but the core of the Harvey Girls was made up of farmer's daughters and women from small-town America. They came from families that had come to Kansas, Missouri, Illinois, and Oklahoma to set up new lives. A large percentage—possibly as many as 50 percent—of the Harvey Girls were

The railroad trestle at Raton Pass in 1900 was a primitive structure in the middle of isolated, thinly settled mountain country. (Credit: Las Vegas Citizens Committee for Historic Preservation, Donnelly Library)

Santa Fe railroaders, Raton, New Mexico, 1894. (Credit: Arthur Johnson Memorial Library)

In 1894, the Raton Harvey House had five Harvey Girls, a head waitress, a manager, his wife and children, a cashier, a chef, a cook, a baker, several baker's helpers, a desk clerk, a housekeeper, housemother, and a busboy. (Credit: Arthur Johnson Memorial Library)

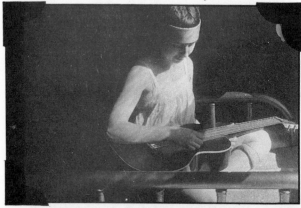

The women's dormitory in a Harvey House gave many rural girls the same experiences of shared life found in college dormitories. Unknown Harvey Girl, Gallup, New Mexico, 1920. (Credit: Ellen Jones)

La Posada, Winslow, Arizona, the last great Harvey House built by the Santa Fe in 1930. (Credit: University of Arizona Special Collections)

from rural America, the daughters of American pioneers, the first ones born in the new country of the land rushes, the homesteading acts, the farm country of the Great Plains. These families were the people by whom the new American West was built, upon whose efforts to relocate their lives on isolated homesteads, American society inched its way across the prairies toward the Pacific Ocean. They were often poor, always struggling, sometimes desperate. Many of their daughters found a way to help through hard times by working in the Harvey system. Some fathers and mothers were grateful that their daughters became Harvey Girls instead of housemaids or dime store part-timers. Others were reluctant to send their girls off to work as waitresses in some distant town along the railroad. But financial concerns, not social position, were the motivating factor.

For rural women, Harvey offered a kind of "higher education." College was out of the question for almost all of them. As Harvey Girls, they could travel and work, as well as meet and learn about people from many parts of the country and the world, and explore life beyond father's front gate or the local parish hall. Many of these rural women were disappointed with life farther west and returned home. But an equal number[31] never looked back and contributed to the development of communities in Arizona, New Mexico, California, Texas—anywhere the Santa Fe Railway had laid its rails.

Bertha Spears had already worked hard most of her life when she signed on with Harvey at the age of twenty-four. Born in rural Oklahoma in 1908, Bertha was raised with five brothers and sisters in a clapboard house with a stoop porch. "We had little patches of crops that couldn't nearly support us. The whole family worked their life away on those fields and still couldn't make a living at it."

Bertha went to a country school, working at home until her father would allow her to leave and go find work in a nearby town. "I went to a little town twelve miles from home and worked as a housekeeper. I was barely eighteen. Then I heard about work at a TB hospital so I went there." Bertha's family gave up trying to make their homestead work in the late 1920s, and Bertha went with them to Texas looking for a new start. After working hard to set up a new place, the depression began: "Things went from bad to worse. The first year we didn't make anything, and in 1930 we had to sell all of our stock. Then my mother died."

Bertha's father moved the family back to Oklahoma where they worked as tenant farmers. It was while in this unlikely position, as the daughter of a tenant farmer working long hours under the Oklahoma sun, a region fast turning into the Dust Bowl, that Bertha's life took a turn up and finally out of the difficult world of farming. The farmer for whom Bertha's family was working had a daughter home for a visit. Bertha remembers her first sight of that young woman, dressed "like a city lady, confident, worldly, and not stuck like I was on a farm in Oklahoma." The event changed her life:

Her name was Audrey and she was very beautiful and glamorous. She worked in Santa Fe and was just about my age. She was watching me. One day she asked me if I wanted a job with someone named Fred Harvey. I'd never heard of anyone named Fred Harvey but I figured if I could live and look like her, I would be happy to work for him. I told her I'd go anywhere in God's world for a job away from that farm. She wrote away to Kansas City and within a few weeks I had a railroad pass and a job in Winslow, Arizona. I honestly never believed anything that good would ever happen to me.

I had listened to my daddy all my life but now I was old enough to decide something for myself, so I took the job. He thought I had gone to the dogs when I left, but he didn't try to stop me. I got on the train and headed west, all alone. I didn't know anything about Harvey Houses; I just knew I was going out of Oklahoma. A woman got on the train in Clovis, New Mexico, and we got to talking . . . it turned out she had been a Harvey Girl and she took me under her wing the rest of the trip. She made me feel so good. When we arrived in Winslow, she handed me over to the bellboy. It was late at night, and he took me to a room in La Posada where I slept in the most elegant room I had ever seen. There was hand-carved furniture and beautiful rugs and paintings.

I was told to be at work at 8:00 the next morning. Even without an alarm clock I was up and ready on time. I was taken to the basement for my uniforms, and then to the dormitory, upstairs in the old Harvey House across the tracks from La Posada. I had my own room and I loved it all right away.

Bertha worked as the relief girl and was often sent out to the Grand Canyon, or to Williams or Ashfork, and even as far as Gallup, New Mexico, and San Bernardino to replace vacationing Harvey Girls and fill temporary vacancies:

I was called 'Tex' by everyone because they thought I was from Texas. I worked the lunchroom and the dining room, and although it was hard work, especially in a new house that I wasn't used to, it was a special job to be a relief girl.

I requested to be sent to California one year and after I got there, to San Bernardino, I was real disappointed. California just wasn't what everyone said it was. So I went back to Winslow.

From her years of home sewing and mending on the farm, Bertha had become a fine seamstress and often made clothes for the other Harvey Girls. She also made clothes for her baby sister back home, which she sent along with most of her earnings back to Oklahoma to help the family out:

I never saved much. It all went back to them. I spent all my vacation time at home on the farm. I worked just as hard during vacation as I did in Winslow. But I was happy. Harvey gave me confidence. Getting away from the farm helped me. Before, I was a timid, green little country girl. When I first went to Winslow, I was afraid to walk downtown, or past a crowd of people. A few years later, I was a different person.

I remember one man coming into the lunchroom at La Posada who reminded me of my daddy. We used to say there were two kinds of people: the train people and the bus people. This man was off the bus. Well, we served everyone the same, of course. This one man from the bus was watching me with a real disapproving eye. Maybe he'd never been in a fine lunchroom. Anyway, another man at the counter, a train passenger, left me a dime for a tip. The man from the bus was astonished when I put that dime in my pocket. He thought it had been left by accident and that I was stealing! You should have seen the look on his face! Those were the bus people.

Bertha never moved back to Oklahoma. She married a railroadman in 1942, and quit work as a Harvey Girl so that she could set up her own sewing shop. Bertha knew many people in Winslow, and her sewing was well known, so she had a large clientele. One of her special customers was Mary Colter, an architect and interior designer who worked extensively for Harvey throughout the Southwest (see chapter 7).

Many rural communities in the early 1900s provided schooling only up to the eighth grade. Young women like Gladys Porter—as well as men— had to leave home and move into town if they wanted to attend high school. Her family lived with ten children on a struggling farm near Guthrie, Oklahoma, where there were Santa Fe shops and a Harvey House. A small town like Guthrie had very few employment opportunities for young women, and Gladys, at the age of fifteen, knew that working as a Harvey Girl was the best job she could find there.

Gladys was hired by the local manager in 1920. He knew she was underage. It was not unusual to find underage Harvey Girls in small houses; as more and more houses opened on the line the demand for women increased and local hiring became common. Often, the only women available were very young. The primary source for Harvey Girls was still through the main offices in Kansas City and Chicago, but managers often needed more help and so interviewed applicants themselves. Locally hired women were given the same standards and rules—they had to live in the dormitory even if their families lived nearby. Hundreds of them became professional Harvey Girls, working out on the line all over the Southwest.

Gladys planned to work and live at the Harvey House, but also to continue to go to school. But she soon liked her job so well she did not attend classes, making financial support of her family a priority:

I felt protected and looked after as a Harvey Girl in those days, which I needed being so young. The staff was like a big family to me. I was never homesick, but my family had moved to town by then and I could see them whenever I wanted. Because I had come from such a large family, I had had no exposure to the nicer things in life. I didn't have any social skills and working as a Harvey Girl taught me how to be hospitable and caring. I also learned how to function in an elegant atmosphere I would never have been exposed to otherwise.

She was given special permission to work on the floor even though her hair was not "up to the Harvey standard":

> *We were supposed to have long hair worn in a hairnet. I had had my hair "bobbed" and after the superintendent said it was okay for me to work, I was told I was the first girl with short hair ever hired. I was also the youngest.*

Gladys remained a Harvey Girl in Guthrie for six years, never opting to leave that house and work out on the line. She did work in different Harvey Houses in Oklahoma and Texas when there were conventions and large affairs that called for extra Harvey Girls to be sent in by train for a day. In 1927, Gladys married a local man whose family had made the land run in 1889. Gladys raised a family and in 1940 returned to school, eventually becoming a registered nurse. "Working for Harvey in those early years was a great education in itself for me. I learned about people, about showing maturity early in life. I would be happy to do it all over again!"

California was the land of milk and honey to a rural Arkansas farm girl named Bertha Parker. Born in Oklahoma in 1902, and raised in a log cabin in Arkansas, Bertha managed to attend the University of Arkansas for a few semesters before family finances forced her to leave and find work. "There wasn't any work at home; there wasn't much work anywhere. My ambition was to somehow get to California. Everyone thought California was the place to go in the early 1920s."

Bertha heard of the Harvey Houses in 1925, and against her father's wishes sent off a photo and application to Harvey's offices in Kansas City:

> *My father thought there were only bad people working along the railroad. But my mother saw there was nothing else for me to do. Besides, when I was sent a railroad pass to Las Vegas, New Mexico, to work as a Harvey Girl at the Castañeda, I knew it was a lot closer to California than Arkansas, and I wouldn't be stopped.*
>
> *There were a lot of Harvey Girls in Las Vegas from Arkansas. And I found the railroadmen to be very nice, not rough like people back home had said. We had our own community at the Castañeda, and I didn't wander too far.*

After fulfilling her six-month contract in Las Vegas, Bertha went home to Arkansas for a vacation, knowing she would be hired again whenever she was ready to begin work. But during her vacation, and sooner than she might have chosen, she was told by the Kansas City office that there was an immediate need for Harvey Girls to work over the summer at the Grand Canyon. "Arizona was even closer to California so off I went!"

Bertha did not leave the Canyon at the end of the summer and head for California. Instead, she married a young man who drove the Canyon touring cars and together they set up house in a canvas tent on the rim of the Grand Canyon. Bertha's husband, Charles Maddux, was a native Arizonian whose parents had met in Kingman during the first years of the gold and silver rush. After two more years of work at the Canyon, Bertha and Charles headed back to Kingman, where they started their own trucking business near the mines:

> We lived out on the desert and in the summer you could fry an egg or poach a chicken on the tin roof of our house. There were a lot of miners out on that desert in the 1930s, and it was a very rough time. But I never wanted to go back to Arkansas. Most of the Harvey Girls I knew did the same as I—married cowboys or Harvey and Santa Fe men, and stayed out west. Even the real classy women, like one of the head waitresses from back east, married ranchers and stayed west.

The Park sisters, raised on a farm in southern Missouri, became Harvey Girls and managed, over ten years, to move their entire family—mother, father, and three brothers—with them west to California. Jesse, the older sister, saw Harvey's newspaper advertisement in Kansas City, where she had gone to find work as a secretary after business school. She answered the advertisement and was invited to come into Harvey's offices for an interview. Two women interviewed before Jesse were told there were no job openings, but Jesse was asked by Harvey's people where she wanted to go and work? She left for New Mexico the next morning.

Jesse worked seven days a week in Vaughn, New Mexico, for the next two years. When she went home to Missouri for a visit, her sister Addie decided to return to Vaughn with her. Harvey management often wel-

Harvey Girls like Chicago-based Kelly were often the best-dressed young women in the community. Because room, board, and all travel expenses were cared for by Harvey and the Santa Fe, Harvey Girls were free to spend their often substantial savings on fine clothes. However, many sent their paychecks home, or retired years later with large bank accounts that sent them to nursing or "normal" school, or helped buy land for a new life as a wife, mother, or business woman in the Southwest.
(Credit: Olive Loomis)

Harvey Girl and later manager Joanne Stinelichner George with the Santa Fe crew at Canadian, Texas. Harvey Girls and Santa Fe men were the best of friends and built a network of mutual admiration and respect from one end of the Santa Fe to the other. (Credit: Joanne Stinelichner George)

Addie Parks with her future husband, Harvey chef Frank Bassett. (Credit: Addie Bassett)

AT and SF depot and Harvey House, Emporia, 1910. (Credit: Kansas State Historical Society)

comed the sisters of Harvey Girls, and Addie was hired in New Mexico. After a year together in Vaughn, the Park sisters asked for a transfer to Barstow: they had heard that Harvey Girls in California were given a day off each week. The year was 1927; Jesse was twenty-three and Addie was twenty-one. Addie made her home in Casa del Desierto, the elegant Barstow Harvey House, for the next forty years. Jesse married a railroad man in 1934.

Starting salary in 1927 for Addie and Jesse was fifty dollars a month plus room, board, and laundry. Ten years later, in the middle of the depression, Addie was only making thirty dollars a month, plus room and board. "But it was all pocket money. We didn't need very much working in the Harvey House."

Addie and Jesse loved their new lives in California, and on frequent trips home, passed on their enthusiasm to their family. Because they were good friends with Santa Fe railroadmen, after years of shared hours at the Barstow lunch counter, they were able to find jobs for each of their brothers: one became an engineer, another a conductor, and the third a car clerk. In 1938, Addie returned home to help her parents sell their farm, pack up their household, and move to Barstow, where they lived until they died.

Country girls became city women in the ranks of the Harvey Girls. The story is told again and again by women who look back and see themselves as "green little country girls" who became worldly, well-traveled women, moving easily from one Harvey House to the next, from one state to another.

Olive Winter Loomis, like many others, overcame her parents' disapproval to become a Harvey Girl in 1918. Born in 1894, her parents had made the Oklahoma land run, but grew to dislike the tough life of homesteading in that territory, and moved to Arkansas to farm. With her six sisters and three brothers Olive worked the farm until an older sister returned home from Topeka with news that there was a job for Olive at a new dime store. Olive left home, but the dime store job only lasted ten days. She resorted to the Topeka newspaper for job listings, where she saw Harvey's advertisement. She put in an application and was soon out on the line in Emporia, Kansas:

I didn't know any Harvey Girls. All I knew was that Harvey would train a little farm girl like me. I was put under the care of the head counter girl who took care of me like my mother. Some of the girls were homesick. Not me! Here I was a country girl, going to picture shows, barn dances, drives in the country in cars with other girls, doing things no one knew about on the farm.

Olive worked at the Emporia Harvey House during World War I, when there were two or three troop trains arriving for meals each day, making for a hectic schedule in the dining room seven days a week. Olive remembers one trainload during the war in particular, made up of several hundred convicts. The men were brought into the dining room only after the Harvey Girls were ushered out, and were served by the male employees. At the meal's end, each convict's pockets were emptied, revealing many pieces of Harvey silver.

Olive worked nineteen years for Harvey. She married twice and was widowed twice. Her first husband was a Harvey chef, and together they worked and lived at many different Harvey Houses in Colorado, Arizona, and Kansas. After his death, Olive returned home to care for her sick mother. She remained in Kansas, marrying a farmer whose land bordered her own:

I have special memories of all the Harvey Girls. They were special women, doing a special job in lovely places. Whatever you did, everything was done with care. You never forget that. You are always a Harvey Girl, all your life.

It was not uncommon for entire families, even over several generations, to work for Harvey. The Klenke family's involvement with Harvey began in the 1880s and continued into the mid-1940s. F. H. Klenke, a German immigrant, came to Kansas with two other men in 1877 and bought Santa Fe Railway land on which they planned to establish a colony of homesteaders. During the first three years, the Windthorst Community of German immigrant farmers suffered the hardships of all Kansas farmers during the drought. No crops were planted, and the families faced starvation. At that time, the Santa Fe Railway offered men in the community jobs laying track.

Grandfather Klenke accepted a job and was gone for months at a time laying rails west for the Santa Fe.

Henry Klenke, the eldest child, began to work for Harvey in 1887. He was seventeen, and was hired to work as a yardman and pantry boy in Harvey Houses in New Mexico. New Mexico was a long way to go to find work, but there were few alternatives in Kansas after the drought and the grasshoppers. It meant the menfolk were often gone for two to three months at a time with the railroad. But with the money Henry Klenke made over the next nine years with Harvey, he was able to return to Kansas, marry, and purchase a half section of land.

Henry Klenke and Mary Bernadine Buttenboehmer Klenke raised six daughters and two sons on their farm south of Bellefont, Kansas. Fred Harvey stepped back into the Klenke family's lives when the eldest daughter Katie's husband died in the "flu" epidemic of 1918, leaving her a young widow with a four-month-old son. Katie had finished the eighth grade, and when she decided she must go to work to support her son, her father suggested she go into Hutchinson and look for a job with Harvey. Another daughter, Mary, a few years younger than Katie and also an eighth-grade graduate, decided to go with her. In 1919, Henry Klenke boarded a train from Bellefont to Hutchinson with his two oldest daughters. He took them to the elegant Bisonte Hotel, and although he did not know any of the Harvey people working there, he understood their methods of hiring and standards of work and hoped they would accept his daughters. To his delight, Mary and Katie were both hired, fitted for uniforms, and set to work as Harvey Girls that same day.

The Klenke sisters lived on the third floor of the Bisonte. Working six days a week, Katie returned home to Bellefont on her day off to visit her small son. Both sisters returned to the farm for the harvest, at which time Katie met an old boyfriend. They married soon after. Josephine, the next sister in line, had recently finished the eighth grade, and was sent back with Mary to Hutchinson. She stepped into Katie's former job, wearing her uniforms, sleeping in her bed, and working her station in the Bisonte dining room. Josephine was only fourteen. The night before leaving home, she was called in to see her father. She remembers:

This was the first time I had a private talk with my father. 'Josephine,' he began, 'you have been a wonderful daughter and now you are leaving home. We want you to come back to us just as good as you are now. Mother, your grandmother and I have made many of your decisions up to now as to what you could do and where you could go. Now you will be making those decisions. Know who you are going out with. Never accept a ride if someone drives up to the curb and offers you one. Their intentions are not good, and you know you could get a social disease. Remember your home is always open to you, unless you marry out of the church and give up your religious training.'

Josephine worked in Hutchinson for two and half years before asking for a transfer to Needles, which, she remembers, was much like going to Europe is today. She also worked in Dodge City and Newton as head waitress. In 1925, Josephine joined the Mount Saint Mary convent and became a nun, Sister Valeria, and a certified nurse.

Mary Klenke remained with Harvey until 1942, never marrying, and working at houses in Kansas and New Mexico. But Mary was not the last Klenke daughter to join Harvey. Johanna, only sixteen, was ready for life beyond the farm, as was her older sister Philma:

I wanted to leave. All young people want to leave at that age. In 1926, Philma and I drove to Dodge City, hoping to get hired at Harvey's. It was frightening and exciting. We'd never worked away from home, and the manager must have known we were as green as grass. But we were hired . . .

They put us right to work. Fortunately, Gladys, the head waitress, came over and helped us get dressed—there was all this paraphernalia to put on. We were used to the shorter skirts in style then, and we couldn't figure those things out—all those aprons and blouses, everything so stiff, and then black shoes and stockings. The shoes were definitely not what I was wearing in those days!

We were put in the lunchroom and shown how to take orders. People were very pleasant, but oh, when the train came in! There would be customers clammering at the counter, some with those tin buckets for coffee, yelling for refills—you just had to ignore them, and go on with the people seated. I remember going back to

Henry Klenke escorted his eldest
daughter, Katie, a widow with a small
son, to Hutchinson for her interview
with a Fred Harvey manager in 1919.
(Credit: Johanna Klenke)

Left, Philma Klenke, Elizabeth Keihl,
center, far right, Johanna Klenke, Dodge
City, 1927.
(Credit: Johanna Klenke)

Harvey House lunch room, Vaughn, New Mexico, 1901. (Credit: Santa Fe Railway)

The Emporia, Kansas, lunch counter was often the training ground for new Harvey Girls.
(Credit: Kansas State Historical Society)

Hazel Williams was fourteen in 1917, but she
managed to secure a job as a Harvey Girl
until she dated an employee and was fired.
(Credit: Hazel Williams LaDuke)

the kitchen that first day to give our orders, and there was even
more commotion back there, waitresses running in, yelling orders,
running out. The cooks looked very hot. Well, Philma and I put
in our orders and when those cooks heard our timid little voices
they stopped dead still and said, 'Well, I'll be damned if we don't
have a couple of dumb-bells from the country.'

But we mastered it all, thanks to the head waitress. We weren't
really sheltered girls, but we had to learn how to handle all those
people and the rush!rush!rush! You had to face the reality of those
trains real quick to survive. There were three trains a day,
morning, noon, and night, and we worked a split shift, six days a
week. On our day off, we went home to the farm—Dad would
come for us in the car.

Harvey management set up a seasonal system for farmer's daughters
whereby they could return home to help during the summer, especially
during harvest time. Their positions in Harvey Houses were temporarily
filled by schoolteachers who were invited to make extra money during the
summer months and fall weekends and holidays. This system worked very
well, and demonstrated Harvey's willingness to accomodate the needs of
rural families who needed the income their daughters could provide as
Harvey Girls, but who also needed extra hands at home during times of
high farm production. "I always wondered what they did when we left,"
Johanna says. "I didn't know until years later that we were replaced by
schoolteachers in the summer."

Johanna worked as a Harvey Girl until 1930, when she left to study
nursing. Philma also had left work as a Harvey Girl to become a registered
nurse in 1927. Johanna recalls:

Harvey had given me a sense of independence, but also of
security. A Harvey Girl was taken care of, yet still felt like she
was on her own. Life as a Harvey Girl prepared me for
nursing—same discipline, same living with other girls in a dorm.
Nursing was easy after working at Harvey's! It was different than
working as a waitress; the training was very intense. At the time,
I don't think Harvey Girls were aware of how professional they
were.

Opal Sells had no trouble finding a job as a secretary after business school; her problems began afterward, when her boss in Little Rock, Arkansas, informed her that she would also serve as his girlfriend, "part-time" because he was married. It was 1924, and Opal quit her first job because she "wouldn't sit on the boss's lap."

Opal's family was among the first pioneers of West Texas. She was born in 1900, and was the last child to leave home: her two sisters married, and her brothers went to look for oil when she was still a young girl. Opal remained on the farm caring for her invalid mother. "I remember covered wagons stopping near our farm. Mother gave them fresh eggs and milk, and then they moved on."

In 1919, after her mother's death, Opal was sent to Dallas to attend business school by a wealthy uncle. But after two unsuccessful and frustrating attempts to work as a secretary—her second job in Amarillo turned out much the same as the first—Opal began looking around in the newspaper. A beautiful, stylish, well-educated woman of twenty-four, Opal was told by her friends not to answer Fred Harvey's ad:

> *People said to me, "Don't be a waitress; you'll be at the bottom."*
> *But I had heard of the Harvey Girls, about the great food, about*
> *all the girls going west from back east. So I went in to see a*
> *manager at the Harvey House in Amarillo. He said to me,*
> *"You're the first girl who has walked in here today who wasn't*
> *chewing gum. You look like our type." He hired me that day and*
> *I began work the next morning. I was real nervous—they had*
> *such a reputation. You started out right from the beginning. No*
> *nail polish, no gum, skirts a certain length from the floor and*
> *then the rules in the dormitory. People said it was degrading to*
> *work in a restaurant. Not so in Fred Harvey's.*

Fred Harvey, the Santa Fe Railway, and the Southwest became Opal's life. She worked her way up to head waitress, and lived in many Harvey Houses in eight states until she retired at age sixty-nine. She was among those Harvey Girls chosen to teach the "Harvey way" of serving at the new Cleveland Terminal, and also at the Chicago World's Fair Harvey House in the 1930s. She married a railroadman in 1949, but continued to work for another twenty years:

The thing I really appreciated about Harvey was the way they
treated you—like you were their own flesh and blood. "Our
Harvey Family" the managers and supervisors called us. And
they hand-picked everyone, so it was a real nice family.

Ellen Mae Hunt also attended business school before she became a
Harvey Girl, but unlike Opal, she found very little work for secretaries in
Missouri in 1920. Born on a Kansas farm in 1901 and raised with seven
brothers and sisters, Ellen had to find work when she was nineteen. "I had
seen ads in the newspapers when I was at school that said Harvey was
looking for girls to go west and work. It sounded like an adventure. I
thought a lot about it. New Mexico sounded like a faraway place." In 1922,
after returning home when a temporary secretarial job ended, Ellen wrote
a friend she had known in school and they decided to meet in Kansas City:

My friend and I were interviewed by a Miss Steel and were both
hired. We were twenty-one years old and had no idea what we
were getting into. We were put on a train the next day, and sent
to Gallup, New Mexico, for training. I had never seen anything
like it—saloons on every street. I had never even seen
whiskey—Kansas City was dry—and I'd never seen anyone
drunk. It was quite an adjustment. I was scared at first, but it
didn't take long before both of us loved working for Harvey.

Homesickness among Harvey Girls, especially those from rural homes,
was very common. Women who worked in Harvey Houses near home
visited their families on a regular basis. Those who were hired and sent
immediately out to houses on the line had more to contend with, but the
system was set up to encourage women to overcome difficulties of separa-
tion. Usually, young women were allowed to work close to home for their
first year or so. When they were eventually sent out to another house
farther away, they already knew how they would be treated and cared for,
and had a sense of identity within the Harvey system. However, there were
many instances when very young women were sent far from home for their
first job because there were houses that needed help. The only consolation
for these women was knowing they had a guaranteed rail pass home at the
end of their contract.

May Etta Arnold was twenty-one when she was hired as a Harvey Girl in Chicago, and sent to what felt like the other side of the world: Needles, California. May Etta was looking for an adventure in 1929: "I was from Kentucky; my father was a carpenter. I needed work and Fred Harvey sounded like an adventure. It was!" On June 20, 1929, the temperature in Needles was 120 degrees in the shade. May Etta had signed a six-month contract and was a few weeks short of finishing when she asked to be let go. Harvey Girls were paid bonuses for working the summer months in Needles, but even so, May Etta wanted to go home. She missed her family and hated the weather. The manager agreed to let her leave early, probably knowing that a few weeks vacation at the right time could keep a well-trained Harvey Girl on the payroll. May Etta returned home, visited loved ones and friends, and soon found she wanted to get out on the line again and work. She asked for another contract, and was quickly sent to Seligman, Arizona, where she worked another year before marrying a railroadman.

Immigrant women found an open door at Harvey's offices. They had to pass the same application and interview requirements as did all Harvey Girl applicants. But once within the system they were entitled to the same professional and personal considerations as everyone else. There was no discrimination in job locations, transfers, or pay.

Turn-of-the-century immigrant women traditionally took the worst, most demeaning and difficult jobs open to women in America. Immigrant women could be counted on to take the jobs white American women would not.[32] But in the Harvey House immigrant women found a reprieve from this assumption. Harvey traditionally hired his chefs from Europe, importing dozens of prominent and well-schooled bakers, cooks, and head chefs in the course of the years. There was a preponderance of German, Italian, and French spoken in Harvey House kitchens all over the West. Chefs were among the most highly paid and respected individuals in the system: after all, their magnificent cooking skills made the Harvey House food famous. At the very least, an immigrant woman could find work as a salad girl in a kitchen where the head chef and his assistants spoke her language. And it was certainly possible for a young woman from Europe to find herself a Harvey Girl, later a head waitress, and eventually even a full-fledged manager, with all the esteem, pay, and mobility of her male counterparts.

Elizabeth Alice Garnas was born in Yugoslavia in 1909. Her father was a coal miner working for a German company that sent him to work in the Gibson, New Mexico, mines. In 1911, Alice's family joined him in New Mexico, but soon after were forced to leave Gibson when her father lost his arm in a mine accident. Alice attended a few years of high school in Albuquerque before being told it was time to leave school and find work to help support the family.

At the age of seventeen, Alice went to work as a maid in Albuquerque. The woman of the house was a former Harvey Girl who suggested Alice go downtown to the Alvarado, the Harvey House, and talk with the supervisor about becoming a Harvey Girl. Alice knew nothing about Harvey, but she wanted a better job. After an interview and application placed at the Alvarado offices, Alice was offered a job in Vaughn, on the eastern plains of New Mexico.

Vaughn was a railroad terminal and division point, and most of the people living in the community were railroad people. There were also cowboys and ranchers in town each day, on wagons and horseback. It was 1926 when Alice arrived, and although it was dusty, isolated, and small, Alice loved Vaughn and her new life as a Harvey Girl:

> *I was respected and protected and the management at the house was wonderful. I thought about asking for a transfer—other girls wanted to go to the California Harvey Houses—but I really liked life in Vaughn. We fed a slew of people for the morning, noon, and evening trains, but we had time to have fun, too. A bunch of us girls would get together and take a picnic out into the sand hills. That was our recreation: hiking and more hiking. I loved it. But you must understand that to many Harvey Girls, sent in from Kansas City and Chicago, Vaughn was a shocking place. There was no place to go, nothing to do. Just Vaughn and those wide plains on all sides—cattle country. Many girls left after six months. It was a rough country. But it was for me.*

Local ranchers were regulars at the Harvey House lunch counter, especially as the cooking skills of the house's German chef and baker gained a wide reputation. The prices were reasonable, and even in the middle of the hot New Mexican summer there was homemade ice cream. There was no competition for service, food, or price for hundreds of miles.

Charles Lindbergh inadvertently found himself a customer at the Vaughn Harvey House in 1928, when he was forced to land his plane on the desert near town because of engine failure. With his mechanic, he waited several days for parts and assistance in the hotel across the street from the Harvey House, taking all of his meals in the Harvey dining room. "The town just went plum crazy," Alice remembers:

> *The Harvey Girls practically fought over who would serve him. I wasn't that interested and stayed out of the arguments. The manager found me later that evening and said, "Alice, you will be in charge of Lindbergh's table." And that's what I did for the next few days. They were very friendly and very nice to me, although Lindbergh was very shy and quiet. I couldn't blame him—everyone in town hovered about him. He must have felt stranded in the middle of nowhere. He was!*

Alice's father died and she left her job to return to Albuquerque to help settle family affairs. As soon as her obligations at home were completed, she returned to the Alvarado and asked for another job. Alice was sent down south to Belen, New Mexico, where she became reacquainted with a railroadman she had known before in Vaughn. They married in 1929.

Elizabeth Hazlewood was a first-generation American when she was brought by her parents to Oklahoma in a covered wagon in 1899. She was two years old and her father, a Russian immigrant, had come with his family from South Dakota to try farming farther south. He moved the family on to Texas from Oklahoma, hearing "it was rich down there," but found, like thousands of others, that this was mostly false advertising. The family farmed outside of Canadian, Texas, in the Panhandle, but it was a terrible struggle, and soon the four girls and one boy had all moved into town to find work. Elizabeth married when she was eighteen and had two children before she was widowed ten years later. She was supporting her family as a cafe waitress in Canadian when she heard there was a better job at the Harvey House.

There were few Harvey Girls sent in from other Harvey Houses to the

Charles Lindbergh was charting a coast to coast air mail route in 1928 when he was forced to land near Vaughn, New Mexico. (Credit: Alice Garnas)

Alice Garnas visited Lindbergh and his plane on the desert during his three day "visit." (Credit: Alice Garnas)

Lindbergh's attempts to get his plane back into the air were closely watched by Vaughn residents. (Credit: Alice Garnas)

Main street, Seligman, Arizona, 1933. (Credit: Katheryne Krause Ferguson)

Chefs, cooks, and bakers, Syracuse, Kansas. Harvey chefs were legendary. La Fonda chef Konrad Allgaier was once the chef for the Kaiser Wilhelm; when the late Kaiser's grandson came to the United States, he visited Allgaier in Santa Fe. (Credit: Joanne Stinelichner George)

small lunch and dining room in Canadian. Many local married women were hired to work in the 1920s and 1930s, and they were allowed to maintain their own homes. Single women were still required to live in the Harvey Girl dormitory.

For a widow with small children, the job offered security and a much-needed extended family. Elizabeth's daughter, Sis, remembers her visits to the Harvey House every day after school when she and her brother waited for their mother to leave work:

> We were treated like royalty. The baker kept the broken cookies in a paper bag for us and everyone was always giving us sweets and food. It was a big family, our family. The manager and his wife took care of us just like we were their own.

Elizabeth remembers worrying about her small children because of the proximity of the Harvey House to the railroad tracks, and the busy rush when a train came in. She claims she never took a vacation, and she doesn't remember travel passes being offered to the local Harvey Girls. "It was just a good, clean job for a woman. It was very strenuous, but a clean woman—a woman who didn't smoke, curse, or drink—could get a good job if she could keep up with the work."

Coal mining brought Violet Bosetti's Italian grandfather to Kansas in the 1880s, where her mother was born in 1895. Violet's father came to America by boat from Austria in the early 1900s, also looking for work in the Kansas coal mines. The Bosettis married in 1911, and Violet's father dug coal until his death in 1924. Violet was eight when he died, and she learned, along with her eleven-year-old sister, what hard work was all about:

> My mother gave me a little red wagon and every day after school I did errands for people. In the winter, I had orders to take the wagon down to the railroad tracks and pick up the coal that had fallen off the trains. I wasn't to return home until the wagon was full. Otherwise, we would freeze. In the summertime, I filled the wagon with ice, also from the trains. The railroad was the most important part of my life.
>
> My mother worked at many jobs—at a laundry, a beauty shop, a business college, and finally in a doctor's office. The doctor's

*office was near the railroad station, and this one railroadman
must have seen my mother and I around there every day. He
pretended to have a cinder in his eye one morning and went into
the doctor's office. He married my mother a little while later.*

*My stepfather knew about the Harvey Houses and when I was
twenty, after leaving nursing school (it was a Catholic school and
the nuns were annoyed with me because I was an Italian
Protestant), he suggested I try Harvey. I went in to see a Miss
Steel in Kansas City and she said I was unsophisticated, but they
would hire me anyway. I was sent to Gallup, New Mexico, in
1936. After I learned the Harvey system, I was sent to
Albuquerque, to the great Alvarado.*

Violet married a railroadman in 1940. "You know, all those Harvey Girls
were really just railroaders themselves at heart. We were all fascinated by
the trains."

Joanne Stinelichner became a Harvey manager after years as a Harvey
Girl. She came alone to the United States from Germany in 1916. Joanne
was twenty-two, and she went to live with an aunt in Milwaukee. Although
her father tried to persuade her to come home to Germany, even calling
her long-distance on the telephone, Joanne was headstrong and felt that
what she wanted was in America:

*I wasn't working yet. I was just going to school to learn English.
And I was doing things with other girls—going skating and to
social events. One of the girls I knew was a schoolteacher . . .
With another friend of ours, a beautician, we headed for Chicago
after writing ahead for interviews. A Mrs. Simmons interviewed
us. I was last. I was dressed real nice, with rosy cheeks and nice
hair. I spoke some English, at least enough to catch on. They
hired all three of us, but I was the only one who stayed . . . I had
never been in a Harvey House, but I liked the people and the work
right away. The manager in Hutchinson was Irish and he liked
me right away.*

Joanne worked in Kansas until 1918, when she took her first vacation west
to New Mexico and Arizona:

It was easy to travel alone, even for a woman. People on the trains were friendly and asked me about my life as a Harvey Girl. Everybody knew about the Harvey Houses. Even the cowboys were nice—the movies were kind of extreme about Oklahoma and New Mexico cowboys. They weren't that wild.

For the following decade, Joanne worked in Harvey Houses all over the Southwest. She married a Harvey chef named John Thompson, had a child, became a headwaitress, and was widowed, all in those ten years. Joanne was promoted to house manager in 1927, in Guthrie, Oklahoma. Her daughter was four years old, and she continued to work for Harvey until 1948, putting her daughter through college while managing Harvey Houses from Kansas to California (see Chapter 5).

Many Harvey Girls claim they joined up in search of adventure, but the majority of these women were simply in search of work. The women considered the true adventurers in the Harvey system were those who may not have needed to work, but who used Harvey to come west where they hoped to find life that was a little different than what they had always known before. These women were not numerous, but many Harvey employees and Santa Fe people remember one or two of "those Eastern high-class women" working as Harvey Girls out in the desert somewhere for a year or two.

In isolated Vaughn, New Mexico, Alice Garnas met a Harvey Girl who had come west from Washington, D.C.:

She was our headwaitress and she had been a secretary at the White House. She was very classy. I asked her one day while we were out hiking on the desert why she had left a good job like that to come to a place like this and waitress? She said her lifestyle and the pressure of her job had begun to get on her nerves. She wanted a change and so had gone to Chicago and asked for a job with Harvey. I'm sure they did not hesitate to hire her. And she got the change she was looking for.

After being told by a London eye specialist that she would lose her sight before she reached middle age, Janet Ferrier, a teenager in Aberdeen, Scotland, set out to see the world. Janet came alone to America where she worked in resorts up and down the Eastern seaboard in the late teens and early twenties. While working in Florida, she met another young adventurer named Alice Stackhouse, a twenty-year-old New Yorker who had overcome her parents' objections and left home immediately after high school to see something on her own. Alice remembers:

> *I was a great disappointment to my parents because I wanted something more than my own home and family. I really wanted to see the world, to be out on my own. My parents tried to talk me out of this, but they couldn't. Even so, we remained very close over the years.*

Alice and Janet found they had much in common, including their individual desires to go west. They heard from a hotelkeeper about the Harvey Girls:

> *We inquired about it and found out they hired girls from the East and sent them out West to work. We went to Chicago and were hired on there. It was a perfect system for Janet and me. They liked to hire two girls together—they hoped they'd stay longer that way—and then send them to the same house as roommates. It worked very well for a lot of Harvey Girls who signed on together.*
>
> *On our days off we liked to go out tramping through the mountains and forests. We'd put on our boots and pants and take off with other Harvey people into the wilds. It was a wonderful life. We worked real hard but then we could do what we wanted. We often organized camping and hiking trips for Harvey people. That was Janet's and my specialty, especially in the thirties when we were working at the Grand Canyon.*

Alice and Janet saved their salary and tips until they had enough money to take off from work for several months at a time. "We'd quit knowing they would hire us back on again when we were ready." From the 1920s until their retirement in the 1960s, Janet and Alice worked at Harvey Houses in New Mexico, California, and Arizona. They traveled to Africa, India, Australia, New Zealand, and all through Europe. Janet Ferrier never lost her eyesight, and Alice Stackhouse lived to the grand old age of one hundred.

Where Harvey Houses were located in communities with colleges or universities, the daily schedule often accomodated Harvey employees who wished to attend classes. The two most notable examples were found in Albuquerque and Las Vegas, New Mexico, where Harvey employees were often students at the University of New Mexico, and at New Mexico Highlands (formerly New Mexico Normal School). The latter was a college located in a northern New Mexico town surrounded by hundreds of miles of open country and mountains with rural communities scattered in between. Young men and women often came into Las Vegas from ranches seeking work by which to support themselves while studying for a degree.

Working full-time as a Harvey Girl and going to college was a difficult, but not impossible, undertaking. There were compensations at the Harvey House not found at other jobs, including peer support and a sense of community not unlike that found in a college dormitory on campus. However, the long hours of physical work with classes squeezed in between trains and meals, with time after work set aside for studying, hardly fulfilled the average American girl's dream of college life. But for most of these young women, it was the only way to go to school.

Bernice and Alice Myers were raised on a ranch in Levy, New Mexico, outside of Las Vegas. Their parents had been homesteaders, and although they had succeeded in keeping their ranch, times were hard in the 1930s and if Alice and Bernice wanted a college education, they were going to have to work for it:

> *Alice and I came into Las Vegas and spoke with the manager about a job at the Harvey House. He found out we were planning to go to school and he said it would be fine. He even said we could work part-time when it wasn't busy. But it was always busy. We managed to go to class between meals, and we had maid service in our rooms, so we didn't worry about housekeeping. But there was no time to study. If there hadn't been a study hall at the college I would never have studied at all.*

Bernice became a headwaitress in the three and a half years she was a Harvey Girl at the Castañeda. She remembers that her parents had mixed feelings at first about their daughters becoming waitresses:

> *They learned that we were different as Harvey Girls. We were*
> *expected to look and act differently than other waitresses. And*
> *most of the women in Las Vegas were very high class. There were*
> *only six local Harvey Girls when I was there; the remainder, some*
> *twenty or more, were from Kansas and other states.*

Tips at the Castañeda were enough to pay for books, and Alice and Bernice's salaries paid for their tuition. During vacation, many Harvey Girls from Las Vegas opted to work extra days at the houses in Santa Fe and Albuquerque where their help was often needed for special events, and where tips were very high. Bernice remembers that one night of work at La Fonda in Santa Fe paid her enough in tips (thirty-one dollars) to pay for a semester of books.

> *It was absolutely the only way my sister and I would have ever*
> *afforded a college education. And I always felt my training as a*
> *Harvey Girl was as important to my education as my years at*
> *college. I learned about people, about hard work and*
> *responsibility, about discipline. And the people I worked with*
> *became my family. It was a very close group. There were Harvey*
> *Girls and chefs, cooks, busboys, who stayed in Las Vegas together*
> *working for many, many years.*

In Bernice's last year of school, her health broke. A doctor told her that the stressful schedule of life as a college student and a headwaitress was too much for her, and she would have to choose between the two. Instead, Bernice took the state teacher's exam, quit work and school, and with a teacher's certificate, left Las Vegas to find work as a schoolteacher. In the year that followed, she married a railroad engineer and moved to Kansas.

As explained earlier, there were many Harvey Girls of European and Mediterranean backgrounds, but American minority women—black, Indian and Hispanic—were virtually excluded by the Harvey system. Black waiters were found in the Kansas City Harvey House, and later on in Harvey dining cars operated on the Santa Fe Railway. Black women were found working as maids in Harvey Houses, or as kitchen help. In many Harvey House locations, particularly in Oklahoma and Texas, segregation was an accepted part of restaurant and public life, and many houses had separate eating areas for black patrons. Usually these were the black conductors and porters who worked on the trains, and while train passengers and Santa Fe Railway personnel ate in the lunch or dining rooms, the black employees ate in a designated area, served by the busboys, not the Harvey Girls.

Indian and Hispanic women, easily the predominant races in many communities in New Mexico, Arizona, and parts of California, were also not solicited for work as Harvey Girls, although there were instances in which they were hired. Albuquerque employees remember one Isleta Indian woman who was a Harvey Girl at the Alvarado. No facts, no dates, and no name are available. In Arizona, oral historians claim there were Harvey Girls hired from local reservations during World War II, when a severe shortage combined with increased meal traffic left the local managers desperate. If there were many Indian women who worked as Harvey Girls, this was probably the result of unusual circumstances.

Hispanic women, like Indians, were only rarely found working as Harvey Girls, although this changed noticeably during and after World War II. Hispanic men worked throughout the Harvey system as bellboys, busboys, kitchen, and maintenance workers, even as maître 'ds. But before the 1940s, Hispanic Harvey Girls were so few as to be invisible.

Bertha Spears remembers one Hispanic in Winslow, Arizona, whose presence on the floor in the 1930s was not invisible to certain train passengers and Santa Fe Railway men:

> I was assigned to train the first Hispanic woman hired by
> the house manager. She was a wonderful person; the manager
> knew it, and I knew—a whole lot of people at the Harvey
> House knew it. But the railroadmen threatened to leave if
> she stayed and worked. The manager ignored them. She stayed.
> And that was that. Things changed a little at a
> time.

Farmer's daughters, first-born Americans, eastern adventurers, single women, wives, college women, even a handful of minority women—these were the Harvey Girls. They came from all parts of the United States and Europe, with all kinds of expectations and needs. But once accepted as Harvey Girls, they all shared a broad range of common experiences. The following chapter illustrates the realities, as well as some of the romantic and fictionalized ideals, of life within the Harvey system.

CHAPTER · 5

Life Along the Main Line

Y OUNG WOMEN INTERESTED IN BECOMING HARVEY GIRLS—be it for a summer or a lifetime—were placed in a rigorous training program soon after acceptance into the Harvey system. Most Harvey Girls were trained in one of the houses in Kansas. Kansas was the "home" of the Harvey system, although corporate headquarters were moved to Chicago in later years. In Kansas communities, Harvey Girls and Harvey employees were met with openness and acceptance.

Topeka was often used as the training ground for new waitresses. Topeka was a railroad town and nearly everyone worked for, or was related to someone who worked for, the Santa Fe Railway. Young, inexperienced Harvey Girls found friendly faces across the counter while learning the ropes in the Topeka Harvey lunchroom. The Santa Fe depot was the center of community activity in the early days of this century. Young and old residents alike gathered daily to watch the trains come in.

"I remember going down to the old depot where the oldtimers used to sit," Lyle Rouse, son of a Santa Fe railroadman, remembers:

> *It was like sitting in the bleachers in Wrigley Field listening to the old-timers waiting for old number forty-four. They had a lot of old stories, those railroadmen.*
>
> *My father worked for the Santa Fe for forty-three years. He used to have a pass on the railroad, but we didn't take as many trips as people might think. We would eat at the Harvey House sometimes—there was an ambience about it, the dining room and the girls. It was a very respected institution. The girls were very professional; you wouldn't even think of making a casual or cute remark to one of them. If they weren't treated with respect, the manager would let you know about it.*
>
> *There might have been some people in the community that thought of the Harvey Girls as saloon girls, but not many. They were immensely respected in Topeka. In a small community like this, the Harvey House was the most elegant place to eat. People knew how much discipline all the employees lived under, how tight an organization it was. It wasn't just based on money and tips—the motivation was different in the Harvey House.*

Even so, training was an exhausting and nerve-wracking experience. The thirty days of required training in Topeka, Emporia, and other Harvey Houses, consisted of full-time hours and duties. The women worked without pay during their training. Uniforms were properly donned the first morning, or evening, on duty, and the rules of the house and dormitory were effective immediately. The pressure of the train rush, the absoluteness of the serving rules, the adherence to certain codes of behavior toward customers and fellow employees, made the first weeks as a Harvey Girl a time of great readjustment for most women. The rigors of training were meant to scare off timid women and flush out those who could not carry their own weight in the house.

The management at most Harvey Houses did want the young women to succeed and gave encouragement and assistance. Headwaitresses were chosen for their competence and efficiency, but also for their ability to keep the staff on the floor organized and happy. Many young Harvey Girls

remember their first headwaitress with a mixture of awe at her professionalism, and affection for her motherly guidance during the first hard days
on the floor.

Katheryn Krause Ferguson, wife of a Harvey manager, knew many
Harvey Girls during her husband's twenty years in the system:

> *They were outstanding ladies chosen so carefully by the Harvey*
> *people. I remember in Emporia in the 1920s, a group of new*
> *Harvey Girls were trained for thirty days without pay. They were*
> *given meals and a room, but not until after they had learned the*
> *whole system were they paid for their work. Every one of them*
> *made it.*

Opal Sells Hill (see Chapter 4) worked for more than four decades for
Harvey, eventually as head waitress. But she claims her career nearly
ended during her first week of training in Amarillo:

> *I was just being trained. I was pretty nervous and jumpy. I was*
> *standing at the lunch counter—fortunately a train wasn't*
> *in—when this little mouse ran out and up my sleeve. I hate mice*
> *and I screamed and jumped up onto the counter. That's when the*
> *manager walked in. Well, I just looked down at him and then*
> *climbed off the counter and went back to change out of my*
> *uniform. I figured he would ask me to leave and I wasn't waiting*
> *for him to say it. But then he came in and told me different; he*
> *talked me out of leaving and I stayed. I stayed for forty-five years!*

Upon completion of the training program, Harvey Girls were sent "out
on the line," often to a small house in Kansas, sometimes to the farther
regions of New Mexico, Arizona, or California. Because women who had
worked within the system for a year or more could request to be transferred to a particular location as long as space permitted, new Harvey Girls
usually worked in the small Kansas houses, or in the less popular houses
of Texas and Oklahoma—small towns rumored to have little social life and
poor tips. But after doing their initial time at these small Harvey establishments, most women who remained for several years were able to work
their way into the larger houses in the Southwest where the glamor and

excitement of the burgeoning tourist industry, and the money behind it, could be found. Several Harvey Houses—those at the Grand Canyon, the Castañeda in Las Vegas, and El Garces in Needles, California—had the reputation of being enjoyable communities within which to work and live. Requests for work positions at these houses were frequent, and employees often remained for years. But a Harvey Girl with perseverance could eventually live and work in the place of her choice.

The Harvey "family" of employees was headed by superintendents, headquartered in St. Louis, Kansas City, and Chicago, and included managers and their families, who lived in the Harvey House, chefs, cooks, bakers, butchers, Harvey Girls, busboys, newsstand managers, kitchen maids, and dormitory house mothers. It was a large extended family of individuals who worked long, hard hours together, ate together, and shared dormitory life and days off. This friendly, familial atmosphere was encouraged at Harvey Houses. However, dating among employees—most especially for Harvey Girls and any other Harvey employee—was strictly forbidden. This rule was outwardly obeyed, but extensively ignored, for fifty years. Depending on the personality and temperament of a manager in a given house, Harvey Girls caught dating a fellow employee could find themselves married and still working as Harvey Girls, transferred to another location, or fired.

Because of the closely knit relationships that existed between employees in most Harvey Houses, many managers were very lenient about this rule, established by Fred Harvey himself in the 1880s. At places like the Grand Canyon, where the Harvey House was located miles from any kind of community, fellow employees were the only steady companions anyone had. But where and when the rule was enforced, in true Harvey style, there was no room for fudging.

Young Hazel Williams grew up in rural Kansas, and became a Harvey Girl at the age of fifteen, lying about her age to her manager. "I wanted to get out and find something of my own," Hazel remembers. "I got on a train for Dodge City in 1918, to go and live with my older sister." When Hazel got a job as a waitress at the Harvey House, she left her sister's apartment and moved into the dormitory:

> *Everyone knew I was young and they took care of me. I became a real good waitress at the lunch counter. I was proud of how fast I could work when the train came in, calling out those orders. We*

*never had pads, but kept all the orders in our heads. We were
there to work and everyone loved it.*

*I didn't want to leave Harvey's, but I got fired for socializing
with a young busboy. He was sweet on me and wanted me to go
out with him. The manager had seen us talking and he pulled
me aside and said, "Hazel, I have to tell you, it's a Harvey rule,
you can't keep company with an employee." I said I didn't know
and that I was sorry. Well, one night the young boy came and
begged me to talk with him out on the steps of the dorm. I said
okay, and we sat down and talked. The housekeeper saw us and
tattled. They didn't just fire me—they said they had a good job for
me in Syracuse, Kansas. But Syracuse didn't have my sister and
my family nearby. I said no. I was told I would have to leave.*

However, secret romances between Harvey employees and Harvey
Girls were widespread. Addie Park (see Chapter 4) remarks that "where
there's a will there's a way" and dated fellow employee Frank Bassett, the
chef of the Barstow Harvey House, for seventeen years before marrying
him: "Frank was here in Barstow when I first arrived. We began dating
immediately, but we both had family responsibilities and then World War
II came, so we didn't marry for seventeen years."

Addie and Frank decided to marry in 1944 during Addie's vacation. Frank
was able to get ten days off so they decided to hop a Union Pacific train
from a neighboring town where the Harvey House crowd wouldn't see
them. After marrying in Las Vegas, and a honeymoon at Big Bear Lake,
the couple returned to work as usual:

*About noon one of the girls noticed my ring and she let out a yell
and dragged me all the way around the counter showing the
railroadmen and everyone. That first night we spent at the Harvey
House, Frank slept in the girls' dormitory. The next day, Irwin
Krause, the manager, had one of the guest rooms with a bath
fixed up for us. And that's where we lived until Frank retired in
1954.*

Joanne Stinelichner (see Chapter 4) also dated a Harvey chef, John
Thompson, on the sly:

The night watchman at Syracuse was a friend of mine and he would let me in and not tell anyone. One time, a friend had a car and we went out, John, the friend and his date, and myself, for a big ride in the country. We got lost. Here we were, almost eleven o'clock, and we didn't know how to get home. We all knew we'd be fired. When we finally got back to town, very late, I timidly knocked on the door. The watchman said, "You'd better sneak upstairs and I won't report you." That's how I dated my future husband!

John and Joanne were married in the manager's apartment in Syracuse. They were both allowed to go on working as before, and were given a room together in the house:

Later I became pregnant in Waynoka, Oklahoma, where we had been transferred. Soon after, we were sent out again to Galveston, Texas. I didn't tell anyone I was pregnant, so I could keep working. Eventually people knew, but I worked up to the end of the ninth month. I was on the floor in Emporia, Kansas, when my water broke!

The Harvey system, for all its rules of behavior and codes of ethics, was flexible and even individualized to accomodate its long-term employees. Joanne Stinelichner proved herself so invaluable an employee, she was given in-house child care services upon the death of John Thompson in 1927. Their daughter, Helen, remained upstairs with a maid or another Harvey Girl while Joanne worked her shift downstairs.

Joanne worked as a head waitress for many years, and eventually became a house manager:

It was unusual for a woman to be a manager, but I loved it—managing the entire house, hiring, firing, buying food, everything. I relieved a manager and that's how it started. I was never a Harvey Girl again, unless someone needed temporary help. I was sent wherever the head office needed me: Guthrie, Canadian, Topeka, Amarillo, Slaton, Clovis, San Bernardino,

Galveston, Dodge City. It was wonderful. I put my daughter through college that way.

I took care of the girls. They were like my family, my daughters. Some were very young—one lied and was only fourteen—they would get homesick and I'd arrange to get them a pass home. After a few weeks home, they'd be back, anxious to work again. The Harvey Girls were very happy women. I only fired two Harvey Girls and one cook. That was in Guthrie in 1929. Thelma, a young waitress, and her roommate, an older waitress, asked for a raise. When they didn't get it, they tore up their room. I fired them. Thelma said she had come under the influence of the older girl—we talked and laughed about it a few years later.

The cook I fired was a young boy in Canadian, Texas. He came into the dining room one day and said, "Mrs. Thompson, I've made two batches of mayonnaise and they won't mix." We made our own, and the cooks had to beat it by hand. I went into the kitchen to look at it. He gave me each of the ingredients he had used, one at a time: the powder mix he gave me to mix the mayonnaise was fly poison! I practically fainted! I had to say, "Pack your bags, otherwise I will have to arrest you. You have to leave." He was not a local boy, but I had to fire him and send him home. My gosh, all that poison!

The managers and chefs were highly paid, well-trained individuals who commanded a great deal of respect from fellow Harvey employees. Managers moved every two years or so, sometimes more frequently, until they established seniority and were given permanent positions at the better houses like the Alvarado in Albuquerque, or Casa del Desierto in Barstow. Although most were college educated, with a background in business and management, there were managers who had worked there way up from the very bottom of the Harvey employee structure.

Irwin Krause was typical of the best managers in the Harvey system. Fresh out of college in Springfield, Missouri, Krause joined Harvey in 1925 and worked first as an assistant manager in Sapulpa, Oklahoma. Krause was moved frequently during his twenty-two years with Harvey, and became a superintendent before his death in 1947. His wife, Katheryne, and their daughter, Alice, moved with him all over the Southwest, living in Harvey Houses in Barstow, Kansas City, Emporia, Colorado Springs . . . the list is formidable and includes very nearly every house open from the 1920s through the early 1940s.

Managing meant overseeing every aspect of the house—the kitchen, the personnel, the account books. Managers' families were always given comfortable living quarters, some of which were elegant apartments. Maid service was provided at the larger houses for the manager's quarters as well as for the Harvey Girls' rooms. A manager and his family were given a paid vacation once a year, with meal and train passes provided as well as lodging at any Harvey House.

"You needed those vacations," Katheryne Krause Ferguson remembers:

> . . . Some of the places we were sent to! Seligman, Arizona, was one of the hardest. We were sent there in the mid-1930s and were there for six weeks. The day we arrived, Alice and I went for a walk down the main street. There was a grocery store, a post office, and a lot of sand. It was the middle of the Arizona desert. Mr. Krause had to take inventory as soon as he arrived at a new house, so he wasn't with us. When he was done, he found us and said, "Let's see the town." Alice and I just looked at each other. We walked with him to the corner, where you could look down Main Street and out to the desert. He said, "That's it?!" That was it. It was a long six weeks, more like six months.

The chef at a Harvey House closely followed the manager in importance. Harvey wanted the best cooks in charge of his food and by the turn of the century, as has already been noted, it was a Harvey tradition to hire European chefs. John Frenden was born and raised in Munich, and joined the Harvey organization in 1927, when he was nineteen:

> My father was the manager of a streetcar line in Munich. I had an uncle in Chicago who promised me a job over here. He worked for Harvey, not as a chef, but more as a recruiter for cooks,

butchers, bakers, most of whom were from Europe. Before I came over, I learned some cooking in France and Italy, waiting for my uncle to get my papers and arrangements for a job and passage worked out. My first job in America was with Harvey as assistant night chef in the Chicago Union Station. The chef I worked under was from Stuttgart, and the whole kitchen was German. Everyone was very friendly and helpful. I went to day school to learn English, and then worked all night.

The Harvey people were like one big family. The people at the top, the superintendents, were really interested in the welfare of the employees, even their children and families. The three Harvey brothers—Byron, Daggett, and Stewart—circulated a lot. You saw them, knew them. It was a family.

All the Harvey Girls were beautiful, high-class women. They always had a crush on the chef, very fun and innocent. They weren't supposed to date Harvey employees, but they did. They had to—what do you do at the Grand Canyon, a hundred miles from nowhere? Harvey people were very close.

Managers were moved about a great deal, but chefs usually stayed longer in one location. After all, they made the money for the house. In many ways, the chef was at the top of the system. You never crossed a good chef. Everyone respected him and let him have his way. There were a lot of very good chefs working for the Harveys.

John Frenden worked his way up the Harvey chef system, eventually becoming a head chef in 1959. He married a Harvey Girl he met at the Alvarado Hotel in New Mexico in 1954, and together they continued working for Harvey in houses in New Mexico, Arizona, and California until they retired in 1973.

The hierarchy among the Harvey Girls themselves was methodically assigned: a new employee began at the bottom, which meant the poorest station in the lunchroom, and worked her way up to the more prestigious positions in the dining room. Hard work, not simply months of service, earned one a better place in the house. Many Harvey Houses used badges to indicate a woman's standing. Opal Sells Hill went from badge number fourteen to badge number one in one year at the Amarillo Harvey House. Opal was an exceptional worker, which aroused the jealousy of another Harvey Girl who had been there longer than Opal:

> *Every month the manager gave a box of chocolates to the neatest, cleanest Harvey Girl. We weren't supposed to wear makeup but sometimes someone would sneak it. Well, I kept getting the chocolates, month after month. I was newer than a lot of the girls. One girl got real mad. She went to the manager's wife and told her stories about me. The manager called me in. I said, "Mr. L—, I know who's been talking about me. She thinks you're making a favorite of me by giving me the prize." The manager called in that young woman and told her to pack her bags. She was on the next train out, sent to work at the Harvey House in Waynoka, Oklahoma.*

Opal remained a Harvey Girl at the Amarillo Harvey House for four years. She later worked in Kansas, in New Mexico, at the Cleveland Union Terminal, and at the Grand Canyon. She married a railroadman in 1949:

> *I got to know so many railroadmen. They were fine people, and I thought about marrying one more than once. But not until John Hill came along did I get serious and marry!*

There was always much socializing and dating between the Harvey Girls and the Santa Fe railroaders. Former Harvey Girls will tell you that the men who worked for the Santa Fe were their best friends, their biggest admirers, and would defend the reputation of the Harvey Girls any day of the week. Bernice Black McLain, a Harvey Girl in Kingman, Arizona, in the 1920s, remembers, "We could *not* date Harvey employees, but we could date railroadmen. The men who worked for the railroad had a real respect for the Harvey Girls. They treated us well and there were many marriages."

Younger Harvey Girls often avoided getting too close to the marriage-minded railroaders, but a good many dated and married them just the same. Harvey Girls and Santa Fe men formed a close social network that existed into very old age. Writer Edna Ferber remembers her father saying that

Kingman, Arizona, Harvey employees. (Credit: Mojave County Historical Society)

Harvey Girl Ellen Hunt Jones on the California desert near Barstow with fellow Harvey House employee Ira Ball, 1923. In 1917, the Kansas City Journal claimed there were already some four thousand children named Fred or Harvey due to the extensive marital liasons between Harvey Girls and railroaders and Harvey employees. (Credit: Ellen Jones)

*Italian immigrant "Gregory,"
cook at El Navajo, Gallup, New
Mexico, in the 1920's.
(Credit: Ellen Jones)*

*Las Vegas, New Mexico, Harvey couples socialize on a day off.
(Credit: Walter Reichenborn)*

the western railroad brakemen and Harvey lunchroom waitresses were the future aristocracy of the West. " 'Fine stock,' he used to say. . . ."[1]

Some railroadmen even claimed they were part of the "deal" offered to single Harvey Girls:

> *I know a lot of things about the Toad [a section of the Santa Fe Railway in southern New Mexico] and the Harvey Houses, and I know a good many rails married Harvey Girls. They used to say that the Harvey employment agent guaranteed the girls a fireman on a six-months' contract, or an engineer on a one-year contract.*[2]

Permission from the house manager was required before a Harvey Girl and a railroadman could date. Dating of any kind by the Harvey Girls had to be cleared first with the manager, especially in the early years of the this century when a young woman's virtue could be in question if she were merely seen alone in the company of a man.

Joe Rison, a brakeman and later a conductor on the Santa Fe line between Gainesville, Texas, and Purcell, Oklahoma, in the late teens and early twenties, recalls:

> *We (the train men) used to go to a lot of parties with the Harvey Girls. The girls would pack a picnic and several couples would go off to a park. I was pretty close to marrying one—Ann. She was a French girl from back East. She was very pretty and very sweet. She left home because her father remarried and she didn't get along with her stepmother.*
>
> *I saw Ann in the dining room at Purcell and one day I just popped my head into the window from the station platform and said, "How about going to a movie with me when I get back?" She thought about it and said, "All right." Well, the trip the next day to Gainesville and back was so late I figured the date was up. When I got there she hollered down from her upstairs window that she would be down in thirty minutes. So I sat down and enjoyed my meal and then we went out. She had to get special permission from the manager to go out with me and she couldn't be out after a certain hour. There was no show—we had missed it—so we sat and talked. I sure thought a lot about her.*

Violet Bosetti (see Chapter 4) quickly learned to discriminate between the varying types of opportunities offered by the Santa Fe men:

> *On my first day of work at the Alvarado the manager said to me,*
> *"We'll guarantee you a good railroadman for a husband." Many*
> *of the girls married railroaders. You learned that brakemen were*
> *a dime a dozen, engineers were good, but men in the*
> *communications department, like telegraphers, were* very *good!*

Social contact between the Harvey Girls and house customers was discouraged, especially in the grand hotels where customers might come and stay for several months on vacation or business. Often the Harvey Girls were the recipients of unsolicited attention from hotel guests, and young Harvey Girls were grateful for the rules against dating that offered them a quick and inoffensive way out. Effie Jenks frequently found herself the object of a guest's admiration. She remembers one guest who approached her when she was still young:

> *Another prominent man in Albuquerque tried many times to date*
> *me but I always declined because I was not sure of his intentions.*
> *He later became a millionaire and once, years later, he came to*
> *La Fonda while I was working there. He grabbed my hand and*
> *held it, to which I did not protest. He said, "Effie, why didn't you*
> *let me do this years ago?" I said, "I was too bashful."*

In communities where the Harvey House was a favorite haunt for local ranchers, cowboys, and businessmen, the girls were often invited to participate in community and church events. "In the railroad towns," Katheryne Krause Ferguson remembers,

> *places where the railroad had made a stop that turned into a*
> *community, like Kingman, Winslow, and Seligman, the railroad*
> *and Harvey people were the cream of the crop socially. And in*
> *other towns, I was always asked to join the women's clubs and*
> *organizations. The girls didn't get to know the communities as*
> *well as I did. They worked so terrifically hard.*

Effie Jenks, although popular and well known in both Albuquerque and Santa Fe social circles in the twenties and thirties, and through World War II, believed there was still a negative public attitude toward waitresses that surfaced now and then even with respect to Harvey Girls. Effie married a prominent mining engineer, and like all the Harvey Girls in Albuquerque, enjoyed the annual dinner in their honor given by the mayor. Nevertheless, she still felt removed from the "social elite" of the city:

Waitresses were not social climbers or they would not be waitresses. Every waitress recognized the line of demarcation. It did not matter how much education, money, or scholastic achievement a waitress may have had; she was still not received. She might have been invited to many homes of the social elite, but she was still not what was termed "received."

When the Harvey Girls did find time to socialize, they often caused a stir among the local women who undoubtedly thought Harvey Girls were paid far too much attention. Myrtle Short came to the Castañeda from Illinois to be a Harvey Girl in 1926. She remembers that the Harvey House was a wonderful place to live and the community welcomed the Harvey Girls to social events:

Sometimes the Harvey Girls caused a lot of jealousy among the local girls, especially at dances. Sometimes after a dance where one or more Harvey Girls had been socializing with a lot of the local men, young women from Las Vegas would come into the lunchroom and find fault with everything we did—the toast was too brown, the eggs not the way they ordered them—petty things. We'd just grin and bear it. We had to be nice to everyone.

The Harvey system's reputation as a "matrimonial bureau" grew almost as quickly as the Santa Fe across the deserts and mountains of the West. Between 1883 and 1905, 8,260 Harvey Girls are said to have married railroadmen, ranchers, cowboys, and probably fellow employees—chefs, busboys, clerks, cooks.[3] By the early 1900s, legend has it that some four thousand babies had been named Fred or Harvey or both. One newspaper writer noted Harvey's contribution to family life in the West:

Fred Harvey, a remarkable man who has been running the eating stations on the Santa Fe Railway ever since it was built, is responsible for a great deal of the growth and a great deal of the happiness in this part of the country. He has done more than any immigration society to settle up the Southwest, and still continues to provide wives for ranchmen, cowboys, railway hands and other honest pioneers. . . . The successful results of his matrimonial bureau are found in every community. It must not be forgotten that a precedent for Mr. Harvey's enterprise was established by the first English settlers in America. Two cargoes of wives were sent out to the colonists of Jamestown by the Virginia society in London, and were sold to bachelor colonists for 120 pounds of tobacco per wife, while Mr. Harvey does not even charge a commission.[4]

Will Rogers, a frequent visitor to the Harvey Houses during his years of travel on the Santa Fe Railway, was an admirer of the Harvey Girls and their role in the West:

In the early days, the traveler fed on the buffalo. For doing so, the buffalo got his picture on the nickel. Well, Fred Harvey should have his picture on one side of the dime, and one of his waitresses with her arms full of delicious ham and eggs on the other side, 'cause they have kept the West supplied with food and wives.[5]

Many real and imagined romances were spawned around Harvey Houses. Young Harvey Girls were said to have married rich ranchers, industrious businessmen, oil magnates, railroad officials, politicians, foreign noblemen . . . Well, with so many tens of thousands of them, it is all probably true. Writers for popular magazines often glorified such romantic liaisons available in the West via the Harvey Houses. One writer told her eastern readers about Miss Mary Warrington, a New York society girl who joined Harvey to escape a marriage arranged with her father's money to a foreign count. Mary, the story explained, had everything a New York woman of means could ask for, but she wanted none of it, and changed her name to Mary Smith, Harvey Girl. But Mary's high-society parents needn't have worried about their daughter becoming a spinster with no resources. Mary met John Creighton-Smith, the youngest son of an English nobleman, over roast beef, served by herself, on the far desert of Arizona. She married him two months later, and moved to Kenya, where their descendants took their proper place as "top-flight socialites."[6]

Miss Emily Van Vores came from Pennsylvania, and was an orphaned, spinster schoolteacher before she heard of Harvey. Her luck turned when a traveling salesman told Emily about those "branches of heaven" known as Harvey Houses in the desert Southwest. Emily wrote to Mr. Harvey himself for a job. She worked as a Harvey Girl only eight months before she found herself standing side by side with the owner of a Colorado copper mine, saying, "I do."[7]

Many a young man riding the Santa Fe formed a fondness for one or more Harvey Girls met and left behind at the Harvey Houses along the way. They were friendly faces in an often lonely land. Typical of the somewhat bad but sincere poetry left anonymously by those who were enamored of Harvey's "women of good character" is: "The fairest of all sights, it seems to me, was a Harvey Girl I saw in Albuquerque."[8]

In the 1940s, Metro-Goldwyn-Mayer made a movie glorifying Harvey and his girls, based on the novel *The Harvey Girls* by Samuel Hopkins Adams. The film starred Judy Garland, Preston Foster, Chill Wills, Angela Lansbury, Marjorie Main, and Cyd Charisse. Although flattered by the attention and importance given their profession, most real-life Harvey Girls scoffed at the depiction of their lives found in the film. The realities of hard work were not sufficiently represented, claimed Harvey Girls. "And then there wasn't all that much singing and dancing!"

The musical had such romantically inclined songs as "The Santa Fe and Topeka," "In the Valley Where the Evening Sun Goes Down," and "Wishing on a Load of Hay." "Set in the imaginary western railroad town of Sandrock," the film's promotional material said, *"The Harvey Girls* is a fast-moving epic set to repercussions of a fight typical of the west in the late 1800s—a battle between the civilizing influences of the Santa Fe Railroad and the Harvey House, as opposed to the lawless rule of outlaws, gamblers and crooked officials of the early west."[9]

There was plenty of romance and glamor in the film's depiction of the Harvey Girls, which contrasted their supposed squeaky clean image with the "tainted" one of the local dance hall girls. Harvey Girl Effie Jenks recalled MGM's attempts to substantiate the position of the Harvey Girls in the Southwest prior to the film's release in 1946:

Publicity men from Hollywood came out to Albuquerque trying to find Harvey Girls who had made good marriages. The records didn't reveal any marriages with Rockefellers or knights of finance and they were afraid the "good marriage" story was all a myth. I volunteered my own marriage as rebuttal: my husband, Thomas Harry Jenks, was a descendant on his paternal side of a Welsh king who fled Wales and settled in England; on the maternal side, he was the descendant of Sir Rowland Hill, author of the English postage stamp and one of England's outstanding statesmen. My husband was also the first cousin to Jerome K. Jerome, England's celebrated playwright. My Harry was a mining engineer, a graduate of Oxford, England, and was sent to the United States by an English mining firm. Among his friends were Herbert Hoover, Theodore Roosevelt, and Howard Taft. Roosevelt and Taft both invited him to the White House, and upon my husband's death in 1941, he was listed in the Encyclopedia of American Biography. *I myself was born of peasant Danish ancestors who immigrated to this country looking for a better life for their children.*

Popular literature claimed that the queens of the dance halls were jealous of the Harvey Girls who moved into town with the Santa Fe. One story claimed that at Jim's Palace near Williams, Arizona, a dance-hall girl named Queenie Le Grand's business was falling off after the arrival of the Harvey House and its pretty waitresses. Determined to do something to save her business, Queenie washed off her makeup, dressed in plain clothes and went to the Harvey House seeking a job. Telling a sob story about being stranded in Arizona after her father died, she found that Fred Harvey, a big-hearted man, could not turn her away. "The application is highly irregular," he told her, "but I cannot in conscience turn you away only to risk your becoming like that infamous woman, Queenie Le Grand—a fallen woman." "Fallen!" Queenie is claimed to have screamed. "No such thing—I was pushed!"[10]

The day-to-day details of the real Harvey Girls lie somewhere between

The 1944 film, "The Harvey Girls," starred Judy Garland. Byron Harvey, Jr., Fred Harvey's grandson and later president of the Harvey empire, was paid twenty-five dollars for his appearance as a railroad brakeman in the MGM film about the Harvey Girls. (Credit: c. 1945 Loew's Inc., Ren. 1973 Metro-Goldwyn-Mayer Inc.; photograph courtesy University of Arizona Library Special Collections.)

Byron Harvey, Jr., acted as consultant to the film's producers, MGM. Here he is shown in his costume as a Santa Fe brakeman with director George Sidney. (Credit: Hospitality Magazine)

The Bisonte dining room, 1926. "At one end of the room a wide arch gave one a glimpse into the lunch room, where behind polished counters, neat waitresses dressed in the inevitable Harvey black and white, passed back and forth, presiding over their domain in a manner of quiet and polite assurance that can scarcely be discerned in the manner of any other corps of waitresses in the United States . . . The waitresses of the Harvey system are not servants. They put plutocrats to shame at times by their unfailing politeness, and their refusal to notice the condescending airs of such would be aristocratic travelers as are occasionally transported . . ." Albuquerque Morning Journal, July 29, 1911.
(Credit: The Kansas State Historical Society)

the glamorous image evoked by newspaper and magazine stories, and the drudgery found in the work of all waitresses everywhere. Kansas is a good place to look for the details of the lives of ordinary Harvey Girls, because Kansas was their original home.

Historians say Kansas's difficult years created a spirit of individualism. Until 1895, the entire history of Kansas was a series of disasters—hot winds, border wars, droughts, grasshoppers, and the skirmishes of man.[11] Even as late as the 1930s, Kansas seemed to wear a sad face to outsiders: "Western Kansas, in the middle of the 1930s," Ernie Pyle wrote, "was the saddest land I had ever seen."[12]

After eight years of drought and struggle with the grasshopper plague, Florence, Kansas, established itself as a thriving community of tents and open-air shops serving 1,400 residents beside the Santa Fe tracks. Harvey chose Florence, a railroad community founded by the Santa Fe in 1870, to be the site of the Clifton Hotel. The Clifton was built to resemble a fine English home with fountains and candelabra in the surrounding yard, and an elegant dining room and luxurious guest accomodations inside. In 1879, when the Clifton was enlarged, it became one of the largest buildings in central Kansas. In one six-month period, the Clifton housed 2,300 guests. But the Harvey House did not exclude local citizens from its comforts: there was an "eating stand" where customers could enjoy a more inexpensive lunch than that served in the dining room[13]; and the Clifton offered bath nights (featuring rainwater!) to local residents for twenty-five cents.[14]

The Clifton needed seven Harvey Girls and usually hired at least four of these from the local community. Additional women were sent in from Topeka or Kansas City. The house served three trains daily, each averaging about fifty customers. Meals were served family-style, ten people to a table. A train passenger paid seventy-five cents for dinner; railroad crew members ate for twenty-five cents.[15]

Despite its beautiful interior and landscaping, and its popularity among local residents and train passengers, the Clifton closed in March of 1900: faster trains changed the Santa Fe's daily schedule. Meal stops at Florence became unnecessary, and Newton's Harvey House, the Arcade Hotel, soon took over the service the Clifton had provided.

As the Clifton was closing, another Harvey House of equal beauty was under construction: the Bisonte Hotel in Hutchinson. The Bisonte, built at the turn of the century, was part of a new chain of Harvey Houses designed to attract tourist "stopover" traffic in addition to serving meal trains. Other Kansas Harvey Houses built for this same purpose were the Sequoyah in Syracuse and El Vaquero in Dodge City. Although Hutchinson was hardly a resort town—like many railway communities, its long, broad streets ended where the open prairie began, and its isolation from the rest of the civilized world was relieved only by the tracks of the Santa Fe—with the building of the Bisonte Hutchinson did offer train-weary customers a quiet, restful reprieve from the rigors of early cross-country travel.

At the turn of the century, Hutchinson had a population of nine thousand; by 1910, sixteen thousand residents enjoyed its churches, schools, musical societies, and the comings and goings of the Santa Fe passsenger trains through the Bisonte's station.

Joanne Stinelichner was a Harvey Girl in Hutchinson in 1916 and 1917. She remembers the Bisonte as one of the nicest hotels she worked in during her thirty-two years with Harvey. Johanna Klenke (see Chapter 4) also recalls the outstanding quality of life and work at the Bisonte: the hotel had a friendly, community atmosphere enjoyed by both the staff and guests. Even house discipline was humorous and low-key:

> We were allowed to eat almost anything in the kitchen except the fruit that was just in season. So when fresh cranberries came in, they were against the rules. The cooks kept them in these huge crock jars in a large refrigerator. When they weren't looking, the Harvey Girls used to sneak in there and scoop them out with the dipper. Well, one of the cooks must have seen us—we ate a lot of those cranberries—and when the cranberry jar was empty, they called the girls into the kitchen. One cook said, "Come in and let me show you something in the storeroom." They took us over to the jar and there at the bottom, in the few cranberries that were left, was a dead mouse. Of course, they had planted it there, just for us! It worked, for a while anyway!

The town of Hutchinson was badly flooded on July 13, 1929. Opal Sells Hill was working at the Bisonte at the time, living with the other Harvey Girls in a dorm that was across the street from the hotel. The only way to get to work during the flood was to find a strong man and be carried:

We packed up our clothes and then we rode piggyback on the men's backs across the water, which was up to their knees! We had to stay over at the Bisonte for two or three days until the water subsided.

One summer afternoon in the 1930s, the dorm was beseiged by fire. Opal was sitting outside on the porch swing when she smelled something burning:

I stood up and looked around back and could see a blazing fire! A lot of girls who worked the night shift were sleeping upstairs, so I ran inside and called and woke them all. It scared them so bad they ran out of their rooms and down the stairs right over me! I was knocked right down, skinned both of my knees—they even knocked the heels of my shoes off! They nearly killed me. I thought later I might have just as well have set there [sic] on the porch until someone else told them about the fire.

The exact date of the opening of the first Harvey House in Emporia, Kansas, has not been established. It was sometime in the 1880s, a decade after the Santa Fe had reached the rural community. The Harvey House was built of brick, with train sheds to protect the passengers as they disembarked from the train for the dining room.

John Preston Brady was born in 1910, ten miles southwest of Emporia. When he was sixteen, he met a friend who was working at the Harvey House; the boy said he was quitting his job as a Harvey busboy, and that if Brady went right in and applied, he could probably get the job:

Harvey had jobs for young boys as busboys, dishwashers, or pot washers. My job as busboy included ringing the gong to bring the people off the train into the lunchroom. I always knew exactly what time that train was due. I also boiled the water first thing every morning and made the coffee with two of the girls. I had to polish the brass railings on the counter, and then mop the floor. The manager would come in and inspect the restaurant area before a train came in, and he could spot a speck of dust a mile away!

I also took care of whatever the girls needed during a meal—carrying trays of dishes and things like that. I was not in the lunchroom at any time during a meal. After the train was out, everyone cleaned up. The girls did the counters, and I did the floors. And then everybody was off until the next meal train. If a train was late, we waited. The routine never varied—everybody did their job.

Brady was also responsible for getting box lunches to the black porters and conductors on the train because they were not allowed in the Emporia lunchroom:

It was a large operation in Emporia. Everyone who worked there stayed there, upstairs. The waitresses were on one end of the hotel, and the men on the other end. It was great fun living up there, although we were all under strict scrutiny of the manager. We had to be in by eleven each night, and they kept very close records of where everyone was in a well-disciplined, friendly way. It was my first time away from home, but it was the best place for a young boy to be.

I worked seven days a week and made thirty-five dollars a month plus room and board. We all became great friends at the house, but if the manager thought one of the guys was interested in one of the girls, well, it was a no-no.

We served four trains a day—two at noon and two in the evening. They were en route from Chicago to Los Angeles and back. The trains were loaded in those days. The movie stars used to take those trains—especially the El Capitan that stopped here—and local folks used to come down and watch to see who got off. Shirley Temple, Will Rogers, Jackie Cooper, Gloria Swanson, and many, many more were seen on the Emporia platform.

Most of the employees at Emporia, excepting the chef, the baker, and the manager, were local Kansans:

We had a stockroom man sent in from Topeka. And there was this salad man they hired as he went through on a freight train.

He was a terrible-looking guy when he arrived, but when he got some food in his stomach, and got some sleep, he was a handsome man. One of the best-looking Harvey Girls fell in love with him. Well, a few months later, some of the guys started missing suits of clothes. The manager suspected the salad guy and sent the maid to search his room. She found five or more suits of clothes pinned up under his mattress. The police arrested him and put him in jail downtown.

He had worked almost a year and everybody kind of liked him—we even went to visit him in jail. And he was a good salad man, real fast. But he was stealing all along. Everybody found they were missing something.

The Harvey Girl who had fallen for him felt real bad for a while. But everybody was nice to her. The guy disappeared after he was released. He was just another railroad bum.

Emporia was a division point and the Santa Fe was the chief employer in town for many years. On the edge of the Flint Hills, Emporia had lots of cattle and lots of cowboys. There were large stockyards near the railroad and cattle buyers were always passing through town. John Brady remembers:

Oil had been struck twenty miles from Emporia, so there was a lot of money around, and that meant a lot of gamblers and bootleggers. There was prohibition in those days, and even selling cigarettes was illegal. Even though there was a lot of activity in Emporia, once you were outside of it, there was just miles and miles of prairie. My father's farm was twenty miles from town, on the edge of civilization.

In the twenties, people who came on the train from New York through these parts were looking to be scalped by Indians. My wife's uncle came here from Chicago and got off the train and said, "Why, you have trees out here, haven't you?"

The baker at the Harvey House made his own home brew in the bathtub in his room upstairs:

He never could get it bottled because everybody who worked in the house would come up and drink it right out of the bathtub! The manager didn't know about it until about twelve batches later. He got to smelling it all over the house. A customer finally asked about it and the manager found it in the bathtub and closed the operation down!

Olive Winter Loomis (see Chapter 4) was trained in Topeka and then shipped out to Emporia. During World War I, Olive remembers the Emporia Harvey House was often crowded with soldiers:

I was in the dining room and it was busy, busy, busy. I roomed with the headwaitress of the counter, and although she was a little wild, she took care of me like my mother. She used to sneak around after hours but she wouldn't allow me to! She was going with this important railroad official. He was single, but they never got married. When he was gone, she went out with one of Emporia's important businessman's sons. The man must have reported it to the manager, because she was sent on.

It was unusual for a girl to be wild in Emporia. We had to be in at nine. I liked it because even though there were rules, I could do things like go to picture shows, things you couldn't do in the country.

There was a railroadman who had a car and he used to take a bunch of us girls out for a ride in the country. He always had us back by nine. I wasn't used to riding in cars. It was new for me. On one of those trips he drove into a farmer's gate and bent it real bad. We all had to chip in and pay for it.

The food at the Emporia Harvey House was outstanding. Fresh fruit was sold at the newsstand, and the restaurant was famous for its homemade ice cream and sherbets, rolls, breads, and pastries. Even the Thousand Isle dressing was an object of culinary conversation:

It was made fresh from the very beginning . . . good olive oil, yolks of eggs, so much salt, so much sugar, so much mustard, and they'd whip that up into mayonnaise; then they would take

little green onions and chop them fine, hard-boiled eggs and
pickles, and then some ketchup—it was out of this world! . . . We
used to serve quarter-heads of lettuce to each guest. We had these
little salad dressing boats and we'd pour it on for the guests
ourselves. Oh, I tell you, the service we used to give them![16]

In the late 1800s, Kansas had as rough-and-tumble a group of cowtowns as was ever found in North America and the rest of the world. Eastern Kansas had established itself as a civilized territory by 1870, but western Kansas was developing a reputation for violence and lawlessness in cattle towns such as Abilene, Wichita, Newton, and Dodge City that would take decades to overcome. With the railroad and the Texas cattle trade came colorful characters and outrageous incidents that gained extensive notoriety in the nineteenth century and later. Kansas was—and is—farm country, and while the cowboys and outlaws were getting most of the press, quiet homesteaders and farmers were making Kansas into a peace-loving, community-oriented state.

With the arrival of the rails Texas cattle by the hundreds of thousands came to Abilene, Wichita, Newton, and eventually Dodge City. Their trails of beaten dirt could be four hundred yards wide, gradually making a huge, sunken rut on the Kansas prairie. By 1873, 450,000 head of cattle, mostly of the fearless, unpredictable breed known as the Texas longhorn, were shipped over the railroad out of Kansas. The transient cowtown population of cowboys and herd bosses, cattle-selling Texans, prostitutes, and saloon-buffs, created an atmosphere of hitherto unmatched chaos on the Kansas frontier. Although the heydey of each of the great cattle towns was short-lived, their chaotic beginnings would follow and often overshadow their development for years afterward.

While the citizens of Florence, Kansas, were enjoying English-style elegance at the Clifton Harvey House in the 1870s and 1880s, Newton's residents, neighbors on the main line west, were seeking ways to overcome the general bedlam brought on by the cattle industry of the 1870s. Called "Bloody Newton, the wickedest town in the West" because of the alarming number of deaths reported on its streets in the 1870s, Newton seasonally hosted hundreds of cowboys fresh off the trail. The young cowhands, often miles from home, had new money in their pockets and long-tempered desires in their trail-weary hearts. They were ready to indulge in reckless and even juvenile behavior in the local saloons and dance halls. Newton's streets and bars became the setting for their party at the end of the trail, and there was little the local populace could do.

Only the departure of the cattle industry could change Newton and that is exactly what happened. By the 1880s, after the industry had long left Newton's shipping yards empty and moved to Dodge City, the residents of Newton were determined to overcome their town's past history and earn it a place in modern Kansas. Policemen in uniform were introduced to replace the old sheriffs, so infamous for their duty on both sides of the law. Without the cowboys and accompanying quick-money businessmen who catered to them, Newton began to assert control over its streets and population. The Old West of horses and cattle drives might be romantic in dime-store novels back east, but out west it was becoming a tiresome burden.

Fred Harvey must have been sympathetic to Newton's efforts because in 1900 he chose Newton to be the location of the Arcade Hotel. The Arcade was a coup for Newton, and passenger trains stopped several times a day at its platform. But several years later Harvey further graced Newton by moving his district headquarters there from Kansas City. This meant the construction of a major dairy, an ice plant, meat locker-rooms, a creamery, a poultry feeding station and produce plant, a carbonating plant for bottling soda pop, and a modern steam laundry. Newton became the hub of Harvey passenger service.[17]

From Newton, supplies were shipped out to other Harvey Houses all over the Southwest. Laundry from the other houses was sent in by train. By 1921, Newton's laundry cleaned four million pieces a year. The Arcade Hotel and the Harvey district operation employed hundreds of Newton's residents. Harvey was an integral part of Newton's emergence as one of Kansas's major modern communities.

The railroad was the fastest, easiest mode of cross-country transportation, and many famous people disembarked on Newton's platform. Though often only for a cigarette or a short walk, Newtonians were treated to glimpses of Clark Gable, Mae West, Gary Cooper, Cary Grant, Bing Crosby, Joan Crawford, Jimmy Durante, and many others.[18]

The original Arcade was replaced by a new Harvey hotel in 1930. The new building was designed to be an exact replica of Shakespeare's home in England. The following year, as the railroad schedules and service

The 1929 flood, Hutchinson, Kansas. (Credit: Opal Sells Hill)

Lunch room, Arcade Hotel, Newton, Kansas. (Credit: Kansas State Historical Society)

El Vaquero, c. 1910, Dodge City. Two giant sundials in the Dodge City station told newly arrived Santa Fe travelers they were now in the Mountain Time zone, heralding the first glimpses of the Rockie Mountains that would begin to rise off the Kansas plains in the next hundred or so miles. (Credit: Johanna Klenke)

The Emporia, Kansas Harvey House staff, 1929, Irwin, Katheryne and Alice Louise Krause center front. Even Harvey busboys were trained in the"Harvey way:" one young busboy watched a crippled customer struggle to open a ketchup bottle. The man's wife called for help; the boy tested the bottle, but when it moved easily, pretended he could not budge it. He took the ketchup back into the kitchen and returned saying that only the head chef, "who was really powerful," could open the bottle. (Credit: Katheryne Krause Ferguson)

demands of the Southwest changed with the coming of the depression, the superintendent's office and headquarters were moved from Newton to Albuquerque.

"West of Kansas City, there is no Sunday. West of Dodge City, there is no God!"[19] Such was the widely circulated belief back east, and even out west, concerning Dodge City, Kansas. To this day, if there is one town in the history of the Americas that brings to mind the worst images of frontier violence, it is Dodge City:

> For a decade, Dodge City handled more live cattle than any other market on earth, and has preserved more of the tradition of that turbulent, brawling era than any other cowtown of that region.[20]

Newton quickly outgrew its uncivilized and rowdy reputation, but Dodge City, a third of Kansas away, took forty years to clear its name of the lawless notoriety developed in its first fifteen years of existence. As in Newton, Dodge City residents knew the cattle trade was a temporary livelihood and sought farmers and businessmen to settle in their community. But in Dodge it was an even more difficult task. Gunmen such as Bat and James Masterson, Wyatt Earp, Wild Bill Hickok, Bill Tilghman, and "Mysterious" Dave Mathers were famous for shooting first and talking later. Dodge City's Boot Hill was the community's most famous attribute.

Although Dodge's daily violence was probably exaggerated, there was a large transient population, along with many saloons, gamblers, and prostitutes. The town sought a cleaner image as early as 1881, when the infamous Masterson brothers, the town's sheriff and marshal, and the league of deputies who worked with them, were run out of town by the new mayor's posse, and gamblers and prostitutes were fined for illegal activities.

The Santa Fe rails reached what was to become Dodge City in 1872. Before the town smelled of cattle, it smelled of buffalo hides. Dodge was a mecca for buffalo hunters, located near the great plains of buffalo grass favored by the great, roaming herds. During the first winter after the arrival of the railroad, 200,000 buffalo hides were shipped east from Dodge. Before a proper depot and buildings for businesses could be erected, the streets were filled with wagons, horses, and traders with all variety of supplies from the East. But within only a few years, the buffalo herds were dwindling and the industry they had supported was dying.

In 1874, the Santa Fe helped Dodge City begin the switch from buffalo to cattle, building stockyards and arranging freight shipments around the Texas cattle drives due from the south. By 1877, Dodge was second only to Wichita in the Texas cattle trade, shipping 22,940 head of cattle, and claiming over one-fourth of the Santa Fe's total annual freight shipments.[21] Dodge City was well on its way to becoming the undisputed and widely celebrated cowboy capital of the world.

"The cowboy spends his money recklessly," observed a visitor to Dodge in 1884. "He is a jovial, careless fellow bent on having a big time regardless of expense. He will make away with the wages of a half year in a few weeks, and then go back to his herds for another six months."[22]

Harvey opened the first Harvey House in Dodge City in 1896, operating a lunchroom out of a boxcar placed on stilts near the tracks. The architecture was crude, the town even cruder, but Fred Harvey's food and service was not. A cowboy was allowed in for a meal, but he had to respect the same coat rule as the genteel eastern visitor.

The boxcar was replaced by the elegant El Vaquero Harvey House at the turn of the century. The hotel and restaurant offered customers refined service and food. But Dodge was still part of Kansas, and Kansas was still on the huge, rolling prairie land of the Midwest. In 1925, even paved streets and the conveniences of the Harvey House could not take all of the frontier feeling out of Dodge City and environs. One Santa Fe railroader remembers:

> Most rooms in the early day Harvey Houses, and this includes those at Dodge City . . . were without bath. . . . The tradition of Saturday night bath was still exerting some influence, and a toilet just down the hall, instead of in the back yard, was a real improvement. . . .
>
> This separation of sleeping rooms and toilet facilities probably saved my life on one occasion, although I do not offer this argument in favor of such a plumbing layout.
>
> One evening in the late spring of 1925, I got into Dodge City about nine P.M. and in company with a commercial traveler,

walked up to the desk in the Harvey House and asked for a room. Only one was available, naturally without a bath, but the night clerk said his room would be unoccupied until after breakfast, and one of us could have it. The matter was settled, however, when the salesman decided he would go up to the O'Neal House, and I took the available room.

It was a warm, still night, with a little lightning in the southwest, but it didn't seem to be in a washout producing area, so I raised the window, pulled down the shade to keep the platform light out of my eyes, and turned in. About one A.M. I woke up and decided to pay a visit to the men's room, which was a few doors down the hall. . . .

When I returned to my room and opened the door, the knob was jerked out of my hand, and the screen blew off the window. Unable to close the door with one hand, I had backed against it, trying to force it shut, when something struck it from the other side and I was knocked the length of the room, finally coming to rest on my hands and knees against a chair. . . .

The lights in the hotel had gone out but I could see the sky through a hole in the roof and ceiling.[23]

Joseph Noble, the author, suffered a bruised hip in what was later identified as a small tornado which struck the brick chimney adjacent to the hotel and hurled a brick through the second story. The hall and part of Noble's room were filled with brick, and the door to his room was torn from its hinges. His bed was covered with brick and masonry.

El Vaquero, for all its charm to customers, was not a favorite among Harvey Girls. Opal Sells Hill claims it is the only house she ever requested a quick transfer out of: "I was there in 1933. There were lots of cowboys and noisy cows. It was too wild for me and I said, 'Get me out of here!' I left after six months." Joanne Stinelichner says El Vaquero had the reputation of being a "workhouse":

There was nothing close to an eight-hour day in Dodge City. There were more trains coming in there all the time because of the wheat and cattle. I didn't find it any rougher than other towns, just very, very busy.

Hazel Williams (who was fired for talking to a busboy on the dorm steps) was only fifteen when she worked at the Dodge City Harvey House, but she liked Dodge in 1918:

Western Kansas was thought of as wild but it was unfair, even back in those days. You could go anyplace, even a young woman. It was the same as Hutchinson or any other Kansas town. Of course, the smell of the cattle was terrible. Some days you could hardly stand it if the wind was blowing right. But the cowboys were okay; they weren't trouble.

Newton and Dodge City may have challenged the Harvey system and its ability to bring gentility to a railroad community, but Kansas City, Kansas, was a made-to-order Harvey town. For many years, Kansas City was Harvey headquarters, with the offices of the Harvey brothers, and the head employment office, in the Union Station. The great Harvey dining room at the Union Station opened in 1914, and could seat an unprecedented 525 people.

"The opening was a glorious occasion," Cora Winter recalled in a 1946 interview with the *Kansas City Star.* "Everything was bright and new, and there were yellow chrysanthemums all over. We had a horseshoe-shaped counter then, decorated with shiny fruits. All the tables had white cloths, and the chairs had cane seats."

Miss Winter said the uniforms were just like Judy Garland's in the movie, except for the bow in the hair: "We weren't allowed to have bows. Instead, all the girls wore their hair the same way—parted in the middle and drawn to a small knot at the nape of the neck."

In 1926, Kansas City Harvey Girls worked only in the lunchroom. The dining room had waiters in black trousers and white coats. The coat rule was enforced in Kansas City, with a supply of coats kept on hand for those who ventured in without one. Men and women were forbidden to smoke in the dining room, a rule that was in fact enforced. In 1922, an elegantly dressed lady lit a cigarette and was asked to leave by the manager.[24]

The Harvey House in the Union Station was very popular among city residents. Many local businessmen were known to take time off daily to wander down to the lunchroom for a cup of Harvey coffee and a chat with the waitresses. Patrons had favorites whose tables they always managed to sit at. In Kansas City, a waitress who had been at the house less than three years was "just beginning."

"The Union Station Harvey House was the highlight of Kansas City," Myrtle Tyler remembers:

> *It was a busy place with lots of big parties. The New Year's eve party held every year brought out everyone in Kansas City. They would have to lock the door. When someone left, they'd let someone else in.*
>
> *All kinds of girls worked there—some with children to raise, others who were taking care of their parents, some who worked parttime and went to school. Quite a few were in nurse's training, but we made so much more as Harvey Girls than as nurses![25]*

In the 1920s and 1930s, Kansas City socialites often paid a late-night visit to the Harvey House after the theater. Favorite late-night snacks were cream cheese and bar le duc, caviar sandwiches, Harvey's famous huge, hot cinnamon rolls and coffee, or chicken a la king:

> *Before the war, couples in evening clothes came in for supper after concerts and musical shows. Often a few would start singing or humming the recently played tunes. Others would take it up, and guests on both sides of the counter would join in the chorus.[26]*

At the western end of Kansas was little-known Syracuse. The Sequoyah Harvey House was a favorite among Harvey employees from the time it opened in 1908 until it closed in 1936. Built in the Spanish Mission style found also at El Vaquero, the Sequoyah's grey stuccoed arches and inviting, shaded walkways made this small community on the high plains of western Kansas an oasis beside the Santa Fe tracks:

> *The building was of Spanish design with wide arches, with a walled patio that opened off the dining room and lobby. The patio was planted with flowers and had a fish pond shaded from the hot sun by large cottonwood trees. . . . East of the Harvey House, the area was planted to blue grass [sic] with the attractive beds of*

bright flowers placed in spots in the lawns. . . . This made a refreshing place for tired travelers to rest.[27]

Katheryne Krause Ferguson remembers the Sequoyah had the "most beautiful yard anyone had ever seen in those parts. It was two blocks long before the platform. I've seen people get off the train, take their shoes off and walk around and around on that grass."

The Sequoyah opened with a large banquet for Santa Fe Railway officials, Harvey people, and Syracuse residents:

Friday evening, July 24, 1908, the banquet . . . celebrating the opening of the Sequoyah Hotel, the Santa Fe Railway's new $100,000 depot hotel, was given in the elegant dining room. . . . The tables were decorated with cut flowers in vases, smilax and ferns, and wreaths and festoons of the same adorned the walls. The room was lighted by . . . electric lights in frosted globes descending from the ceiling. . . . The effect was most pleasing . . . and could hardly be equalled outside of the environs of a center of wealth and luxury.[28]

The favorite pastime of the citizens of Syracuse, like their peers in small towns all over Kansas and America in the heyday of the great trains, was to gather at the platform on a warm afternoon to see who disembarked from the train. Will Rogers, Herbert Hoover, Clara Bow, Ann Sheridan, and Leo Carillo all appeared on the Sequoyah platform, and Franklin Roosevelt waved from the rear of one of the passing trains.

The Sequoyah was the favorite child of Syracuse, Kansas, and was the hub of all social and business activity:

Resolved: That we do hereby beg to express to the officials of the Atchison, Topeka and Santa Fe Railway on behalf of the citizens of Syracuse generally, the deep feeling of gratitude and appreciation of this magnificent building, which was not built for a day, but for all time, as a monument to the generous and broad business policy of the managers of the Santa Fe system.[29]

In 1908, who could have foreseen the events of the 1930s and their effect on the great Santa Fe and Harvey Houses in places like Syracuse, Kansas?

As the Santa Fe moved across Kansas to Colorado, and to New Mexico, Oklahoma, and Texas, Harvey Houses opened every hundred miles or so. Life for Harvey Girls sent out from Kansas to work in these young territories and states of the Southwest varied from town to town, region to region. In one community they could be the toast of the town; in the next, they were accused of being prostitutes. Often the character of an area was reflected in its attitude toward and treatment of the young women who worked in the local Harvey House.

New Mexico was the home of sixteen Harvey Houses, five of which were among the grandest in the system—the Montezuma and Castañeda in Las Vegas, La Fonda in Santa Fe, the Alvarado in Albuquerque, and El Navajo in Gallup. But most New Mexico Harvey Houses were the typical lunch and dining facilities by the tracks, usually of brick, with living quarters for the staff upstairs or in a building nearby. These Harvey Houses, in places like Raton, Deming, San Marcial, Belen, Vaughn, and Clovis were constantly busy with railroad crews, and also served as social centers for the small and often isolated young communities they were part of. They opened all up and down the Santa Fe line from the 1880s until the early part of the 1900s. Like Kansas, much of small-town history in New Mexico is interwoven with the Santa Fe Railway and the Harvey Houses.

Coming from the north and Raton Pass, the Santa Fe directed its tracks toward the city of Santa Fe, where it seemed logical enough to create a major stop. But it was not to happen this way. The Atchison, Topeka and Santa Fe Railway never laid its main track into its namesake. There are two supposed explanations for this: one claims that the citizens of Santa Fe supported a rival railroad before the Santa Fe was established in New Mexico, and that the Santa Fe later snubbed the little city, laying its main line substantially east of her; the other story claims that the city of Santa Fe made an all-out effort to secure the railroad's consideration, but lost after the railway's surveys showed the route would be too mountainous. When the main line could not be laid into Santa Fe, a spur was promised, completed on February 16, 1880.[30]

In 1880, Lamy, New Mexico, was the site chosen as the junction from which a spur track from the main line would be laid into Santa Fe. Lamy became a town overnight. Fifteen miles southeast of Santa Fe, in the foothills of the Sangre de Cristo Mountains, the Santa Fe Railway built maintenance yards, section crew housing, and a depot and Harvey House. Lamy never boasted more than three hundred residents, but in 1910, it had the "oasis in the desert," El Ortiz Harvey House.

El Ortiz once enjoyed the distinction of being the "littlest hotel in the littlest town" in the Southwest. Harvey people called it the Honeymoon House, because some sixty-two young managers were sent there between 1910 and 1938. It was an architectural gem. The Spanish-Pueblo-style building was designed by Kansas City architect Louis Curtiss, and the interior was the masterpiece of Harvey designer Mary Colter. El Ortiz was a one-story structure built around an enclosed courtyard. The feeling was of a small inn or Spanish hacienda, with less than ten guest rooms, all with doors onto the patio, "whose perimeter in the growing season was a verdant scene of hanging vines and split-log planter boxes."[31] Colter selected each piece herself: the heavy carved Mexican furniture, Navajo rugs, Spanish religious paintings, and *santos*—every item in the hotel. The result earned a wide and faithful audience of admirers. The hotel even became a favorite gathering place for locals charmed by its peaceful, old-world ambience:

> *People even motored to Lamy for breakfast! T. T. Flynn, the pulp magazine writer par excellence, who lived in Santa Fe a few years ago, said he often worked on his story-writing all night, and then motored to Lamy for coffee and doughnuts. The trip pepped him up.*[32]

Owen Wister, author of *The Virginian*, stayed at El Ortiz and wrote the manager that it reminded him of

> *a private house of someone who had lavished thought and care upon every nook. . . . In the patio of this hacienda, pigeons were picking in the grass by the little center fountain. This little oasis among the desert hills is a wonder of taste to be looked back upon by the traveler who has stopped there, and forward to by the*

traveler who is going to stop there. The temptation was to give up
all plans and stay a week for the pleasure of living and resting in
such a place. [33]

William Jennings Bryan was a guest at El Ortiz in 1918. William F. Cody—
"Buffalo Bill"—is reported to have said, "This little hotel would have made
a nice little ranch house," and to have "toasted his booted toes at the huge
fireplace, and stroked his bushy eyebrows as he contemplated the pictures
of bullfights."[34]

One newspaper writer discovered the charm of the littlest hotel by
accident:

Traveling over the line of the Santa Fe a few days ago, the writer
found himself held over at Lamy, a junction point on the main
line. Three hours of waiting were staring him in the face, and a
drizzling rain outdoors made the prospect a little worse than
dismal. On sight of a Harvey House, with a peculiar sign before it
marked "El Ortiz" he picked up courage to believe that the
evening might be pleasant in spite of the murky weather.

A cold wind had come up with the rain, and the glow of a log
fire in the open fireplace of the large hotel living room, gave a
cordial welcome that caused the rain and the hours of waiting to
be forgotten. Lights in well designed mission electroliers gave the
room its illumination, and a number of men and women who
had entered to enjoy the warm comfort of the attractive room
seemed very little concerned about the hour at which their train
was scheduled to leave.

The latecomers had not recovered from the astonishment
produced upon their entrance into the living room, and looking
around at old Spanish engravings on the walls, exquisite pieces of
hammered copper decorating the stone fireplace, rare old furniture
made of brass, leather and Flemish oak . . . they exclaimed again
and again, "Who would have expected to find such a beautiful
room, and such a building in this isolated place?" As no one had
expected it, except those who knew the perfection of the Harvey
system by previous experience, there were no replies advanced to
those wondering interrogations. [35]

Because of its relative isolation, El Ortiz was often passed by in favor of work at La Fonda in Santa Fe by young Harvey Girls. Older Harvey Girls, less interested in the sort of social life offered at larger Harvey Houses in active urban centers, often chose to work at Lamy.

In 1919, a young woman named Lenore Dils stepped off the train in San Marcial, New Mexico, to begin work as a stenographer for the Santa Fe Railway. She found a community of railroad workers, ranchers, homesteaders, gamblers, saloonkeepers, and Harvey people.[36] San Marcial was a town that kept its Old West flavor well into the 1920s. The main street was "wide, dusty and unpaved," and provided parking spaces for "Model Ts as well as hitching posts for horses."[37]

San Marcial was a very old, albeit tiny, community of adobe houses by the Rio Grande when the Santa Fe chose it for a division point in 1881. A railroad depot, company houses, and a gleaming, bustling Harvey House soon came to the still remote region of southern New Mexico. For many years, four passsenger trains passed daily over this stretch of track, called the Horny Toad Division by railroad personnel because of the inordinate number of horny toads found covering the tracks in the early years. (These creatures were frequently swept off the rails by railroad crew members to prevent the train wheels from slipping.)[38] Situated between Albuquerque and El Paso, San Marcial and its Harvey House became an important and busy place on the New Mexican desert.

Lenore Dils later wrote a book, *Horny Toad Man,* about her years in San Marcial, and her hours in the two-story Harvey House. A red building beside the Santa Fe tracks, the Harvey House had a "long, empty veranda across the front, and a few shreds of parched grass striving to live inside the picket fence."[39] Inside were the standard Harvey shining mahogany counters, gleaming chrome-plated coffee urns, sparkling crystal glassware, and pastry display cases. The San Marcial Harvey Girls were from as far away as Switzerland:

The Harvey House was probably the brightest, most modern place in town. . . . A world away from the food prepared over a campfire on the range, or at a fly-infested, greasy restaurant run by some vino [sic].[40]

El Ortiz, Lamy, New Mexico. A.T. and S.F. railway president Edward P. Ripley is credited as the "father" of El Ortiz; he decided the small hotel should be built at the junction named for Archbishop J.B. Lamy, a Catholic prelate and pioneer educator, and subject of Willa Cather's DEATH COMES FOR THE ARCHBISHOP. (Credit: Santa Fe Railway)

The westbound Super Chief leaving Lamy for Los Angeles. Additional locomotives and their crews were kept at Lamy to move trains through Glorieta Pass. The ten-mile upgrade took one hour with assistance from mountain engines, equipped with lowered wheels for traction, hooked one in front and two behind. (Credit: Santa Fe Railway)

The San Marcial Harvey House. San Marcial, New Mexico, 1920, was the old west of wide, dusty streets, Model T's and horses. Two thousand people left the town after the 1929 floods. Seventy-five residents escaped the water from the Rio Grande by climbing on the flat and coal cars of the only train at the station, and with the water over the train's axles, left town for the last time. Called the Pompeii of New Mexico, San Marcial was inundated by seven feet of silt.
(Credit: Santa Fe Railway)

The Kingman, Arizona, Harvey House, 1905.
(Credit: Mojave County Historical Society)

San Marcial had grown to become a large railroad town when it was destroyed by two major floods in 1929. The first flood, on August 13, damaged the adobe and frame buildings in the town. Residents immediately began to rebuild. However, the second flood, on September 24, brought ten feet of water from the Rio Grande into the heart of town. The only buildings still visible above the torrent were the second floors of the Harvey House and the depot. Those residents who did not leave town in time were marooned upstairs in these two buildings. Some thirty-one people waited out the tide in the Harvey House; another thirty huddled upstairs in the depot.

The second flood completely devasted the town. It was never rebuilt. San Marcial simply ceased to exist. The first floors of the depot and the Harvey House were filled with silt, and what few buildings were left even partially standing were soon torn down. For many years, the residents of San Marcial, mostly career railroaders and Harvey employees, held annual reunions to reminisce about their days in the lovely town by the Rio Grande. Today, San Marcial exists on no maps, and its streets and town limits are indistinguishable from the desert.

Mohave County, Arizona, was famous for its gold and silver mines in the 1860s. When the Santa Fe reached Kingman in 1883, the town quickly became the established shipping and trading center for the entire mining district of Mohave. The first depot was only a boxcar, but this was soon replaced by a two-story wooden building.

Kingman's citizens included many fortune hunters from the East Coast and Europe. Claims were recorded by the hundreds in Mohave County from the mid-1860s until the turn of the century. Ranching was also possible in this section of the Arizona desert, but not like it was in Texas and Kansas: here cattle had to be kept near the few sources of water, and herds were raised to provide meat for the railroad crews, and later for the early settlers of Arizona.

Double track was not laid on this section of the Santa Fe until 1920, at which time train traffic was exceptionally heavy. Each stop—Kingman, Seligman, Ash Fork, Williams, and Winslow—received at least two assigned meal trains a day.

The Kingman Harvey House was completed in 1901. At that time, Kingman boasted, and rightly so, that its Harvey House was "the largest west of Kansas City and east of Los Angeles."[41] (This was not an honor it would have for long, as the Santa Fe was engaged in building the Alvarado in Albuquerque.) A meal cost seventy-five cents—expensive for those parts at that time—but the rate was the same at all Harvey Houses. The Kingman Harvey House was, from its inception in 1901 until it closed in the 1930s, *the* place for Kingman residents to go after a party or show. Although it allowed no dances, the dining room was used for banquets, parties, and Rotary Club meetings.

Because of the great shortage of women in Arizona in the early years of the twentieth century, almost no Harvey Girls were hired locally. Until World War II, Harvey Girls were sent from Kansas to serve in the Arizona Harvey Houses. Although they were said to be in high demand in a community like Kingman, attending numerous dances and parties with local residents, the Harvey Girls were not necessarily treated with the respect this might imply.

One former Kingman Harvey Girl, Bernice Black McLain, remembers that the employees were still treated "like all waitresses—not very well" in the 1920s. Bernice came to Kingman from Topeka, after a training session at El Navajo Harvey House in Gallup, New Mexico:

> *Kingman and the desert looked terrible to me! I was used to trees and flowers and grass, all the things I grew up with in Nebraska. There was nothing here but sand.*
>
> *I left home in Nebraska when I was 19, in 1926. I went to visit a cousin who was living in Topeka and that's where I heard about Harvey. My mother and family didn't think too much about me becoming a waitress, but I wanted to work. Girls weren't supposed to work in those days unless they had to, but I wanted to. I was different. My friends wanted to stay home until they got married. Not me.*
>
> *I signed a six-month contract at Kingman. There weren't a lot of trains stopping for meals there, just two a day. There were lots of railroadmen, however, and ranchers and miners. Kingman was a very big mining town.*
>
> *I lived upstairs in the Harvey House. I kept saying I was going to leave for good after six months. Just before I left, the manager asked me to stay. I said, Oh no, not me! So I went home and*

*after three weeks, I missed the desert so much I wrote and asked
if I could return. They said yes, and I returned and stayed here a
long, long time.*

*The Harvey Girls here had a very good life, but a lot of us
resented the way people in the community looked down on
waitresses. We thought Harvey Girls were very different from
waitresses. . . .*

*It was a great situation for me as a young woman. I liked
traveling and I liked the freedom to be on my own. It wasn't like
being stranded out on the desert. Everything was cared for and a
woman could save money. . . . Harvey encouraged young girls to
leave home—I would never have gone so far otherwise.*

Bernice worked as a Harvey Girl in Kingman, the Grand Canyon, and at
Winslow, Arizona, before marrying a railroadman when she was thirty-two:
"That was pretty old to be getting married in those days!"

Needles, California, named for three pinnacles of rock on the California
side of the Colorado River, was a division of the Santa Fe Railway. Harvey
first opened a house in this desert community in 1887, later building the
fine El Garces Hotel in the early 1900s. Needles was a town Harvey people
either liked very much, and chose to remain in a long while, or disliked and
left as soon as possible. Besides its extreme heat in the summertime,
Needles, before World War II, was a very isolated town. It was a major
railroad town, with plenty of people and activity surrounding the Santa Fe,
but it had little contact with other communities.

"You couldn't run to the next town for entertainment," Katheryne
Krause Ferguson recalls of her life in Needles in the 1930s:

*Before airplanes, it was a very isolated place. But I loved Needles.
I thought it was a great place to live. People were thrown together
for everything. People did a lot of things together and became very
close. There were a lot of Harvey picnics and outdoor events.
There wasn't much turnover in Needles. People came and they
stayed a couple of years. Many of the Harvey Girls settled here,
marrying railroaders or ranchers. The Harvey Girls were accepted
by the community in Needles, and were never looked down on.*

Route 66, the main artery west by automobile, passed through Needles. Katheryne remembers, "It was a big stopping-off place in those days. We saw a lot of people traveling across the country by train and by car."

Hazel Redenbough came to Needles in 1923. Born in Topeka, Hazel was raised by an aunt and uncle after her parents divorced when she was a baby. Both of her parents were circus entertainers, and Hazel eventually followed in their footsteps, but not until she had worked for Harvey for six years:

I told the Harvey people in Topeka that I was 18, but I was really only 14. My uncle was a laborer and very poor. I had to work. I couldn't afford an education, but I got one with Harvey!

I was trained at the Topeka lunchroom and then sent out to Kansas City. I was what they called a relief girl, and was sent to houses where people were on vacation. I worked in Newton, Albuquerque, Belen, Clovis, Raton, and finally Needles.

I loved the dorm life. I was a natural clown and also a musician so I was always performing for the Harvey employees.

I was the only blonde in a dining room with twenty-eight Harvey Girls. And do you know, nearly every single unmarried man in Needles proposed to me! There were an awful lot of single men in Needles, mostly with the railroad. I finally got engaged to a young man who was an engineer with the Santa Fe. His father was a big lawyer in Nebraska. We were engaged for a few months, with the manager's approval, of course, when he started to grow this mustache. He kissed me one night and that mustache made me mad. I asked him to shave it off—I told him I wouldn't marry him if he didn't. Well, he wouldn't shave it, so I gave him back his ring.

The biggest thrill I ever had was when William S. Hart, the famous western silent-movie star, came into the dining room. He sat at one of my tables and when I served him he said, "I'd like to stick you in my pocket and take you home and let you play with my ponies." He patted me and left. I looked under the plate after the train had gone and found a silver dollar!

We treated all customers the same. Sometimes you'd get

Head Waitress Clara (Rebel) Quartier worked in Oklahoma and New Mexico before moving to Kingman where she made her home. "You could be fired for carrying a glass of water in your hand . . . There were no ifs, ands, or buts—you minded or you lost your job."
(Credit: Mojave County Historical Society)

The Harvey House at Needles, California, 1907, before El Garces was built. (Credit: Santa Fe Railway)

Ponca City in 1889 was one of the few "communities" found along the new Santa Fe track.
(Credit: Santa Fe Railway)

Registration before the Cherokee Strip "run," 1893. Those registered appear to have the evidence stuck under their hatbands.
(Credit: Kansas State Historical Society)

Hundreds gathered at the A.T. and S.F. depot in Arkansas City the day before the first "run," awaiting special trains that would take them into Indian Territory on April 22, 1889.
(Credit: Kansas State Historical Society)

someone who was needy—Groucho Marx was like that. The coffee wasn't hot enough, the service not enough, nothing pleased him. We'd give those people special attention, but otherwise, everybody was treated the same. . . .

The most unusual Harvey Girl I ever knew was my roommate in Needles, Sally. She was from North Dakota. I loved her. She weighed no less than 230 pounds. They hired her because she had such a fine personality, like Kate Smith. Of course, in Needles in the summer, it was nothing to be 120 degrees in the shade. Sally had difficulty with the heat. She'd get dizzy and all, and go downstairs and sit in the cooler, the refrigerated area, till she felt better. One day she didn't make it. All we had were ceiling fans, and she was upstairs in our room. I saw her on the bed and hurried downstairs for help. But when we returned, she had died. We kept it a secret from the new girls. Sally was only twenty-two. They sent her body home on the train.

Hazel left Needles to go into show business: "Harvey gave me the security and education I needed to go on in life. I was only twenty when I left. I met my husband, the great King Felton, a magician, in a show I was in two weeks after I left Needles. We were married for thirty years."

The Atchison, Topeka and Santa Fe Railway played a key role in the opening of Oklahoma Indian lands to white settlement in the 1880s. Before 1885, the U.S. government blocked settlement of the Unassigned Lands of the Oklahoma Panhandle and central Oklahoma. Farmers and ranchers from Kansas and other bordering states anxious to try the fertile soil often crossed into the territory and settled illegally. Called Boomers, these squatters were determined to establish white colonies in Indian Territory. They were probably supported by the Santa Fe, who wanted to build across Okalahoma and needed a population of white farmers and businessmen to justify its effort.

In 1885, Washington began to change its mind about white settlement in Oklahoma. In 1886, the Santa Fe began building across Indian Territory toward Texas and the Gulf of Mexico. The Santa Fe built through the large tract of land between Arkansas City, Kansas, and Gainesville, Texas. This area was not assigned to any tribe (thus, the Unassigned Lands) and so promised the first opportunities for white settlements.

The Santa Fe established stations every ten miles across Oklahoma. Most of the land was still wilderness and the only "communities" were shanty towns set up by the Santa Fe: Guthrie, Purcell, and the future Oklahoma City. These towns served the railroad crews, United States troops, and Indian agents. Oklahoma and the Santa Fe still awaited the go-ahead from Washington to begin official opening of the Indian Territory.

The word came from President Benjamin Harrison in 1889. The territory would be opened in land "runs" whereby specific tracts of land would be available for claim staking. The first run, on April 22, 1889, like those that followed, was partially orchestrated by the Santa Fe. The railroad offered special trains to settlers. At the sound of a pistol, the Santa Fe trains began their run into Indian Territory alongside hundreds of people on horseback, in buggies and wagons, even on foot. These trains ran slowly, allowing homesteaders to leave the cars without injury. Many settlers chose sites within the designated "towns" of Guthrie and Oklahoma City, while many more chose ranch and homestead sites on the open prairie. It was easy to stake a claim: a qualified man (twenty-one years of age or older) or woman (single, twenty-one years of age or older, widowed, or legally divorced or separated), put down a stake bearing his or her name and then entered the claim at one of the United States land offices in Guthrie or Kingfisher, Oklahoma. A small fee was charged for formal entry. Non-American homesteaders could also enter a claim if they had declared their intentions to become legal United States citizens.

Twelve thousand people staked claims that April day. With eleven trains containing a thousand people each suddenly descending on Indian Territory, the area that is now Oklahoma literally grew overnight from wilderness to populated farm and ranch land. Oklahoma City was a small depot surrounded by flat prairie one day and a city of thousands of wagons and tents and dugouts the next.

The second run for homesteads was in October 1891, and involved twenty thousand settlers on additional "surplus" Indian lands. The third run into the Cherokee and Arapaho lands was in April of 1892 and brought twenty-five thousand newcomers to Indian Territory. The final Oklahoma land run was in September of 1893 into the no-man's-land of the Oklahoma

Panhandle. One hundred thousand people rushed for forty thousand available claims.

The Santa Fe had its desired population by 1900: where there had been no available customers in 1886 (the railroad claimed Indians were not good trade customers), by 1900 there were 400,000 ranchers, farmers, and small-town businessmen and women.

Guthrie was named the first territorial capital of Oklahoma and was one of the main stops on the Santa Fe's route between Texas and Kansas. Harvey built a Harvey House in Guthrie in 1903. It was a small house with a lunch and dining room, but in Oklahoma at the turn of the century, it was the best the Territory had to offer. One story of the Guthrie Harvey House's first year of service has survived despite fifty years of secrecy. First published in the Wichita *Morning Eagle* in May, 1953, the story involves a Santa Fe employee, live Oklahoma toads, and the famous Harvey coffee.

Mr. Snyder, a brakeman working on a Santa Fe freight train, pulled into the Guthrie depot for a meal at the Harvey House and saw live toads jumping around a water tank near the tracks. Snyder decided to pocket a few of the creatures, and then walked into the Harvey House where the waitresses and busboys were making their final preparations for the incoming passenger train. Everything was neat and ready, including the coffee cups, which would be filled as the customers walked in. Without attracting anyone's attention, Snyder managed to remove the small toads from his pockets, placing one in each empty coffee cup.

The train came in, and the Harvey Girls filled the cups with scalding coffee. The passengers sat down, saw the toads, some still struggling in the coffee, and pandemonium followed. Fresh cups of coffee were immediately served, but many customers would have neither coffee nor food, but left the dining room to return to the safety of the train.

It was no laughing matter at the Harvey House. The manager, John W. Wiker, was furious and began an immediate investigation of house employees that turned up no answers. The general attorneys of the Santa Fe Railway in Oklahoma were called in, but they found no leads, either. The issue finally was dropped, with no conclusion or satisfactory answer found until 1953, when retired Santa Fe station agent W. L. Ingham related the story to Corb Sarchet for the *Wichita Morning Eagle*. [42]

Gladys Porter (see Chapter 4) worked as a Harvey Girl in Guthrie in the

1920s. Born in 1906, her parents had both come to Indian territory as children in the 1890s. Gladys's grandfather worked at the Santa Fe round-house in Guthrie. Guthrie was in the middle of the great oil-field country of Oklahoma, and in the midst of struggling farms and small-town business-men lived the wealthy oil men. Gladys served several of them: "I met and served T. B. Slick, who was a wealthy oil man out of Oklahoma City. He would drive over to Guthrie to have dinner and would always leave me a five-dollar tip." Gladys also knew a Mr. Ursle, brother-in-law of Mr. Slick, who was later kidnapped and held hostage in Texas. After the ransom was paid, Gladys remembers that Ursle's kidnappers were caught because Ursle remembered hearing an airplane overhead at the same hour every day, enabling the FBI to locate the farm where he was held by using flight patterns and schedules:

> I also served the FBI men who were in Guthrie posing as oil scouts while investigating the Hale and Rampsey case. Mr. Hale was a local banker who was appointed by the government to be the "great white father" to the Osage Indian people in Osage, Oklahoma. When a great number of Osage Indians mysteriously died, and their financial holdings ended up in Mr. Hale's hands, the government decided to investigate. Rampsey was Hale's brother-in-law and was in the scheme with him. But when the evidence turned up, Rampsey turned state's evidence. Hale was convicted.

Gladys married a local Guthrie boy in 1927 whose family had made the land run in 1889. On her last night of work, the Harvey House cash register was robbed:

> I was not in the habit of working at night but I was relieving a girl who was on the night shift. The callboy (the boy who got the crew of the train together) came in for a cup of coffee and told me there was a strange man standing outside the door. He was suspicious of him because he had spoken to him but he wouldn't reply. About the time the callboy sat down at the counter, the man from outside came in with a kerchief over his face and a pistol in his hand. He threw a handkerchief down on the counter and told

In Guthrie, Oklahoma, the Santa Fe distributed seed wheat to new Oklahoma settlers for their first winter wheat crop. The farmers gave the railroad notes for their seed and then paid off the notes after their crops were harvested. September, 1889. (Credit: Santa Fe Railway)

The Fred Harvey women's softball team, Waynoka, Oklahoma, ca. 1925. (Credit: Vernon McNally, City of Waynoka).

Mrs. Ira Fox shown with an aerocar, used to
transport TAT passengers between the Harvey House
(left) and the TAT airport.
(Credit: Waynoka Historical Society)

Amelia Earhart (right) flew through Waynoka on
the first westbound flight of the TAT.
(Credit: Waynoka Historical Society)

Gainesville, Texas. AT and SF depot and Harvey House, c. 1940. (Credit: Santa Fe Railway)

*me, "Give me all your money and make it snappy." He did not
appear to be a tramp. He kept telling me as he held the gun on
me not to look at him, as I kept glancing at him.*

*He only got fifty-two dollars out of the register, as we never kept
much money in at night. The callboy could offer no resistance
because of the gun and the railroad detective had just gotten home
and gone to bed. The robber sent the callboy and myself to a back
room and told us not to come out for five minutes. When we
came out, we both ran to the front door to the telegraph and ticket
office as we were afraid the robber was still around the area. The
telegraph operator called the police and the railroad detective, but
he was never caught. There was speculation that he could have
been a member of one of the now-famous gangs operating at that
time in the area.*

In the 1870s and 1880s, the land of Woods County, Oklahoma, was
Indian territory, called No Man's Land, used by cattlemen driving their
herds from Texas ranches to Kansas railheads. The Oklahoma Territory,
the land of the Cherokee and Arapaho, was first opened for settlement by
the United States government in the land rush of 1889. Woods County and
lands to the east in the Panhandle were opened for settlement in the largest
and most spectacular of the three Oklahoma land runs, the 1893 run on the
Cherokee Strip. One hundred thousand people participated in this run,
stampeding into No Man's Land in buggies, wagons, on horseback, and on
foot. Historians say the confusion was beyond description.

Waynoka (an Indian word meaning sweetwater), in Woods County, was
probably a community of squatters before the land run. The town lies in
a small valley of the Cimarron River. Before the turn of the century, the
area was a favorite hideout for bandits and desperados from Texas and
New Mexico. The Texas Rangers came through from time to time, but until
the Santa Fe Railway made it a division point in 1907, Waynoka was an
obscure and remote community.

Connecting Waynoka to Wichita to the north and Amarillo to the south,
the Santa Fe brought a new population of railroad officials, laborers, and
Harvey employees to a town formerly made up entirely of cowboys, farmers, and a few local businessmen. Harvey began building the Waynoka
Harvey House at about the same time the Santa Fe was building its own

shops and depot area. Harvey chefs, managers, headwaitresses, and Harvey Girls arrived for the opening of the new house in 1910.

Charlotte Shorts lived on a ranch on the banks of the Cimarron River. Charlotte heard about the Harvey House coming into Waynoka when she was a young woman and planned to become a Harvey Girl when it opened:

> *There were some hard times for farmers in the early parts of this century. My dad and mom had already homesteaded in Kansas, and then again in Oklahoma in the Cherokee Strip area near the Cimarron River. But it wasn't a good farm and I had to go to work when I was still pretty young.*

The Santa Fe crews were still working on the shops and depot, and the Harvey House was also under construction when Charlotte came into town looking for a job. She got a job as a waitress at the little cafe temporarily set up near the Harvey House, serving meals to the railroadmen and laborers. It wasn't really the Harvey House, but everybody knew it was the preliminary. Charlotte was planning on getting a job as a Harvey Girl once the house opened. But a conversation with one of the laborers changed all that:

> *I was walking home from a friend's house one afternoon, walking along the new tracks. I met up with this man from one of the crews. We got to talking and he let me know he didn't think too much of me, working in the cafe away from home and all. I got real mad and we got into an argument. He went back and told my boss that I was just a green country girl and didn't belong here in town working near the railroad. I was fired. The Harvey House was almost open, but I had to leave and go back to the farm. It seems kind of funny now, but you have to understand how hard jobs were to come by in those days. And the best jobs were along the railroad.*

Helen McCally's family moved into Waynoka in 1909. Originally a homesteader from Kansas, Helen's father staked his claim outside of Waynoka in 1895, and then returned to Kansas to marry. The family lived on the farm in Woods County for more than ten years, struggling to make the homestead work. But father McCally knew the railroad coming to Waynoka meant jobs, and so he moved the family into town and set up his own business. "Father met the trains with a team of horses and a dray," Helen remembers:

> He would meet salesmen who had come to Waynoka from Wichita or Topeka to sell shoes and suits, cloth, dresses, all kinds of wares. Father would load up the goods as they were taken off the train, and deliver them, and the salesman, to the hotel where local businessmen would look them over. Father did that work for three years. Then, in 1912, he became a brakeman for the Santa Fe. He kept that job until 1925. He quit because they moved him out onto the main line, and that meant he had to be gone from home a lot. He didn't like that. Besides, he was still a farmer at heart, so he and mother moved back out to the old farm.

Helen and her sister Jessie learned very young that the place to be in Waynoka was around the railroad depot:

> It was a great deal to us kids, watching the trains come in. Everybody in town did it, every single day. Mama showed us where to stand, and we'd go down there every afternoon after school and watch all the people and activities around the depot. There was one railroadman who knew us, and he'd take us into the Harvey House for some of their homemade ice cream. We were just little girls. There was nothing like it in the world, nothing!

When Helen was eighteen, in 1917, she became a Harvey Girl:

> I knew I couldn't depend on my father to support me forever. I had the chance to get a job at the Harvey House and I took it. I was the only girl from Waynoka—the other Harvey Girls were from Kansas City and Wichita and other places. I had to live in the dormitory, even though my home was in town. That was one of the rules. And there were lots of rules—about how you spoke to people, about wearing no jewelry, no chewing gum, and more. But we had lots of fun. I worked the seven P.M. to seven A.M. shift,

and slept most of the day. Everybody was friendly at the Harvey House—here and in other Houses I was sent to work at in New Mexico, Texas, and Kansas. I learned a lot, working for Harvey. I came back to live in Oklahoma, but I saw a lot of other places as a young woman, and I loved it!

Jessie McCally became a Harvey Girl in 1919. Although originally hired as a salad girl, not a Harvey Girl, a train wreck on the main line brought an enormous crowd into Waynoka and the manager asked Jessie to go home and put on one of Helen McCally's old uniforms and come to work as a Harvey Girl. "You can't imagine how terrified I was," Jessie says,

having never worked at the lunch counter. And the people were shouting for coffee, pushing and shoving to get a place at the counter. It was a pretty tough way to learn the Harvey system. But I loved it anyway, and worked as a Harvey Girl from then on—in Oklahoma, Kansas, Colorado, even at the Chicago World's Fair in 1934.

Zadie Chapman was sent to Waynoka from Kansas City in 1920. Raised on a farm, Zadie decided at eighteen that she wanted something for her own, and after seeing an advertisement in a newspaper, she traveled the thirty miles from the farm to the city in a wagon and signed on as a Harvey Girl. "I didn't need a job," Zadie says,

I just wanted to work. I wanted to find out some things for myself, away from the farm. I knew a little bit about Harvey and the Harvey Girls, so I knew I'd be well cared for, have a place to live and all. They interviewed me in Kansas City, and the next day gave me a pass for the train and my meals, and sent me off to a place called Waynoka, Oklahoma. They asked me if I'd ever heard of Waynoka? Of course I'd never heard of Waynoka! But I didn't care—it was someplace different, and that was what I wanted.
. . . I used to write a lot of letters home about Oklahoma. I wasn't really homesick, but I had to tell them about Oklahoma,

the terrible wind and sandstorms they had. There were hardly any trees in Waynoka in those days, and very little grass. The sand could be terrible; you can't imagine how bad it was!

Zadie saved a little money and considered her thirty dollars a month plus room, board, laundry, and tips to be a good situation:

Still, there were people in Waynoka who looked down on us, like we weren't nice women because we had jobs. Passengers were always nice, and the ranchers and the railroadmen appreciated how hard we all worked to make an honest living. Even so, there was one section of Waynoka where we weren't welcomed, and it got to some of the girls.

Dan Jones was a night cook at the Waynoka Harvey House in the 1920s. His father had run the Cherokee Strip and still had a farm outside of town. But like so many farmers before them, the Joneses' farm came into bad times in the early 1920s, and they had to send young Dan, just sixteen, into Waynoka to find work. He cooked nights at the lunch counter, serving railroad crews and local ranchers who came in for a late supper or early breakfast. (The Santa Fe depot and Harvey House were open twenty-four hours a day.) "Some of the local people gave the Harvey Girls a hard name they didn't deserve," Dan says:

Not the railroadmen, or the passengers. Just local people who thought they must be "bad" to be single and away from home. People didn't accept working girls then the way they do now.
I got to know all of those girls. They were my best friends. And like women everywhere, some were nice, some were quiet, some were wild once in a while. Since I was the night cook, I'd have to let one in sometimes. They'd stay out past their ten o'clock curfew and get locked out. I'd let them in through the kitchen. There wasn't much for a girl to do here, especially if she was used to Wichita or Kansas City life. They'd get bored. The wildest thing they could do was sneak out at night—climb out an upstairs window and shimmy down a tree, and then sneak back in again!

Waynoka already considered itself a cut above other communities in the Panhandle, with its Harvey House and Santa Fe depot, when another event of major importance to the history and development of the West came its way in early 1929. Like the Iron Horse before it, the "Tin Goose" chose Waynoka to be a major division point on a new air/rail transportation system—the Transcontinental Air Transport, or TAT.

The TAT offered the first nonstop service between New York and Los Angeles, combining the Pennsylvania and Santa Fe railroads with the Ford Trimotors to make a fly-by-day, train-by-night journey across America in forty-eight hours. The TAT began business in July 1929. Passengers traveling east to west on the TAT climbed on board a train in Pennsylvania Station, New York, early one evening; the next morning, they were given breakfast in Columbus, Ohio, where they were put on a trimotor bound for Waynoka. After a day of flying, with several refueling stops, passengers landed at the Waynoka airstrip, where a special bus took them into the Santa Fe station and to the Harvey House. After several hours of rest, including a four-course meal in the Harvey dining room, passengers were ushered onto the Santa Fe train, the Missionary, for an overnight pull to Clovis, New Mexico. From Clovis, the last lap of the trip was again by plane, and after several stops for fuel and another day in the air, TAT passengers arrived in Los Angeles a mere forty-eight hours after leaving New York. Remarkable time, when the alternative was a four-day, nonstop, overland trip by train alone. The same trip could be done on the TAT from west to east, with stops and schedule reversed.

Charles Lindbergh chartered the course across the country, and with Amelia Earhart, served as an officer on the TAT advisory board. Well financed, heavily promoted, using the best aviation equipment and personnel available in 1929, the TAT later merged with the Western Air Express to form Trans World Airlines.[43]

Newspaper stories in 1929 hailed Waynoka as the center of the United States, where all roads—by plane, train, or automobile—lead:

This little city of 2,300 population, until the arrival of the TAT landing field, was a quiet little community of home loving people, little known to the populas [sic] of the extreme east and west but which almost overnight has become known to every city and hamlet between the Atlantic and Pacific Ocean and which we now

*predict is destined to become a commercial center of much
importance, . . . 44*

But many outsiders to Waynoka still saw an isolated frontier community,
out of touch with "modern" America. Anne Morrow Lindbergh wrote:

> *But Waynoka! I have* never *seen a place like it. It is smaller
> than this [Clovis, New Mexico]—has four or five paved streets and
> a hotel (one of the TAT men described it as the "kind you see in
> an old western movie") painted white with a large sign, "Baths,"
> over the front door. . . . We got a room at the Harvey House
> connected with the station and slept well in spite of two or three
> trains going under our window. The Santa Fe Railroad goes by
> there and stops. A small country crowd tumbles out to the
> restaurant and gets a* terribly good meal.
> *It all felt very, very western: the quiet, the lack of pressure or
> touch with progress. . . . 45*

The TAT lasted just sixteen months. The fares were too high; the stock
market crashed and the depression followed. Besides, there was bad press
when a TAT plane crashed in a bad storm. The Santa Fe Railway did
continue its passenger service through Waynoka, but life at the Harvey
House was never again as exciting as it had been in 1929.

The region known as the Texas Panhandle—isolated, known for its sandstorms, mirages, sweeping prairie fires and rolling, treeless plains, and
once home to thousands of buffalo—always had an aura of romance that
linked it more to the Southwest than the Midwest it resembles. It was
already established cattle country in the 1880s; the Santa Fe saw the
market and business potential of this beef and farm area and began laying
track toward a little known settlement called Canadian, on the Canadian
River, in 1886.

This country was a true cowboy paradise, with hundreds of miles of open
prairie called the "Llano Estacado." Settlers and the railroad meant one
thing to ranchers: fences and the dividing up of grazeland. Like all cattle
country, it was a rough area; the Panhandle even had its own Boot Hill

cemetery in Tascosa on the Canadian River. Like their Kansas counter-parts, those buried here had died because of their love of the six-shooter; but at this Boot Hill, unlike the one at Dodge City, a man was buried well beneath the surface of the ground and given a marker with the Lone Star of Texas carved in stone.

Canadian was initially a stop on the first stage lines because there was a shallow crossing spot in the Canadian River nearby. The area surrounding Canadian is reminiscent of the terrain found to the west in New Mexico—large cottonwood trees and dry, angular mesas. After the railroad arrived and built a bridge across the same spot, the town grew quickly, with wooden buildings, town lots, and streets replacing the dugouts and tents. The 1880s brought a saloon, a mercantile store, a press, a barbershop, a blacksmith, and a hardware store. Canadian was on its way to becoming one of the important cities in the Panhandle. Even so, Canadian never suffered the rowdiness of other boom towns, even when oil was discovered in the plains nearby. It was always a civilized place, and the Santa Fe rewarded this community by expanding its facilities in the early 1900s, making Canadians certain their town would soon rival Amarillo as the beef capital of the Texas Panhandle.

The Santa Fe officially announced its intention to construct a Harvey House at the Santa Fe depot in 1909: "Great is the Santa Fe," the *Canadian Record* of October 7, 1909, stated, "and we are proud to be on its line." The new Santa Fe buildings by the tracks were completely destroyed by fire in 1910, but the Santa Fe was undaunted by this setback, and after replacing them, continued construction of the Harvey House. The Harvey House cost the railroad $36,000, and its presence meant trains would stop for the first time for meals in Canadian. The *Record* told its readers:

> . . . *more traffic will be sent this way. In the near future a California train will pass through Canadian, but not without stopping.*[46]

The Harvey House was a two-story brick structure by the track, con-nected to the depot with covered walkways. It did not have any hotel accomodations, but had a dining room and a lunchroom, with employee bedrooms on the second floor. "The most substantially built structure in the town,"[47] the Harvey House was part of a planned system of Harvey

Houses that promised to bring additional passenger traffic through this division of the Santa Fe. Canadians recognized the Santa Fe's influence in the shaping of their community:

> *Time was, perhaps, when a railroad town could not boast of her high class of citizenship. In this instance, at any rate, we class our railroad inhabitants among our very best people. . . . A citizen of Canadian would no more expect discourteous treatment from one of the railroad employees than they would from the gentlemanly cashiers of our banks.* [48]

Canadians old enough to remember say that most of the Harvey Girls at the house were local women. A few were sent in, especially to get the house opened and on its feet. The manager, chef, and baker were never from the area, but many local women found work over the years at the Canadian Harvey dining room and lunch counter.

Una Gertrude Atchison Matthews was born in 1907 in Houston County, Texas. Her father was a farmer, but like many farmers in south Texas in the early 1900s, was forced by terrible droughts to find other work. When Una was still young, her mother died. She was left in her grandmother's care while her father went in search of work in western Texas. In 1923, he found a job with the Santa Fe bridge gang in Canadian. After meeting a woman he wanted to marry, he sent for his family to join him in Canadian. "There were a lot of ranches here," Una remembers,

> *and a lot of cowboys. I was eighteen when my father's job in Canadian ended and my family decided to move on. But I wanted to stay. I had met a cowboy at the skating rink that winter, so after graduation I got a job at the Harvey House and worked all summer there. In the fall I was married, but I went on working just the same.*

Una and her husband Bill lived in their own house in town. Una walked to work until December when the snow and cold made it difficult without a car: "I was working the night shift and Bill finally said, 'Quit!' and I did."

There were twenty Harvey Girls working at the Canadian Harvey House, also open twenty-four hours a day. The house had as many married

Harvey Girls living in their own homes as unmarried girls living upstairs in the dorm. Married couples could live in the house itself if there was room. High school students were also given jobs at the Canadian Harvey House, the girls working as waitresses, the boys as busboys and dishwashers.

In the 1920s, the depot at Canadian was bustling with two to four meal trains stopping each day. Before the roads were paved, all of the county's wheat and livestock were shipped out from the depot. Warren Harrington worked summers as a busboy at the Canadian Harvey House:

> I was responsible for spotting the trains and alerting the chef and the girls. I'd stand out on the platform where I could see up the tracks about four miles. With the first glimpse of the train, I would run back and report to the chef, then I would grab this big brass gong—dish-shaped, about four inches deep and twenty inches in diameter—and whack the daylights out of it with a wood stick with a ball on the end of it. I really gave it a working over. Inside, everything went into gear but quick!

In the following thirty minutes, the Canadian cooks and Harvey Girls served upwards of eighty passengers.

Warren's brothers and sisters also worked for Harvey. His brothers both became chefs and worked all over the line, including the Grand Canyon hotels. Two of his sisters were Harvey Girls, both of whom married Santa Fe engineers. Besides alerting the dining and lunchroom staff of the approaching train, Warren, dressed in black trousers and a black jacket with brass buttons, also served the black railroadmen their meal: "When everyone was inside, I went in and served the colored porters and conductors in an alcove that was just for them. They weren't allowed in the lunchroom in those days."

Canadian became popular with regional sportsmen in the 1920s: "Many, many hunters gathered here," Warren remembers.

> They had safaris here; people would come in from Kansas and even farther east to hunt prairie chicken and quail. I helped clean and ice down as much as two hundred pounds of prairie chicken. We would put them in those big old laundry baskets—hampers on

rollers with wooden tops—clean those birds, put them on ice, shove them on the train where they'd go back to Kansas City or Wichita with the hunters. It was a very big business here for awhile.

Canadian's Rotary Club met at the Harvey House dining room, and school banquets and celebrations were held there. It was the only real dining room for miles.

There was not a lot of social stratification in Canadian, situated as it was in the middle of nowhere with most of its residents sharing similar lives. The Harvey Girls were from local ranches, farms and homes in town. Married Harvey Girls were common, and working mothers accepted.

"In 1926, I had two children and was a widow needing a job," Elizabeth Hazlewood (see Chapter 4) remembers:

I got a job at the Harvey House. I had worked as a waitress before, but it was not like at Harvey's. It was so clean and organized. It was like a big family then and the children loved it. So did I. The children would come down late in the day, just before I got off work, and play with the girls and railroad people. I didn't like them to be there too much because of the steep stairs and the tracks, but the manager's wife used to take care of them. I don't remember any Harvey Girls leaving Canadian and going on to other houses. I didn't. We were all mostly local folks.

The importance of Amarillo, Texas, to the Santa Fe blossomed in 1898 when the railroad built a roundhouse and moved its general offices there. Amarillo had slowly but surely won the title "Queen City of the Plains" to the disappointment of towns like Canadian, making it the cattle-shipping center of the Panhandle by the early 1900s. A larger passenger station and Harvey House were built in Amarillo in 1910, in the standard mission-revival style found throughout the Southwest along the railroad. The Amarillo Harvey House did not have hotel accomodations, but it was part of a large complex that included the offices of the Santa Fe and Harvey employee rooms and apartments, as well as the dining room and lunchroom.

Opal Sells Hill (see chapters 4 and 5) was born in 1900 on one of the first wheat farms in Hall County near Amarillo. Raised with her two brothers and two sisters on an isolated stretch of sage, sand, and prairie grass,

Opal was familiar with the way of life of farmers and ranchers in the Panhandle. Will Rogers was one of many young cowboys who came to the Panhandle at the turn of the century in search of work and adventure: "I got enough money to buy me an old horse and lit out for Amarillo, Texas," Rogers wrote of his youthful days on the Texas frontier:

> This country was thinly settled then—I only passed three ranches
> on the way in. They'd let me cook up a lot of biscuits and some
> jerky—dried beef—and then that old skate and I would amble on.
> When I finally got into Amarillo, the whole country around was
> covered with trail herds waiting for cars to ship them away. There
> was plenty of grass and water everywhere . . . and crowds of
> cowboys in the saloons. [49]

Opal could never be certain if her family's spread was one of the stops young Will Rogers made en route to Amarillo, but his path crossed Opal's later when he was a famous cowboy and she a young Harvey Girl. Opal first saw Will Rogers in downtown Amarillo, where he would draw a crowd with his rope tricks and storytelling: "He was a frequent passenger on the Santa Fe in the 1920s," Opal says:

> All the girls knew who he was and used to go and stand on the
> porch of the Harvey House to watch him perform in the street.
> Everybody watched him. Later, I became the Harvey Girl he
> always requested serve him. We became great friends. He'd call
> me by name when he came into the Amarillo dining room and
> then he'd say, "Bring me some of that corn bread and red beans
> or some of those delicious ham and eggs!" Everybody knew what
> he wanted; and he'd get it, even at dinner time. He was a great
> favorite at the Harvey House.

In 1901, the Santa Fe Railway built a brick, mission-revival-style depot and Harvey House in Gainesville, Texas. This Harvey House was typical of many houses in Texas, with a lunch counter but no dining room facility. Upstairs there was a two-room apartment with a bath for the manager and his or her family, and six rooms and a bath for the other Harvey employees, five of whom were Harvey Girls.

Gainesville, in Cooke County north of Fort Worth, is historically known as that part of Texas where the South meets the West. Gainesville has always shared characteristics of both regions: the cotton, slavery, share-cropping, and confederacy of the South; the cattle, oil, frontier life, Indian population, and grain production of the West. This section of Texas is known for its rolling green hills, good soil, turbulent thunderstorms, sheets of rain, and funnel clouds.

Perhaps it was Gainesville's southern connections—the Harvey Girls were not treated well here. Although Gainesville residents brought their families and friends to the Harvey House for Sunday dinners and special occasions, the Harvey Girls were viewed with suspicion by the local populace, even after a number of them had married into the community.

"There were rumors and gossip around Gainesville," one old-timer remembers:

> *I remember my mother telling me that any woman who lived upstairs in the downtown area was a prostitute, and those Harvey Girls lived on the second floor of the depot! But as I got older I heard about how they were supposed to be such refined women, and the reputation they had, so I knew it was just gossip; just small-town gossip.*

Frances Yarbrough was born in 1905 in Gainesville, and remembers being told never to go into the Harvey House when she was a teenager:

> *There were lots of railroad and traveling men in there and we young girls were told to stay away from them! So the big sport was to sneak in there and order us a ham sandwich! And oh, those ham sandwiches! They took two pieces of real thin bread, buttered it on one side and put ham on top of that. It cost something like a quarter and it was the best sandwich I ever ate.*
>
> *Gainesville was kind of snobby then. Girls didn't work and those that did were in a different social class. They'd work as servants or in stores—mostly German women did that; they'd come in from the country for a job.*

Gainesville was part of the Santa Fe run from Fort Worth to Purcell, Oklahoma, and crewmen assigned to this part of the line were frequent and familiar customers at the Gainesville Harvey House horseshoe counter. Joe Rison (see Chapter 5) spent forty-four years working on this section of the Santa Fe, where his father had worked before him:

> *I began work with the Santa Fe when I was eighteen, in 1916. I was a clerk in the yard office. The depot was always crowded in those days. Gainesville was still quite a cattle town, with stockyards on the north end of the railroad yard. People used to wander down to the station every afternoon to see who was getting off, who was getting on. The busiest time of the year began in April when the stock started arriving.*
>
> *The Harvey folks were real nice to the Santa Fe folks. Sometimes a fellow would be broke and need a meal. He could go to the Harvey House and sign up in the Pie Book—a coupon book is what it was—and he could eat on the line all the way up to Purcell. Then later, the railroad would deduct it from his salary.*

Most Harvey customers were tired travelers grateful for a good meal in a quiet place before climbing back on a train and rattling over another stretch of bumpy track. But every so often a customer, usually a local resident, came in with nothing better to do than find trouble in the Harvey House. Rison watched a brawl begin in the lunchroom over money that one Gainesville resident had given another for whiskey:

> *The man who took the money went and bought the whiskey and then he drank it all up. The other man came after him; he knew he'd be in the Harvey House and they had a big fight in the lunchroom. That was in 1919. Harvey people rarely asked anyone to leave, but they did that afternoon. They kept their establishment decent!*

Helmut Schurig first came to Gainesville as a small boy in 1911. His father, Ernest Emil Schurig was a chef, born in Germany, trained by Harvey in Houston, and then sent north to work in Gainesville. "My father came to Galveston, Texas from Germany all by himself," Helmut says. "He was six years old and had a grandfather living on a Texas farm. He worked and lived on the farm and then got a job with Harvey in the storeroom in Galveston."

Helmut remembers arriving at the Gainesville depot with his mother: "We stood there waiting for my father to find us. He had already moved up here. We went into the kitchen and I remember staring at those huge hundred-pound sacks of flour."

Ernest Schurig worked twelve to fourteen hours a day, seven days a week as chef of the Gainesville Harvey House. If a train was late, he and all the other Harvey employees worked longer. Although he had train passes, he had little vacation time and so the Schurig family rarely used them. The chef was given a room in the Harvey House to nap and change clothes in, but the Schurigs did not live on the premises.

"The meat they served in the Gainesville Harvey House was sent in from Kansas City," Helmut says. "It was top beef, brought in on the train in huge baskets that were two feet by three feet by two feet. Veal cutlets were brought in in buckets. They weren't refrigerated but were shipped directly from the packing plant."

Gainesville was one of those places with water that was deemed inferior for use in Harvey coffee, so it was brought in on tank cars from Fort Worth. Strawberries, blueberries, watermelon, and other fruits were bought locally. Schurig also bought local chickens, eggs, and milk for his kitchen. Helmut remembers that "the house supported a lot of local farmers."

Helmut was the only child around the house and was mothered by all the Harvey Girls:

> *They were all good friends with one another and with me. They were single. If they married, they left. And they married a lot of local farmers and other men from around here, and stayed and raised families. They weren't from Texas, those Harvey Girls; they were from other parts of the country.*

The shape of small towns along the Santa Fe were changed forever by Fred Harvey. Rural communities and the people who called them home were suddenly swept into the forefront of a new age of mass transportation. The world that had once included only a few square miles was now part of an entire continent of people moving from east to west and back again. Many young Harvey employees—men and women from small town America—chose to join the ranks of people moving on, moving out and into, a changing, expanding America. And if they wanted it, they always had, beneath them and beside them, the extended family of the Fred Harvey organization.

Fred Harvey people are always and forever Fred Harvey people and have no life aside from that. Most of them have never known anything else, and probably never felt its lack.[50]

CHAPTER · 6

Life in the Grand Hotels

I N THE YEARS between the turn of the century and World War I, the American West became the tamed wilderness in which upper-class Americans and Europeans sought adventurous excursions and leisurely vacations. Tourism as an industry became a major source of income as thousands of Americans came west looking for the romantic heroes and heroines and mythical Old West towns made popular in the new western literature of such writers as Owen Wister, Charles F. Lummis, and Mary Austin. The railroad provided these travelers the means by which to see much of the Old West in as little time as possible via excursion trains. These trains offered Pullman cars and were often very luxurious, but they also made stopovers at hotels located within sightseeing distance of major western attractions—national parks like the Grand Canyon and the Petrified Forest, and cultural attractions such as the picturesque Indian pueblos found in New Mexico and Arizona.

Harvey and the Santa Fe Railway were quick to realize the potential of this booming interest in the West. After 1900, the Fred Harvey Company and the Santa Fe began expanding their services to attract the new stop-over passenger traffic. Luxurious hotels with extensive facilities were built to provide railroad travelers with resort-like accomodations along the Santa Fe line. Although these hotels all handled overnight customers, their primary function was to develop and help expand tourist clientele through extended visits to various communities along the railroad in the Southwest.

Mary Elizabeth Jane Colter gave many of these new buildings the extra-special touches they needed to become more than railroad hotels. Colter was chief architect and interior designer for Fred Harvey from 1902 until 1948. She had a keen eye for authentic southwestern building design and decoration, be it in the grand scheme of a building like La Posada in Winslow, or in the minute details of a one bedroom suite in La Fonda in Santa Fe. Today, Colter is recognized as having been among the first to have seen the importance of Indian and Spanish design and architecture in southwestern culture.[1]

With Harvey, Colter promoted and paid homage to Indian art, using the finest examples of such age-old crafts as weaving, sand painting, and pottery throughout her hotels along the railroad. The time for national appreciation of Indian life, past and present, had arrived: archaeologists and anthropologists were discovering the importance and beauty of Indian culture in numerous ruins throughout Arizona and New Mexico, and in the life of the living pueblo cultures of the Southwest. National public interest in Indian artifacts had been generated by a display of Mesa Verde (site of extensive prehistoric cliff dwellings and ruins in southwestern Colorado) artifacts at the World's Columbian Exposition in Chicago in 1892. Museum curators and private collectors were beginning to search for similar items.

Ford Harvey, Fred's son and president of the company, became interested in marketing Indian art after one of his New Mexico managers, Herman Schweizer (who had climbed up the ranks from news agent), began collecting and selling the pottery, jewelry, and weavings of local Indian artists to patrons of his Coolidge, New Mexico, Harvey House. In 1902, the Fred Harvey Indian Department was formed. Ford Harvey hired his brother-in-law, John Frederick Huckel, a Harvey executive married to Fred Harvey's daughter Minnie, to head the new enterprise. Minnie and John Huckel, like Schweizer, had already begun their own collection of Indian arts and crafts. Ford Harvey, the Huckels, and Herman Schweizer were pioneers in the field of southwestern art appreciation and acquisition.

The opening of El Tovar at the Grand Canyon offered a magnificent setting for the display and sale of Indian work, and the Alvarado in Albuquerque had an entire room devoted to Indian arts and crafts. Schweizer, already something of an expert concerning Indian art, began touring reservations in Arizona and New Mexico to locate the finest examples of Indian work to sell at various Harvey Houses. From the Navajos, Schweizer commissioned new silver work for public sale using "pawn" silver designs for authenticity. He bought museum-quality baskets from the Pimas and Papagos of Arizona, and turquoise and silver jewelry from the Zunis and Navajos.

Schweizer bought only the best and soon Harvey shops had a reputation for showing and selling collector-quality Indian arts and crafts. The Harvey Indian Department also had an honest reputation among its Indian craftsmen and women, offering fair prices and a ready, year-round market that encouraged the Indians to pursue ancient artistic traditions. American tourists and art collectors also had the opportunity to watch Indian craftspeople at work at Hopi House at the Canyon, and in the Indian Building workshops at the Alvarado in Albuquerque. Slowly, the American public learned of the beauty and historical importance of the ancient crafts of the southwestern Indians.

The Santa Fe and Harvey soon incorporated an Indian motif into all of their advertising. Exotic paintings of Navajo and Hopi lands and people decorated Santa Fe brochures and Harvey literature. In the 1930s, Mary Colter created an exclusive line of china for the Super Chief, decorated with thirty-seven different Mimbreño designs derived from the thousand-year-old pottery found in southern New Mexico Mimbres sites. Today, pieces from this china set are highly valued collector's items.

Harvey and the Santa Fe soon began another venture to promote and expand tourism in New Mexico and Arizona. The railroad brought the adventurous public from the East into the deserts and Indian country of the West in the 1920s, but the Wild West was still only a landscape and lifestyle glimpsed fleetingly and with little explanation from a train window. Although good roads were scarce, the automobile was the only means by which to take those passengers interested in a more intimate look into the heart of Indian country and to the many natural scenic attractions of the Southwest.

In 1924, New Mexico businessmen tried to organize an automobile sightseeing program in Albuquerque to promote New Mexico's beauty and culture. But they were not successful; they needed the help of an established organization and turned to Harvey and the Santa Fe in 1925. Harvey and the railroad were already offering automobile tours to the Grand Canyon, and knew of the potential tourist traffic stopover tours promised. Transcontinental railroad passengers obviously enjoyed the time off the train and a chance to see southwestern wonders up close.

A trial automobile detour was run on March 27, 1926, from Albuquerque to Santa Fe to Las Vegas: the roads were terrible, the journey was long and difficult, but with Harvey food and Harvey accomodations at the Alvarado, La Fonda, and the Castañeda, the trip was a success and the Southwestern Indian Detours were officially begun.

The Detours were arranged so that a passenger planning a cross-country trip on the Santa Fe Railway could purchase a ticket in Chicago or Boston for Los Angeles that included a stopover at the Grand Canyon, Gallup, Albuquerque, or Santa Fe. All the details of his or her adventure to the native pueblos, art colonies, and Spanish communities, or to the rim of the Grand Canyon, were taken care of by Harvey's Indian Detours. In the 1920s, tourists to the Southwest needed reassurance to step off the train into nowhere: automobiles were apt to break down and roads into the mountain and desert outback were usually unmarked, precarious, and passable only by experienced drivers.

Harvey hired Major R. Hunter Clarkson, a Scottish businessman with a knack for organizing large-scale operations, to run the Detours. Yellow Cab of Chicago was given the contract for the cars and coaches, called Harveycars. The tours were organized in one-, two-, and three-day trips from Albuquerque, Santa Fe, and Winslow, Arizona, and in the Harveycar brochures they were advertised as the means by which to reach those ". . . buried cities that flourished when Britons crouched in caves, reach medieval Spain dreaming away the centuries in the mountains of America, and string together age-old Indian pueblos" and "catch archaeology alive."

Erna Fergusson, a native New Mexican writer and successful businesswoman who had operated her own tour guide service in Santa Fe since 1921, was hired by Harvey to organize a courier corps of women to accompany Detour passengers on their jaunts into the Southwest. The Indian Detour Couriers were distinguished twenty-five-year-old women

The Fred Harvey Tour Book for the Indian Detours included this photograph of the potters and pottery of Santa Clara Pueblo, northwest of Santa Fe. Harvey cars brought buyers and admirers from all over the country to Santa Clara and other remote New Mexico pueblos.
(Credit: Las Vegas Citizen's Committee for Historic Preservation Collection)

Herman Schweizer in white suit, in front of the Alvarado Indian Building, ca. 1905. Inside, the main Harvey art collection, built by Herman Schweizer, was kept in a huge safe-like vault. It was known as the "drool room" by insiders, and Schweizer waited twenty-five years before handing over the key to his assistant, J.A. McDonough. Schweizer collected only the best. William Randolph Hearst, when building his own collection of fine Southwestern art, offered Schweizer six-thousand dollars for a rare Indian blanket. Schweizer refused, saying Hearst would then have something better than he had. Among the vault's drawers and boxes of artifacts were housed Mexican lace mantillas, Indian buckskin blouses, rare gems, silver and turquoise jewelry, Indian pottery, and the world's largest collection of buffalo-hide shields. The collection is now housed at the Heard Museum, Phoenix. (Credit: University of Arizona Special Collections)

Native American silversmith working on his craft in the Alvarado Indian Room ca. 1910. (Credit: Albuquerque Museum)

Guests at the Montezuma Hotel (in background), 1900, enjoying a ride up the canyon. Canned foods were not allowed on the tables of the Montezuma dining and lunch rooms. Harvey sent an employee to Guaymas and Hermosillo, Mexico, to find fresh fruit, green vegetables, and shell fish to be shipped north to his hotel near Las Vegas. A contract with the Yaqui Indians brought green turtles and sea celery to the Montezuma. The turtles cost $1.50 a piece, and weighed two hundred pounds. They were placed in a small pool near the hotel for fattening. The daily menu at the Montezuma offered fresh turtle soup and turtle steak. (Kansas City Star, December 24, 1911) (Credit: Las Vegas Citizen's Committee for Historic Preservation)

carefully screened and chosen to serve as hostesses and expert guides on the Harveycars. The women had to be college graduates, and were given crash courses in southwestern art, geology, sociology, architecture, and history.

The Couriers were a physically elegant, intellectually impressive group of women. They wore a uniform that consisted of a long wool skirt, Indian velvet shirt, silver concha belt, and leather boots. With the Harveycar drivers, hand-picked young men who underwent a rigorous driving and endurance test before acceptance, the Couriers escorted the rich, the famous, and the simply adventurous around New Mexico and Arizona. The women were paid $150 a month plus expenses, and $10 more per month if they spoke Spanish. The drivers, who wore English-style riding boots and breeches, cowboy shirts and 10-gallon hats à la Tom Mix, and negotiated some of the most difficult and often frightening roads in America, were paid $125 a month plus expenses. The Couriers and drivers were allowed to date one another and quickly formed an elite social circle in New Mexico and Arizona in the 1920s.

Courier Margaret Moses, a native of Germany, was assigned to act as Albert Einstein's interpreter when he visited the Southwest with his wife in the late 1920s. Moses accompanied Einstein's entourage to the Grand Canyon and to the Petrified Forest of Arizona. Moses remembered Einstein standing and looking at the newly erected plaque at the Petrified Forest. It read, "Six Million Years Old." Einstein remarked, "I believe it is not six million, but sixty million years old."

The depression of the 1930s ended many of the Indian Detour trips in New Mexico and Arizona. Harvey sold the entire operation, excepting the cars at the Grand Canyon, to Clarkson in 1931. Clarkson continued to run the tours out of Santa Fe on a depleted basis until the Second World War.[2]

The young women who were assigned to work as Harvey Girls at the grand Harvey hotels along the Santa Fe lived in some of the most unique and luxurious mini-communities of the Southwest and all America. They still worked as hard as Harvey Girls everywhere—the daily routine was exactly the same. But most of them felt privileged to be part of such truly beautiful and unusual places as the Grand Canyon village, the old plaza of Santa Fe, and the ancient pueblo areas of Winslow and Gallup.

Situated on the very edge of the Sangre de Cristo (Blood of Christ) mountains in northern New Mexico, Las Vegas had the honor of being the only community along the Santa Fe to boast two major Harvey establishments: the Montezuma, built by the Santa Fe in 1882, and the Castañeda, opened in 1899.

Las Vegas's location in northern New Mexico had always brought it historical significance. Indians of the Great Plains and the Southwest met here to trade, and later the Santa Fe Trail brought early travelers and traders to what would become the village of Las Vegas. In 1846, General Stephen W. Kearny used one of the local rooftops to proclaim United States possession of what is now New Mexico and Arizona. By the time the Santa Fe Railway completed tracks near the town in 1879, Las Vegas, although still a popular spot for bandits and other desperados, was a thriving community of sheep and cattle ranchers.

The railroad brought changes to Las Vegas (Spanish for "The Meadows"), setting up New Town on the east side, half a mile from old town Las Vegas. New Town was a boom town overnight, with Santa Fe shops and facilities quickly erected, and tradesmen, merchants, lawyers, prostitutes, cowboys, and desperados moving in to share the new prosperity. The railroad enabled the already strong wool and cattle businesses to flourish. The Denver *Tribune* claimed on November 17, 1879, that the shipments of wool, hides, and pelts out of Las Vegas reached ten million dollars that year. With the railroad, Las Vegas became one of the largest wool shipping centers in the United States, possibly in the world.

Besides its cattle and sheep industry, Las Vegas had something else the Santa Fe wanted: hot mineral springs. In 1880, Fred Harvey himself came to Las Vegas and with the Santa Fe, purchased the hot springs and made plans to build a large health resort. The springs were located about six miles from the main line so a spur was built up the canyon to the site of the hotel, the Montezuma. An enormous castle-like structure tucked up against the canyon where the springs bubbled out, the first Montezuma opened in 1882 and attracted health-seekers from the East through widely distributed publicity material. The hotel, constructed entirely of wood, was four stories high, with a massive tower standing eight stories above the canyon floor. Balconies opened from the 270 rooms, and with bathhouses connected to the hotel capable of serving five hundred people a day, the Montezuma could compete with any of the finest health resorts of the time in the United States and Europe. It was the largest frame building in the country, and the pride of the Santa Fe, but it burned to the ground in 1884. Harvey and the Santa Fe, confident of the continued success of their expensive venture, immediately rebuilt the million-dollar hotel. This second structure also burned and was again replaced before 1899.[3] The popularity of the hot springs and the hotel continued until the late 1890s. But at the turn of the century, travelers to New Mexico were continuing all the way to California without stopovers in Las Vegas, and when El Tovar opened at the Grand Canyon, the Montezuma could no longer maintain the nearly full occupancy it needed to survive. It closed in 1903.

The Montezuma may have drawn the highest class of people to Las Vegas, but the community itself, situated as it was in the still-wild regions of New Mexico, continued to be a stage for more notorious characters. Montezuma Harvey Girls walked the streets of downtown Las Vegas with the likes of Billy the Kid, Doc Holliday, Pat Garrett, Jesse James, Saw Dust Charlie and Little Jack the Cutter. The *Las Vegas Optic* kept its columns full informing the public who was where, be they famous or infamous. It reported that John Carson, son of Kit, was working at the O. K. Barber Shop,[4] and that someone answering the description of The Kid was seen with a Winchester rifle strapped to his back walking the Las Vegas streets on Saturday night.[5] When Pat Garrett left town to become the new sheriff in Lincoln, the *Optic* was the first with the news[6]; and after Garrett shot and killed Billy the Kid later the same year, Las Vegas citizens raised twelve hundred dollars for Garrett's territorial reward.[7]

Because Las Vegas was the major shipping point for cattle from New Mexico and parts of Texas, huge herds were brought in to the valley several times a year. Cowboys who had seen only cattle and prairie for the last six months were paid off and left with nothing to do but visit Las Vegas's gambling houses and dance halls. Like all great cattle towns, Las Vegas became a rowdy camp for the duration. Local citizens knew it was in their best interest not to interfere, and the old plaza with saloons on every corner was vacated by Las Vegans who waited out the end-of-the-trail celebrations at home. Those who dared walk the streets during such festivities did so at their own risk. One old-timer claimed, "If a man asked you to drink, and you didn't, he had the privilege of shooting you."[8]

Most of the more uncivilized visitors to the area patronized the downtown eating and drinking establishments, but on at least one occasion, a group of hell-raising cowboys rode up for a look at the Montezuma. The group was drunk and started shooting up the billiard room. Fred Harvey, who happened to be visiting the hotel, reached the scene just as the boys began to shoot the bottles of liquor behind the bar. Harvey demanded they put up their guns. When asked who he was he replied, "My name is Fred Harvey. I am running this place and I will not have any rowdies here. You are welcome to come here as often as you please and stay as long as you behave like gentlemen, but if you don't behave like gentlemen you can't stay here and you can't come again. Now damn you, put up your guns and take a drink with Fred Harvey!" One of the cowboys began to curse and swear, at which time Harvey grabbed him and pinned him to the floor. "You mustn't swear in this place!" One of the less intoxicated cowboys calmed his friends saying, "Fred Harvey is a gentleman." The rowdies finally sat down to a drink, which soon became an entire breakfast and all the black coffee they could consume.[9]

At the Santa Fe depot in New Town, a small frame Harvey House was built to accomodate train passengers. This small lunchroom was replaced by the first of the elegant beside-the-track hotels built by the Santa Fe and Harvey, the Castañeda, opened in 1899. A two-story, U-shaped brick building with porches running the length of its perimeter, the Castañeda faced the great open plains of northeastern New Mexico. The hotel had thirty guest rooms, a large dining room, and a lunchroom. The Castañeda owned a silver service valued at two hundred thousand dollars that was often sent out to other houses for special dinners.

In June of 1899, the Castañeda became the site for what would become a major annual event in Las Vegas—Roosevelt's Rough Riders Reunion. It began when twenty men from the Las Vegas area signed up for volunteer service in 1898, when the United States declared war on Spain. These men became part of the First United States Volunteer Cavalry, 40 percent of whom were recruited in New Mexico. Under Theodore Roosevelt, this unit went to Cuba, where their fighting brought them great distinction. They returned home as the famous Rough Riders, and they chose Las Vegas as the site for their first annual reunion.

The entire community of Las Vegas met Roosevelt's train at the Castañeda on June 24, 1899. Several days of parades, speeches, bands, dances, and rodeos honored Roosevelt and his men. Although Roosevelt spent all

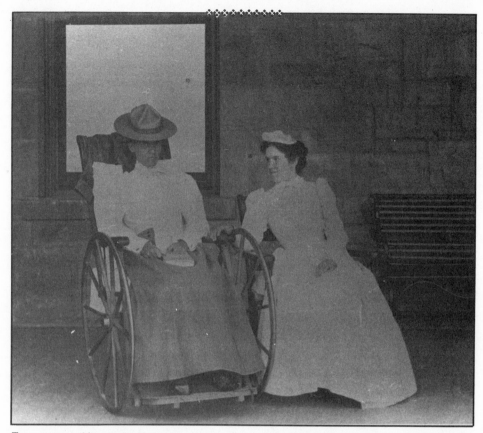

Two women seeking the health benefits of the high mountain air found on the porch of the Montezuma Hotel, 1900. (Credit: Las Vegas Citizen's Committee for Historic Preservation)

A train stopped at the Castañeda platform, Las Vegas, New Mexico. (Credit: Santa Fe Railway)

Theodore Roosevelt and his Rough Riders were met by five thousand people in Las Vegas, June 1899. Roosevelt, then Governor of New York, stayed at the Castañeda Harvey House, although his "Riders" stayed in tents near town. (Credit: Las Vegas Citizen's Committee for Historic Preservation)

The frame and stucco Alvarado shortly after its opening in 1902. (Credit: Albuquerque Museum)

of his waking time with his men at their camp in a nearby park, he had his own comfortable sleeping quarters in the Castañeda.

In the years that followed, the annual event became known as the Rough Riders and Cowboys Reunion, and grew to be one of the largest rodeos in northern New Mexico. Until its discontinuance in 1948, its headquarters were always at the Castañeda.

Despite its rough and tumble days, the Castañeda was a favorite Harvey House for employees. The community of Las Vegas accepted the Harvey Girls, and many Harvey employees remained in Las Vegas to raise families of their own. Marie Haggerty arrived at the Castañeda in 1899, just after Roosevelt and his Rough Riders had enjoyed their first reunion. The beautiful Castañeda was in deplorable condition, the furniture scarred and dirty from the parties held for and by the Rough Riders.[10] Hattie Blethen came to Las Vegas from Memphis, Tennessee, in 1906. She spent the next thirty-six years as a Harvey Girl, thirty of them at the Castañeda. In the early years of this century, Hattie remembers there was a free ball given by the Castañeda for local citizens. The Harvey management finally had to end the annual dance because of the damage sustained each year by the interior of the hotel.[11] Given the opportunity, Las Vegas still showed vestiges of its frontier past.

Bernard Kane's father came to Las Vegas as a "boomer" from Ohio in 1908. He worked as a roundhouse machinist until the railroad had a strike: "At that time, he just up and left his job, walked across the tracks and got a job at the Harvey House as a clerk," says Bernard. Bernard and his brothers and sisters were born in Kansas. In 1927, when Bernard was fourteen, he was hired by an old Harvey friend of his father's to sell ice cream from a wagon on the ramp of the Topeka station. The following summer, after school was out, Bernard went to Albuquerque to work for the same man as a bellhop at the Alvarado. Several summers later, he joined the summer staff at the Castañeda where he worked as night clerk and later as assistant cashier, earning money to put himself through college:

> Las Vegas was a nice little western town in those days, the early thirties. It wasn't a health spot anymore, and the Castañeda was becoming one of the older structures in the Harvey system. The really wealthy people went on to Albuquerque.

The girls had a separate dorm from the men and we were not allowed to fraternize. I was one of the youngest and everyone was very nice to me. Because I was night clerk, I often had to let someone in who was out after hours. I never reported them. I figured if they were sober enough to walk, well . . . !

People in Albuquerque, New Mexico, who know little or nothing about Harvey Houses, know about the Alvarado. Even younger people, and people who moved to the city after 1970, know that the Alvarado was one of the classiest, most romantic, elegant, and authentically New Mexican hotels to ever grace the Rio Grande valley. The Alvarado Hotel no longer stands. There is not a trace of it to be found near the Santa Fe tracks or depot. Most people cannot even say exactly where the hotel stood. They just know it was once the most important building in Albuquerque.

The Alvarado opened in Albuquerque in 1902. Albuquerque, like so many railroad towns, was really two small units: Old Town, founded in 1706, and New Town, one and a half miles to the east of the old plaza, founded by the Santa Fe in 1879. The Santa Fe reasoned that the land near Old Town was forever in danger of flooding from the Rio Grande, and to lay track into the old community also meant diverting from a straight line north to south through New Mexico. So Old Town Albuquerque watched as many businesses, new and old, moved into the tent and shanty town that sprung up overnight near the new depot. Albuquerque would eventually join the two towns, and not placing the railroad offices and yards in Old Town probably saved it from the crowding and modernization that comes to all areas surrounding major railroad yards.

At the turn of the century, Albuquerque was a dusty town with a large saloon and red light district close to the railroad station. The first Harvey House was built by the depot in the 1880s, and was a little red frame building with a tiny lunchroom and kitchen. Although the Alvarado brought the city its first luxury hotel, civilization would come slowly to the city.

The Alvarado's Spanish mission architecture with long, sprawling porches, high arches, and shaded courtyards, cool on the hottest desert afternoon, was in stark contrast to the false fronts of New Town Albuquerque's business district. But Albuquerque's citizens were ready for a bit of civilization: "In those days," said one pioneer father with a sigh,

*nobody cared if a man took a drink or if he didn't . . . a handful
of men were building the town . . . men (who) could visualize a
city behind the frame shanties . . . vast population and a city life
. . . the real pioneer spirit, doing the best you can with what you
have.*[12]

The Alvarado was a frame stucco building with great lawns surrounding
its long brick walkways and private courtyards. When it opened in 1902,
its seventy-five guest rooms, parlors, barbershop, club, and reading and
dining rooms had electricity and thermostatically regulated steam heat.
Designed by Charles F. Whittlesey, the Alvarado claims to have been the
first building in New Mexico to revive the now familiar Spanish mission
style of architecture found throughout the Southwest.

The Santa Fe depot was connected to the hotel by a two-hundred-foot
arcade that gave the two separate structures the appearance of a huge
Spanish mission beside the tracks. Train passengers walked the length of
the arcade enjoying the clear air of Albuquerque's high desert terrain, and
local people quickly adopted the same pastime, going for lunch and a
leisurely half hour's stroll on the Alvarado's promenade, possibly sighting
some famous personage disembarking from the noon train.

Situated between the hotel and the depot was Fred Harvey's Indian
Building, the interior of which was designed by Mary Colter. It was her first
job with Harvey, and the museum/sales shop was to launch the Harvey
Company's full-scale involvement in the promotion and sales of Indian arts
and crafts. Colter arranged both the museum and shop to tastefully exhibit
Indian art objects. There were rooms where tourists could watch Indian
weavers, silversmiths, potters, and basketmakers at work. The whole
atmosphere of the Indian Building was intriguing and authentic, the culture
and lifestyle of the American Indian of the Southwest represented alongside the beautiful art indigenous to it. Although the building was situated
on the main arcade between the hotel and the depot, interest in the Indian
collection was so slight during the first years that Schweizer himself could
be seen daily encouraging travelers to stop and just take a look inside.[13]
But neither the Harvey Company nor Schweizer was discouraged, and new
items from the reservations were constantly scouted and brought in for
sale and exhibit:

Fred Harvey saw the value of this outmoded article when others less discerning were casting it aside for the new, and I think it is no exaggeration to say that Fred Harvey saved from destruction thousands of worthy old specimens of Navajo weaving. [14]

The Alvarado attracted hundreds of stopover visitors to Albuquerque, most en route to California and grateful for a night or two off the train. William Allen White stayed at the hotel in its first decade and wrote to his readers in Kansas about the fine food, elegant and sophisticated clothing and hats worn by the local women, and the lovely music found during luncheon in the dining room: "The Alvarado hotel at Albuquerque is a Fred Harvey place, and is undoubtedly the best railroad hotel in the world. The New Yorkers who have been over Europe say so, and they ought to know."[15]

Albuquerque became a place to shop for Indian wares, cowboy boots and hats, and Mexican crafts and clothing. Downtown Albuquerque grew quickly, and the needs of the Alvarado's expanding clientele brought about the building of an addition in 1922, and more renovations in the 1930s. Mary Colter was asked in 1940 to decorate a new cocktail lounge in the hotel. She designed La Cocina Cantina, decorated to capture the spirit of an early Spanish kitchen. The room was centered around an old white-washed brick fireplace, and was lighted by drop lights in Mexican parrot cages. The lounge opened onto a flagstone patio where a high wall surrounded tables set among flowering potted plants and vines. Colter also designed special uniforms for the Harvey Girls assigned to the Cantina— copies of old Spanish dresses with long swishing petticoats and bright scarves for aprons.[16] "Within and without these new-old rooms and gardens, you are invited to seek your pleasure," the promotional brochure stated,[17] and La Cocina Cantina soon became a special meeting place for tourists and Albuquerque natives alike.

By 1941, Albuquerque was a conglomerate of cross-country travelers, Anglo newcomers, Hispanic and Indian natives, frontier and modern America. The social center for the city was the Alvarado, where those who could afford Albuquerque's best cuisine took their families for Sunday dinner, and politicians took visiting dignitaries for afternoon cocktails. It was still a dusty town surrounded by nothing but sage-covered mesas, but once on the grounds of the Alvarado, where the Super Chief and El Capitan luxury

The veranda of the Alvarado, ca. 1908. (Credit: Albuquerque Museum)

Interior of the Indian Building, ca. 1908. (Credit: Albuquerque Museum)

Fred Harvey's Indian Building located between the Santa Fe station and the Alvarado Hotel.
(Credit: Santa Fe Railway)

Alvarado Harvey Girl Grace Jones in the special uniform used in the cantina and for the governor's inauguration, 1938.
(Credit: Grace Jones)

liners stopped daily, Albuquerque passed for a cosmopolitan city well versed in worldly matters.

Like most Santa Fe Railway employees, Gene Montgomery's daily life included at least one visit to the Alvarado. A telegrapher at the Albuquerque Santa Fe office beginning in 1916, when he was sixteen years old, Gene ate lunch and often returned for afternoon coffee each day at the hotel. Santa Fe employees were given a 25 percent discount at the Harvey House:

> *I first saw the Alvarado in 1909. It was a beautiful place even then, with the mountains visible behind it, the Indians selling their wares near the depot, and the train passengers wandering around the platform. There wasn't much else in Albuquerque; the streets were dirt, it was dusty and there was little grass. I had come from Iowa so I noticed these things, even as a boy. But the Alvarado was simply beautiful.*
>
> *Albuquerque thought well of the Harvey Girls sent in to work at the Alvarado. I knew them well and thought highly of all of them. I never heard one of them complain about their work or life. They were picked 'specially and the management here was very strict with them. They were different from local waitresses—many of them married uptown lawyers and other respected men in the community. One couple, a chef and a Harvey Girl, married and bought land outside of town with money they had saved. They wanted to put down roots here. The Harvey Girl, Grace, started taking engineering classes at the university. She would work at night at the hotel and then go to class all day. She was a very unusual woman. With her husband, she built a home out there on their land. You know, that land later became some of the most valuable land in the city. They had real foresight.*
>
> *A lot of the girls went to local churches every Sunday, and the ministers used to come in for lunch at the Alvarado. The lunch room was an integral part of community life in Albuquerque.*

Because the telegraph office was the only place a train passenger in the early days could send messages, Gene sent many messages for the rich and famous who had an extra hour or two in Albuquerque:

I sent a lot of "I'll be there"–type messages for many famous people: Ronald Reagan, Charles Lindbergh, Shirley Temple, Jackie Coogan, Albert Einstein. When I was still very young, Mary Pickford came in and needed to send a telegram. Albuquerque was the last communication stop between New Mexico and Los Angeles. Well, I had to touch her hand to give her change and I'll tell you, that kept me going for a couple of years!

In 1927, when Bernard Kane first came to the Alvarado from Kansas, he was told it was a misdemeanor to spit on the sidewalks:

Albuquerque was the home for a lot of consumptives, but it was a very nice town. It was my first time working away from home—I was fifteen and worked all summer. I loved the Alvarado. My job was as a bellhop. I would get baggage from the people getting off the train and take it to their room. Then I'd be on call to take them water, whiskey, whatever.

I worked seven days a week. I don't remember having a day off all summer. There was always something going on in the hotel; something was always needed by somebody. We were paid, with tips, about forty dollars per month, plus room and board. In Albuquerque, you could be paid in gold. I didn't need cash so that's what I did. They were fine pieces of gold, worth a fortune today.

All night there was one bellhop on duty. There were often long-distance phone calls for the guests, and those operators from back east used to ask us if the Indians were tame out there? Were things peaceful in New Mexico? We got real tired of this and one night I got one of the little drums from the newsstand and told the operator to make it fast 'cause there was an uprising by some of the Indians in the lobby. She could hear the drum and she honestly believed me! People back east didn't know New Mexico was a state in the union!

Every Fourth of July Albuquerque had a huge celebration with parades and parties, many of which were held in the Alvarado. Tourists flocked to the city to watch the festivities, which included many colorful Indian, Spanish, and cowboy events. Bernard Kane remembers one such Fourth in particular:

> *I remember one wealthy eastern woman who brought her children to the Alvarado for the celebration. She had the kids, who were only about six and nine years old, outfitted to look like cowboys. A man who was traveling with her, a doctor, I believe, bought them the clothes. The main parade went right by the hotel, and the woman and her children were watching from one of the balconies. It turned out that the doctor had given the children real guns and one of the kids, just for fun, decided to shoot one of the guns off. I don't believe he knew it was loaded, but he shot a hole right through the wall of the Alvarado. No one was hurt.*

Bernard was exclusively assigned to serve Charles Lindbergh during his stay at the Alvarado. Only the desk clerk, the manager, and Bernard knew Lindbergh was in the hotel:

> *Lindbergh didn't want any reporters bothering him so his visit was kept a secret. He was up on the second floor and I would take him all his meals. One morning after I had gone upstairs for his tray, a man stopped me at the main desk and said, "I know Lindbergh is in this hotel, could you tell me where?" I said as far as I knew, he was not here. The man looked kind of exasperated and said, "Well, if you should see him, will you tell him Mr. F—— is here to see him. I have an appointment with him." I said alright, if I see him. I told Mr. Lindbergh that this man was roaming the hotel looking for him and that his name was Mr. F——. Lindbergh jumped up, ran out of his room and down the stairs looking for the man. It turned out the man was president of TWA and was there to hire Lindbergh. Lindbergh had just forgotten to say anything about it.*

The Alvarado was a highly requested house in the Harvey system. Until World War II, nearly all Alvarado Harvey Girls were hired out of Kansas

City and were usually women who had worked their way up to positions of choice. All Harvey employees lived in the hotel until the late 1940s, when a union meant they had to move off the premises. Tips at the hotel were good, and extra work at the Grand Canyon and La Fonda in Santa Fe was available to women wanting to make extra money. Many of the women would serve breakfast at the Alvarado, hop a train to Santa Fe—sixty miles north—serve a banquet at La Fonda, and then take the train home to Albuquerque in time to serve the evening meal.

Effie Jenks (see Chapter 5) began work as a Harvey Girl at the Alvarado in 1923 and found Albuquerque to be a warm community that included the Harvey employees in many of its annual activities. Although she was always aware of her "station" as a waitress, Effie Jenks, like many Alvarado Harvey Girls, accepted numerous social invitations and enjoyed the general acceptance of Harvey Girls in women's circles in Albuquerque:

> *When I first came to the Alvarado Hotel in Albuquerque, some of the socially prominent families gave parties for the girls. To a degree this might have been called a patronizing sort of gesture but it was nonetheless a most gracious one. The hostesses used their best linen and silver and we girls were treated like queens. The Mayor and his wife held an open house at New Year's, and a prominent dentist's wife gave an annual tea at which her friend, a woman generally considered to be the social leader in Albuquerque, poured. A doctor sometimes took the girls on his rounds making house calls—he realized the girls didn't often have a chance to ride in an automobile.*
>
> *This was all in the old days when Albuquerque was still a small town and Harvey Girls had waited about everybody in town. This all showed the respect in which the early Harvey Girls were held.*

Bernard Kane was only a teenager when he came to the Alvarado and remembers that the Harvey Girls took special care of him:

> *We were not allowed to fraternize. Of course, I was too young for that. One Harvey Girl I knew, Mary, became the object of one of the hotel guest's admiration. The girls were not allowed to*

*socialize with guests and could be promptly fired for doing so. So
the young man and Mary sent notes back and forth via me.*

*This particular man had ridden up to the hotel one day on a
horse, with a suitcase behind his saddle. I went out and took his
suitcase and tied the horse to a tree after he informed me he
would be a guest at the Alvarado. He gave me a five dollar tip,
which was unheard of in the 1920s. It turned out he was the son
of a very wealthy family in Kansas City, and was just out of
college, spending the summer roaming the mesas, looking for
artifacts, painting, things like that. I was assigned to wait on him
by his own request, and that's why I had to deliver all of his notes
to Mary. Mary really wasn't that interested in him, but it went on
for two or three weeks.*

*His parents sent him a Packard coupe with a Victrola player
on the back seat. It was a very fine car. Still, Mary wasn't
interested. Every time he gave me a note to give to her, he gave me
a dollar. He told me if I could get an answer he'd give me
another dollar. I told Mary about this, and we would split the
dollar for each note she sent back. It all ended when his parents
called long-distance and told him it was time to come home.
Before he left, he told me I could use the car. It was the finest car
in Albuquerque, and I did take it out a couple of times. I don't
know what happened to that car. I've always wondered about it.*

*The bellhops all ate together in a staff dining room. We had
this one Harvey Girl who always served us dinner, and when I
was first there, I noticed that the other guys were getting pie à la
mode for dessert and I wasn't. I asked about this and they told
me you have to get in good with the waitress. The way to do this,
they explained, was to sing her a nice song.*

*All of the bellhops that summer, except me, were
Spanish-American, and the song they suggested was a Spanish
song. They wrote out the words and I took a couple of days
learning it. One night when I thought I was ready, I told the
Harvey Girl I had a song for her. I sang it in front of everybody.
After I finished, she came over to me and dumped an entire tray
of spaghetti and meatballs on me! I couldn't figure out what had
happened. No one would tell me. I finally found someone in the*

laundry who spoke Spanish and I learned I had sung to her about losing her pants, shoes, and shirt. After that, I had trouble getting dinner, let alone pie, from that Harvey Girl!

Grace Jones and a girlfriend were looking for jobs in Topeka in 1929. The only job Grace could find was in a dime store, working four days a week, four hours a day, for $ .15 an hour: "It was not great," Grace remembers:

People were starving. I did that for awhile and then they started laying people off. That's when a railroad friend told us there was a chance we could find a job in New Mexico, at the Alvarado Hotel. We were flat broke, there were no jobs in Kansas, so my girlfriend and I decided to drive to New Mexico. Her boyfriend offered to go with us and we set out in her car for Albuquerque. The roads weren't too bad.

We both applied for jobs at the Alvarado. I had had an aunt who was a Harvey Girl, and that must have helped because I got a job and my friend didn't. She did find work at another restaurant in Albuquerque, but she hated it and decided to drive back to Kansas. I stayed.

I loved the work, the people at the hotel, my room, everything. There were all kinds of people in Albuquerque, and there were Indian reservations to explore. It was something else for a girl from Kansas. On my day off I would go out hiking, or on a tour up north, or horseback riding. It was a very good life.

I worked at the coffee shop. One afternoon I was watching this one man who had strolled in, real nice looking. I was just staring at him and then it dawned on me that he was Don Ameche. I asked him and he said, yes, he was. He was real friendly. I got to see many famous people at the Alvarado. Everyone became accustomed to it. Back in Kansas it was a big deal. I wrote home about the people I served like Bob Hope and Ed MacMahon. I remember Delores Del Rio swinging into the Alvarado lobby with furs and a great big hat. But she was just another customer to the Harvey people.

Violet Bosetti (see Chapter 4) also loved her life at the Alvarado:

*I grew up in six months at the Alvarado. Life there liberated me
from life in Kansas. They treated us like ladies, everybody. I was
assigned to La Cocina Cantina when it first opened. Mary Jane
Colter saw me and pulled me aside and said she wanted to make
a special costume for me to wear in the Cantina. I was not
beautiful, but different-looking—Italian, a Latin type. A
seamstress came in and made me this beautiful dress later worn
by all the Harvey Girls in the Cantina. They were all lovely
women and it made the Cantina very elegant.*

Journalist Ernie Pyle made his home in Albuquerque in the early 1940s
because "here you could actually see the clouds and the stars and the
storms instead of just reading about it in the newspaper."[18] Albuquerque
was the place where Pyle and his wife Jerry could relax and unwind, and
Ernie was a frequent customer at the Alvarado: "In four months, I haven't
been out of overalls more than a half dozen times," he wrote. "And I go
to the Alvarado Hotel's swell 'Cocina Cantina' always in my overalls and
nobody raises an eyebrow."[19]

A hot, sandy railroad junction located on what was known as the Mohave
River Bridge in the Mojave Desert was named Barstow in 1886, in honor
of Santa Fe Railway president William Barstow Strong. Barstow, California,
was another of those southwestern communities created and sustained by
the Santa Fe.

The first dining and hotel complex in Barstow was built of brick the same
year the railroad arrived. Business at the Barstow depot thrived in the
1880s with waves of excursionists from the East seeking sun and profit in
southern California. In May of 1887, the Barstow depot hotel and dining
operations were taken over by Fred Harvey. Harvey bought out the hotel
and restaurant business previously owned by Stackpole and Lincoln, which
included the Barstow complex as well as establishments at San Bernardino
and Needles.

In its first year as a Harvey House, the Barstow restaurant burned to
the ground. The hotel was immediately rebuilt by the Santa Fe, but was
to fall victim to a second fire in 1892. The third structure, with extensive
railroad yards and shops surrounding it, burned in 1908. The community

of Barstow was plagued by fires and floods in the two years that followed, and the last and finest Barstow Harvey House, Casa del Desierto (House of the Desert), was not built until 1910.

In 1910, the Santa Fe began a major renewal program in Barstow, launching the desert junction into the twentieth century at a cost to the railroad of two million dollars. Renovations included miles of new rails, new machine shops, oil and water stations, and a new roundhouse. The construction of Casa del Desierto gave Barstow the most extensive and elegant Harvey House in southern California.

Designed by Santa Barbara architect Francis W. Wilson, Casa del Desierto was a pseudo–Spanish-Moroccan complex of reinforced concrete and brick. In Barstow's otherwise styleless landscape, it was a true jewel in the desert. It was a self-contained village, and was the fifth such luxurious hotel west of Albuquerque.

Casa del Desierto was divided into three main buildings, all connected by covered walkways and spacious verandas with colorful, lush, flowering bushes. The Harvey Girls lived on the first floor of a wing behind the main section of the hotel. The male employees lived in the basement of the same area, while the second floor had more guest rooms and accomodations for railroad employees. The manager lived in a large, four-room apartment in the main part of the hotel.

Casa del Desierto had its own bowling alley, swimming pool, library, and theater for employees, plus a laundry, ice-making and -crushing facilities, a butchering station, and ice cream plant. The latter was the pride of the house, with up to thirty gallons of ice cream made daily. Young Barstow natives could earn pocket money by peddling the ice cream to train passengers on the platform. Barstow's ice cream was also shipped out to Needles, Seligman, Winslow, San Bernardino, even to Los Angeles and San Diego.[20]

Young Harvey Girls seeking life and possible adventure in the desert West found just what they hoped for at the Barstow Harvey House. Barstow Harvey Girls became outdoor enthusiasts and were part of a community whose social life revolved around physical, outdoor living. Tennis, swimming, hiking, and dancing were favorite pastimes of Barstow's populace, and Harvey Girls often donned trousers, heavy boots, and a sturdy hat for excursions into the desert. Like all of the great Harvey Houses, Casa del Desierto offered its employees a tightly knit family atmosphere.

The first train to the Grand Canyon, September 18, 1901. (Credit: Santa Fe Railway)

Casa del Desierto, the Barstow Harvey House and Hotel. (Credit: Santa Fe Railway)

74

El Tovar with Harvey touring cars parked out front; the hotel stocked divided walking skirts and straw hats for female visitors ill-equipped for the rugged hiking and riding expeditions offered around and into the Canyon in the early years of the century. (Credit: Katheryne Krause Ferguson)

An early guest room, El Tovar. (Credit: University of Arizona Special Collections)

Harvey Girls and employees all speak of their days at Barstow with warmth and nostalgia.

Jesse and Addie Park came to Barstow from Missouri, eventually transplanting their entire family to California (see Chapter 4). Addie worked at the lunch counter, a job she loved because of the daily contact with local people and railroaders: "I made many, many friends in the community."

"Meanwhile Fred Harvey and the Santa Fe had discovered the Grand Canyon of the Colorado of Arizona . . ."[21] Harvey and the Santa Fe didn't really discover the Grand Canyon—that honor belongs to a member of Francisco Vasquez Coronado's expedition to the Southwest in the mid-1500s. But they did make the Grand Canyon accessible to modern travelers, beginning in the early 1900s.

In the 1880s, a handful of ambitious sightseers made their way to the Grand Canyon via a long, jolting stage ride from Williams, Arizona, forty miles south of the canyon rim. The Santa Fe's main line passed through Williams, but not until 1901, when the Santa Fe purchased a bankrupt railroad that ran from Williams north to a copper mine in Anita, and extended the track to the canyon, could it offer train service to its new depot on the rim.

The Grand Canyon was largely unknown in the United States, but Harvey and the Santa Fe believed it would one day be one of the greatest natural sights in the world. Located in the isolated desert and Indian country of northern Arizona, it only needed comfortable facilities and adequate promotion. It is fortunate for the canyon that Harvey and the railroad officials behind him were sensitive and appreciative of its natural beauty and set out to build facilities that were not disruptive of the landscape. (The Grand Canyon was placed under the protection of the U.S. Forest Service in 1905, but was not made a national park until 1919.)

Development of the Grand Canyon began in 1903, with the building of El Tovar by the Santa Fe.[22] In the tradition of the great resorts of Europe, El Tovar was an impressive, four-story, log-and-boulder structure "tucked" into the Ponderosa pines near the canyon rim. Most of the logs were Douglas firs brought in by train from Oregon; the boulders were native stone. Described as "the most expensively constructed and appointed log house in America,"[23] El Tovar stretched 325 feet north to south and 218 feet east to west.[24] El Tovar opened in 1905 with one hundred guest rooms, steam heat, hot and cold running water, electric lights, but only one bath for each of the four floors, for which reservations were needed in advance. The hotel cost the Santa Fe $250,000 and was designed by Charles F. Whittlesey.

Over the next two decades, the community at the canyon, centered around El Tovar, grew into an entire village. Once at the canyon, a visitor found all the comforts and conveniences of any small community. El Tovar itself housed, besides guest rooms, a large dining room, a huge lounge, art galleries, a solarium, music room, club room, recreation room, and garden on the roof. It had its own power plant, an extensive fire-protection system, and a laundry that eventually did all the cleaning for the four Harvey operations at the Grand Canyon village. Water for the village was hauled in daily by train from Del Rio, Arizona.

El Tovar had the traditional Harvey kitchen, bakery, and butcher shop, offering the finest meat and baked goods found anywhere in the United States. Bulk storage refrigerators held fresh salmon from San Francisco, celery from Michigan, honeydew and Persian melons weighing up to twenty-two pounds each, apples, pears, and oranges from California, French and Portuguese sardines, Kansas beef, Camembert cheeses, and raw milk from the Fred Harvey dairy at Del Rio.[25]

Promotion of the Grand Canyon began with travel brochures, Fred Harvey advertising, and newspaper stories nationwide. But the canyon's public identity was really bolstered by Santa Fe official Edward P. Ripley's promotion of a particularly spectacular painting of the Grand Canyon by Thomas Moran. The Santa Fe bought the painting, made several thousand full-color lithographs from it, framed them, and gave them to schools, hotels, private homes, offices, and railroad stations throughout the country. The painting portrayed the awesome size and unique colors of the canyon; Ripley reasoned it would inspire hundreds of people to come and view the real thing for themselves. His reasoning was right, and El Tovar became a very busy place, with reservations needed months in advance.

The same year El Tovar opened, Hopi House, built directly across from the hotel, also opened. Designed by Mary Colter, Hopi House was the main sales facility for Fred Harvey Indian arts. Colter's idea was to build a structure that accurately represented the dwellings of the Indians whose history and art were to be exhibited inside. Hopi House resembled the Hopi dwellings found at Oraibi, Arizona, and offered visitors to the canyon a chance to watch native craftsmen weaving and making traditional pottery and jewelry in public workrooms inside. In the evenings, the Grand Canyon village was treated to traditional Hopi songs and dances.

The first two decades of the twentieth century brought a tourist boom to the Grand Canyon, and Harvey had to increase the services available near the rim. In the late 1920s, the old Bright Angel Camp was enlarged to become a small town of cabins capable of accomodating five hundred people. The Harvey employee dormitories were placed in this camp. Because automobile traffic was increasing, a public campground, sponsored by the government, was operated at no cost to canyon visitors, and Harvey opened a garage, a livery stable, and a general merchandise store.

In 1919, when the Grand Canyon was made into a national park, the Fred Harvey Company became official park concessioner. The park already included three structures designed by Mary Colter—Hopi House, Hermit's Rest, a small building that served as a rest area for tourists viewing the canyon in Harveycars, and the Lookout, a rustic but comfortable lounge built on a precipice west of El Tovar, with high-powered telescopes set up on its porches. In addition, Harvey and the Santa Fe built Phantom Ranch, designed by Mary Colter and placed five thousand feet below the rim near Phantom Creek. Hikers and groups descending the canyon by mule stayed overnight at Phantom Ranch, which consisted of cabins, a large dining hall, and a recreation facility.

Tourist traffic to the Grand Canyon either by train or automobile, grew from 44,000 in 1919 to 200,000 in 1929, to over 300,000 in the mid-1930s. At that time, Harvey commissioned Colter to built the Watchtower at Desert View. Modeled after the primitive Indian watchtowers Colter had seen at various ruins in the Southwest, the tower was built of stone with a steel framework hidden beneath to give the seventy-foot-high structure a secure foundation. The Watchtower served as a rest area and gift shop at the eastern end of the Harvey sightseeing tours.

In 1934, Mary Colter built Bright Angel Lodge, a rim-side hotel that was to be more moderately priced than El Tovar. The Lodge opened in June of 1935. The lobby was decorated with every size and style of western hat

Colter could find, including Pancho Villa's famous sombrero. Two thousand people attended a Harvey barbecue; entertainment was provided by Hopi ceremonial dancers and by cowboy singers.

Harvey employees, once hired on to the staff at Bright Angel Lodge or El Tovar, often remained in the community on the rim for many years. An estimated five hundred people lived at Grand Canyon village in the twenties and thirties, and Harvey rules and regulations regarding employee relations here were, from the first, a law unto themselves. Because they were not part of a greater community, and everyone living at the canyon worked either for the Harvey company or the railroad, all community events were initiated and attended by the same group of people. Employees at the Grand Canyon Harvey Houses hiked, danced, worked, and partied together, and rules forbidding such fraternizing were quickly abandoned by early Harvey management.

Bernice Black McLain (see Chapter 5) requested a position at one of the Grand Canyon Harvey Houses after six years at the Chicago Dearborn Station Harvey House. Bernice liked her work, but wanted a change from life in Chicago, where the Harvey Girls lived in their own apartments, and, Bernice felt, the community viewed Harvey Girls much the same as all waitresses:

> *Everybody, believe me, everybody treated us the same as waitresses there. We were considered lower-class, even though many girls married very well. I'll tell you quite frankly, the Harvey Girls were a nice bunch of women.*
>
> *I got tired of Chicago and asked to be sent out on the line again. I requested the Grand Canyon. At the Canyon, you were under contract to begin work at Easter and stay until Labor Day, although I stayed until Christmas. I worked at Bright Angel Lodge, which was new. El Tovar was already old when I worked at the Canyon [the mid-1930s].*
>
> *The Grand Canyon was very busy, even in those days. Some people would come up just for the day—they'd take a train up from Williams in the morning, tour the Canyon, eat lunch, and then take a train back down in the late afternoon or evening. They would take those mules down into the Canyon, or just tour the rim. I liked work at the Canyon. It was very different from all*

the other Harvey Houses—I worked at Kingman, after training in Gallup, and later at Winslow and then Chicago. But the Canyon was different. There were many, many Harvey Girls working there. It was a large community. And it was a glamorous place, the Grand Canyon. We could all socialize together because we were the only people living there. Other Houses were very strict about the girls.

I left the Canyon when I was married. My husband was a railroadman and had come up there to work on a new power house the Santa Fe was building. I was thirty-two years old. I was the girl who was never going to get married.

Bertha Parker Maddux (see Chapter 4) was a Harvey Girl at the Castañeda in Las Vegas when she was told by the Harvey office in Kansas City that she was needed at the Grand Canyon:

I was sent there for the rush—the summer season at Bright Angel Lodge. I worked both the dining room and the lunch counter, and lived in a dormitory across the road from the hotel. In 1926, we were paid forty dollars a month plus room and board. I saved some money—the tips were very good at the Canyon.

The rush began at Easter. We served several hundred people after the sunrise service. Extra girls were brought in from other houses in Arizona and New Mexico. The canyon was a place Harvey Girls wanted to work. It was an established tourist attraction, and people came from everywhere. There were many wealthy people visiting the canyon.

Bertha remembers carloads of Harvey employees driving to Williams to see a show:

We could get permission from the manager to stay out late. It was a sixty mile drive, and we often returned home early the next morning.

We didn't feel isolated at the canyon. It was so beautiful there, and we learned to create our own fun. I went down into the canyon on a mule. It was straight down, there were big curves in the path; it was scary but fun!

Most of the employees were from out-of-state. They came from farms, from cities, everywhere. It was a fun group of people there. The Harvey Girls got to know the local cowboys—they were guides around the canyon, and we had square dances. I could play a little fiddle, and we'd play those old hoe-downs. I remember our headwaitress, a classy woman, married one of the cowboys.

I met my husband at the canyon. He drove one of the sightseeing cars and lived in the boys' dorm across the village. My first date with him was on a picnic that couples went to. I had gone with another boy, and my roommate had gone with the man who became my husband. We got separated; my husband took me home. From then on, we went to the picnics together.

I quit after six months. I was in love. Charles and I left the canyon in his Chevrolet touring car, drove to Flagstaff and were married. After I met his folks in Kingman, we returned to the canyon. He drove sightseeing cars and I worked as an extra Harvey Girl. They gave married employees tent houses in the village—one room, with a pot-bellied stove, canvas walls, a wood floor. We got by. Then they built new houses for everyone. We lived there for two years before leaving to live in Kingman.

Gallup, New Mexico, founded in 1881, was an old station of the Pony Express. Old-timers say the town got its name from the early Atlantic and Pacific Railroad workers who used to say they were "going to Gallup's" on payday.[26] David L. Gallup was paymaster and auditor for the Atlantic and Pacific, later bought by the Santa Fe Railway. Located near the Arizona and New Mexico border, Gallup was an early railroad and coal mining center, and was perfectly situated to become the jumping-off spot for tourist sojourns into Indian country in the early 1900s. Gallup became a popular stopover with the Indian Detours with its accessibility to such places as Enchanted Mesa, Chaco Canyon, Zuni and Acoma Pueblos, Navajo land, the Painted Desert, the Petrified Forest, and Inscription Rock. Gallup seemed a worthy location for one of the last great Harvey hotels to be built, and in 1921, the Santa Fe approved Mary Colter's plans for El Navajo.

Unlike the other major hotels built by Harvey and the railroad, El Navajo was a tribute to the American Indian. The hotel was not built in the Spanish

El Navajo Hotel was a popular departure point for tourists interested in seeing the famous pueblos and reservations in Arizona and New Mexico. (Credit: University of Arizona Special Collections)

Harvey Girl Ellen Hunt Jones waiting for the train home after a day off spent exploring Manuelita, New Mexico. 1923 (Credit: Ellen Jones)

The main room of Hermit's Rest. (Credit: University of Arizona Special Collections)

Lobby of El Navajo with authentic Indian sand paintings Mary Colter introduced to non-Indian America. (Credit: University of Arizona Special Collections)

or California mission revival style of the other large Harvey hotels. Colter took a bold architectural step with El Navajo, blending modern architecture with ancient Indian art.

Colter had established lasting relationships with Indian artists and was able to engage their cooperation in the decorating of El Navajo. She even received approval from the Navajos to use Indian sand paintings as a decorative motif throughout the building. In the early 1920s, very few non-Indians had ever laid eyes on a sand painting, as they were a sacred part of Navajo religious ritual and were destroyed after use.[27]

Two thousand Indians attended the house-blessing ceremony that opened El Navajo on May 26, 1923. Sightseers from as far away as Albuquerque, from Arizona, as well as New Mexico old-timers, Santa Fe railroad and Fred Harvey officials, and some thirty medicine men from various southwestern tribes came to attend the "Blessing of the House, the Ritual for Making Perfect."[28]

Harvey personnel were sent in from Kansas City and from other Houses to put El Navajo into full swing. Gallup and El Navajo's busiest time was the annual Inter-Tribal Indian Ceremonial begun in the 1920s and held each August. Thousands of Indians and tourists attended this event, and El Navajo was the natural center for many activities during the ceremonial. Extra Harvey Girls were brought in by train from Albuquerque, sometimes farther, to work at the hotel during the August event during which the isolated and often mundane community of Gallup became one of the most popular tourist attractions in the Southwest. The Harvey Girls wore festive dresses and skirts for the ceremonial instead of the black and white standard uniforms worn the rest of the year.

The Harvey office in Kansas City sent many new Harvey Girls to Gallup for training before sending them out to other large houses such as the Alvarado or Casa del Desierto. The permanent Harvey Girls at El Navajo were often older, long-term employees well equipped to train Kansas farm women for life and work at one of the elegant Harvey Houses. One such woman was Ellen Mae Hunt (see Chapter 4) who had little idea of what she was getting into when she signed on to work as a Harvey Girl in 1922:

Miss Steel, in Kansas City, asked me if I was afraid of Indians? I kind of was—I'd only known two in my whole life. But I said,

"Oh, no!" Then she told me I was being sent by train to a place called Gallup, an Indian center in New Mexico.

Ellen went to El Navajo with a girlfriend from business school:

We couldn't be roommates at El Navajo. We were sent to two different rooms when we arrived. We were scared. *But when I opened the door to my room, a woman was standing there and she said, "My God, come on in!" She was much older than I; all the Harvey Girls at the hotel were older than we were.*

Gallup wasn't very big yet, although there were many Indians and cowboys on the streets. It looked nice but it was wild. *I'd never seen a town like that because Kansas didn't have saloons. But after I was there a short while, I began to like it.*

. . . I remember when my friend and I were first at El Navajo, we met two nice boys in the pantry. They were Mexican. They liked us and we liked them. But we couldn't go out. The head waitress pulled us aside and said, "We don't do that with Mexicans."

We fed three passenger trains a day. Some people were nice, and some people were not so nice. Many would ask us how we liked New Mexico. In the 1920s, the best people stayed at El Navajo. It was beautiful, and expensive. When I first arrived in Gallup, I felt that people were looking down on me because of my work. But after I had lived there awhile, I stopped feeling that way. Harvey Girls could marry, settle down, in Gallup.

I met my husband in 1925. I worked other Harvey Houses in Barstow and San Bernardino, but I ended up in Gallup because I missed it when I was away. My husband was a Santa Fe man—my friend from Kansas also married a railroader—and Harvey people and the railroadmen all pushed us together. Even the headwaitress told me we should be together. We married in 1932 and lived in Gallup. Robert worked for the Santa Fe until the depression bumped four trains in one day, and Robert's job was taken away. They had a seniority system, and he just went down a notch. In 1935, we moved out to Zuni Pueblo, where we lived and worked as traders until 1959.

I would never have come west if it hadn't been for Harvey.
Think what I would have missed!

"Santa Fe has been advertised, at various times, as the City Different, the Crossroads of the Centuries, the Royal City, the ancient Capital, and the Athens of America. . . . For three centuries Santa Fe has always been aware of itself as something special; not conceited, exactly, just sure of its pre-eminence. . . ."[29]

La Fonda hotel and the city of Santa Fe were famous in their own right long before either Harvey or the Santa Fe came to town. Situated on the southwest side of the Sangre de Cristo mountains, Santa Fe (Holy Faith), founded in 1610, is the oldest European community west of the Mississippi River.

Santa Fe had a historic adobe inn or *fonda* as early as 1609. It was literally the inn at the end of the trail—the Santa Fe Trail opened in 1821—and was the rendezvous for all variety of trappers, gamblers, pioneers, miners, soldiers, merchants, and politicians. The one-story inn had various names over the years: La Fonda, the U.S. Hotel, and later the Exchange Hotel. A hardy and adventurous lot of people patronized the hotel where there was always plenty of liquor, gambling, and colorful incidents befitting northern New Mexico. At least one man is supposed to have been lynched in the back yard of the inn, and a chief justice is said to have been shot in the lobby.[30] A confederate general housed his staff at the hotel and General Grant was given a ball there after the Civil War.[31] In later years, Billy the Kid is supposed to have washed dishes in the kitchen and played the piano in the bar, and at least one Texan rode into the billiard room and shot out the lights.[32]

The old Exchange Hotel was torn down in 1919 to make way for a larger hotel to be built on the same spot. The new building was in the Pueblo style, with four stories of forty-six rooms, terraced roofs, towers, and balconies. The company that built La Fonda in the early 1920s went bankrupt in 1926. The same year, the Santa Fe Railway acquired the property and made it into a Harvey House.

The Fred Harvey Company enlarged the hotel from 46 to 156 rooms with the addition of a fifth floor of deluxe suites and an annex. Harvey brought Mary Colter to La Fonda to completely refurnish the guest rooms, lounges, and dining areas. Colter worked her extraordinary charm on the hotel, replacing the stiff furniture with warm, informal Mexican furnishings. Every item in every room was chosen according to Colter's specifications, and most of the furniture was made in Kansas City; 798 pieces were shipped to Santa Fe and hand-painted to fit the color scheme Colter designed for each room in the hotel.[33]

La Fonda Harvey House opened in 1929. It was an overwhelming and immediate success among the people of Santa Fe and Santa Fe Railway travelers alike. In a community of Hispanics, Indians, Anglos, and tourists, La Fonda became a social center few other local establishments could compete with. The hotel had the great cuisine and service of all Harvey Houses, but it also had a romantic atmosphere and a superb location on the old plaza of an exotic little city that was suddenly of great interest to the traveling world.

Monte Chavez began work at La Fonda the year it opened. A native New Mexican born in Tesuque in 1911, Monte remained a Harvey employee at La Fonda until the hotel was sold by the Santa Fe in 1968. Monte began work as a pantry boy, was soon a bellboy, and eventually served as maître 'd:

> *Most of the bellboys were from Santa Fe with a few sent in from Kansas City. There were twelve of us, and the hotel kept us very, very busy! We were paid a dollar and a half a day, and with tips made about forty-five a month. It was a pretty good job to have back then.*

La Fonda had a steady group of people who lived and worked at the hotel for many years. "Sometimes we'd get a Harvey Girl who joined up just to get a railroad pass west," Monte remembers,

> *but usually the girls stayed for a long time. In the summers, there would be college girls working here, too. It was a very close group, the Harvey people. They were united. We would all go out to dances and parties together, go out around Santa Fe after work.*

Like their counterparts at the Grand Canyon, La Fonda Harvey employees were a community unto themselves. Although they lived within a greater community, and had access to activities and people not connected

A fonda, inn or tavern, has stood on the corner of San Francisco and Shelby Streets in Santa Fe since 1609. (Credit: Katheryne Krause Ferguson)

The lobby of La Fonda, like every room, suite, and dining area, was meticulously designed and planned by Mary Colter when the Santa Fe bought the hotel in 1926 and made it into a Harvey House. The closest passenger station to Santa Fe was Lamy, New Mexico, several miles east of the capital city. (Credit: University of Arizona Special Collections)

La Fonda with Fred Harvey tour buses parked in front of the hotel. From Santa Fe, visitors could go to pueblos and historic ruins all over northern New Mexico, including Taos, via the Indian Detours operated by Fred Harvey from La Fonda.
(Credit: Las Vegas Citizen's Committee for Historic Preservation)

La Fonda Patio. (Credit: Ruthanna Caster)

to the hotel, many of the Harvey rules regarding employee relationships were altered and even abandoned at La Fonda. The Harvey Girls could date Harvey employees, but they had to meet outside of the hotel. "Forty or fifty Harvey people would meet at a place in another part of the city every Sunday night," Monte remembers. "It was a standard part of our social life. The manager knew about it. He didn't mind."

Because of northern New Mexico's large Hispanic and Indian population, and the unusual and often non-discriminatory whites (such as Mabel Dodge Lujan, an eastern heiress and close friend of D.H. Lawrence, who married a Pueblo Indian) who chose to live among them, segregation was less identifiable and often nonexistent in local restaurants and hotels. La Fonda in Santa Fe and the Alvarado in Albuquerque served everyone who walked through their doors with money in their pocket and *reasonable* social habits. As illustrated in the pages ahead, the atmosphere at La Fonda like at the Alvarado, was informal yet elegant, relaxed, classy, and often colorful.

Local women were hired to work as Harvey Girls in Santa Fe, and Monte remembers that this included Hispanic women. All of the girls were treated well in Santa Fe, which was a highly diverse community of ranchers, businessmen, politicians, artists, writers, and out-of-state visitors, all of whom were regular customers at La Fonda. Monte remembers:

> *Every day the dining rooms and patio would be filled with business people and artists sitting around having meetings over lunch. The tips were very good for the girls. All the customers, even those that weren't so wealthy, gave them good tips. It was that kind of place here.*

Many Harvey Girls came from Kansas and the Midwest, married and then remained in New Mexico. "They stood out," Monte says. "They were some of the best-dressed, most attractive women in Santa Fe. I knew them to marry judges, cowboys, ranchers, local politicians—everyone. They were part of the community."

La Fonda Harvey Girls wore the traditional black-and-white uniforms in the dining and lunchrooms, but those working on the outside patio wore colorful Mexican skirts and blouses. These skirts were also worn by all the women during Santa Fe's annual *fiesta*. Celebrating the 1692 Spanish reconquest of New Mexico, the Santa Fe Fiesta attracted hundreds of visitors to several days of festivities held on and around the old plaza. Rowdy parties and general mayhem accompanied fiesta time, and La Fonda historians claim it was common for a pretty girl to ride a horse into the hotel at least once during the festive weekend.[34]

It was at La Fonda that Harvey's "coat rule" finally broke down. The hotel was a haunt for famous and soon-to-be famous artists and Harvey and the railroad used this in their advertising of La Fonda. Because the local painters and sculptors and writers wore a "uniform" of brightly colored shirts and Mexican-type clothing, and refused to change their attire to have lunch in their favorite dining room at La Fonda, the rule was dropped.

Ernie Pyle was amused by Santa Fe and La Fonda's special collection of people:

> *In the thirties Santa Fe, New Mexico had fifteen thousand people, of whom half were Spanish-American. Of the rest about 150 were artists and writers. Which doesn't sound like many in figures, but it's an awful gob of genius. Then there were the governor and the politicians, whom the geniuses didn't recognize. Life among the upper crust centered by daytime in the La Fonda Hotel. (La Fonda is Spanish for "The Hotel," but people don't pay much attention to that. They just go on saying The-the-Hotel-hotel.) You could go there any time of day and see a few artists in the bar, or an Indian that some white woman loved, or a goateed nobleman from Austria, or a maharaja from India, or a New York broker, or an archaeologist, or some local light in overalls and cowboy boots. You never met anybody anywhere except at the La Fonda. You never took anybody to lunch anywhere else. I couldn't see how some of the struggling geniuses afforded it. I stayed at the De Vargas.*
>
> *Most of the artists seemed to be genuine people, living normal lives, though there were freaks and pretenders—people who liked to go dress up like Indians and stare into fireplaces. Many people who go to Santa Fe stay sane. Some go to pot.*[35]

Bernice Myers (see Chapter 4) remembers that the local clients at La Fonda were given special treatment. She waited an entire evening on one group of well-known artists:

They had brought their dog into the hotel and placed him in a chair at the table. The management let them get away with that because they were artists and regular patrons. We put up with a lot as Harvey Girls at La Fonda!

Movie companies from Los Angeles used La Fonda for their production headquarters while shooting feature films in northern New Mexico. Monte Chavez remembers:

We had the crews and stars from such movies as Cowboy, The Texas Rangers, Empire, *and* Route 66. *They were here at the hotel for weeks at a time. But it was common to see famous people sitting in the lounge or eating on the patio of La Fonda. I served Ferdinand of Germany, picked out wine for Igor Stravinsky, and became good friends with Greer Garson. Harvey people were always told not to disturb celebrities or make a fuss about their presence. And they were all left alone to enjoy their visit here.*

Ruthanna Walz began work as a Harvey Girl at La Fonda in 1936. She was raised in Kansas and after graduating from high school, needed to find a job to support herself:

My parents couldn't afford to have me live with them. Those were very hard times. I couldn't find a job in Kansas, when a friend told me she had an aunt who was hostess at La Fonda in Santa Fe, a Harvey House. I lived in Atchison so I knew all about Fred Harvey. I had to do something, so, with a recommendation from my friend's aunt, I went into Alice Steel's office in Kansas City where they hired all the girls, and was hired right away.

I was about nineteen when I left Kansas on a train for New Mexico. It was an adventure! Here I was, a little country girl, raised on a farm, off for Santa Fe! It was unusual to be a single woman alone on the train. There were mostly couples and families, but they treated me very well. The dining cars were all Harvey so everyone knew about the Harvey system and respected what I was going out to New Mexico to do. I really wanted to go

*to college, but in those days, there wasn't the money to just go.
The only other sort of job I could have found would have been as
a housekeeper or babysitter, or as a switchboard operator. After
those sorts of jobs, a Harvey Girl in the Southwest was really
something.*

*I came into Lamy where I was to get off and take a bus for
Santa Fe. I was used to the fertile farmland of Kansas. This was
desert. When I got off the train in Lamy, I thought I had come to
the ends of the earth! I got on the bus and wondered what I was
doing here, driving up this winding dirt road? It was pretty
uncivilized. But it didn't take very long to get used to it. La
Fonda was the elite resort-type hotel. People who came and stayed
there were going someplace. Of course, there were the artists! Some
of them were real characters hanging around the hotel.*

*I roomed with Lona, my friend's aunt, who was old enough to
be my mother and had worked for Harvey for years. The Harvey
Girls lived at the sidewalk level of La Fonda, two to a room.*

The majority of Santa Fe Harvey Girls were single, but those who married
were allowed to continue working at La Fonda. Married Harvey Girls lived
in their own homes in the community.

"In some ways, looking back, it was slave labor," Ruthanna says.

*There was no eight-hour day. If a train was late, you waited, even
up to five hours. But at La Fonda, we made upwards of three
hundred a month just in tips. With thirty dollars a month plus
room and board and laundry, that was very good money in the
1930s. I banked most of mine and saved a lot. We had
black-and-white uniforms, but I often wore the colored, long skirts
for lunch on the patio. We had to own a concha belt to go with
the skirt. It was a beautiful, stunning outfit.*

On her day off, Ruthanna would often join fellow employees for a drive up
to Taos, or to one of the nearby Pueblos: "I went with one of the bellhops.
One afternoon we went up to visit the Castañeda and as soon as I saw it
I knew I wanted to work there someday."

After one year at La Fonda, Ruthanna quit work. After a visit home to

Kansas, she asked Miss Steel in Kansas City if she could be transferred to Las Vegas or the Grand Canyon. She was sent to the Castañeda in 1938, where she met and married another Harvey employee, Warren Caster.

La Fonda was expanded to 203 guest rooms in 1950. In 1949, Mary Colter, just before retirement to a home of her own in Santa Fe, redecorated La Cantinita in La Fonda. Colter called it her "pots and pans" room[36] and decorated it to resemble an old Mexican kitchen, including several huge old copper kettles from the first kitchen of the Topeka Harvey House.

La Fonda never faced closure or cutbacks in staff during the thirties and early forties. But, as illustrated in detail in the next chapter, Harvey Houses large and small were closed during the depression. The advent of automobile traffic and the problems and changes faced by the railroad during the 1930s and through World War II closed scores of Harvey Houses along the main line between 1930 and 1948. Only a handful of them would survive the great transition in American lifestyle and tourism that took place during this era.

CHAPTER · 7

Decline of the Harvey Girls

T HE 1930'S BROUGHT THE INTRODUCTION OF FASTER, more luxurious trains like the Chief and Super Chief to the Santa Fe Railway. Stops in places like Emporia, Kansas, Amarillo, Texas, and Waynoka, Oklahoma, became unnecessary as the new trains featured dining car service. The new train service combined with the advent of better air and automobile transportation closed dozens of Harvey Houses by 1939. Although many car travelers continued to stop at Fred Harvey's for a meal, they did not provide the customer load formerly brought in on the Santa Fe trains. Harvey did supervise most of the dining car service on the Santa Fe, but this did not involve the Harvey Girls. It was the beginning of the end of Fred Harvey along the Santa Fe.

The closing of Harvey Houses in small towns in the Southwest was an event mourned by entire communities. In many of these communities more than half of the residents depended on the Santa Fe Railway or Harvey for income. And everyone in these small towns in the 1930s was acutely aware that the railroad was their lifeline to the outside world. The aura of importance and excitement brought in with the daily trains would never be replaced. The towns Harvey and the Santa Fe had put on the map, made into major stops, were left overnight to fend for themselves. The Great Depression was more than an economic condition in those small communities where Harvey and the Santa Fe suddenly disappeared in the 1930s.

Mary Lou Lewis Urban worked as a Harvey Girl in Waynoka during the summer of 1935. Mary Lou was still in high school, but her father was a railroadman and was acquainted with the Harvey House manager, so Mary was allowed to work at the age of seventeen. She lived at home with her family in Waynoka:

> *It was a good job for a young girl in the 1930s. Being a Harvey Girl was very educating. My father was with the railroad for fifty years. My brother and later my husband and son were railroaders, too. The Harvey Girls were railroaders; a woman couldn't do things with the railroad back then like nowadays.*
>
> *There were only a few Harvey Girls from out of state when I worked in the Waynoka Harvey House. Most were local girls like me.*
>
> *I first quit in 1935 because of the manager. I was walking through that swinging door from the kitchen with a tray of dishes when another person came through the doors the wrong way and hit me. I dropped all those dishes. The manager said to me, "You don't know if you're walking or riding a bicycle." I said, "I know one thing—how to walk out that door." I quit and went home. A year later, another manager who knew my dad asked if I had worked at the Harvey House last year. He asked if I would work again. I went back and worked as a Harvey Girl until the house closed in February of 1937.*
>
> *It hurt Waynoka when the Harvey House closed. We didn't have much anyway; it was a big deal here to go down and see people getting off the train. Everybody went there to eat. There was always a lot of people around—you could meet all kinds of people. And they wanted to know all about the Harvey Girls: what kind*

*of life we had, how we lived. Just ordinary American folks talking
with other folks.*

*After the Harvey House closed, there were still trains coming
through here, but the stops weren't for meals. People would just
get off and then get right back on. Eventually the passenger trains
didn't come here at all.*

The population of Waynoka was cut in half when two hundred families
were moved to Amarillo with the Santa Fe's shops and offices. Before the
Emporia Harvey House closed in 1937, John Brady (see Chapter 5) remembers watching the effects of the depression on local businessmen:

*We had one customer from the Ford Motor Company. He had a
special table where he sat with his paper every evening for several
years. He was a tall, handsome man, with a wife and family in
Emporia. He was a well-known millionaire. He knew all the
Harvey Girls and he treated them very well. After the crash of '29,
he lost everything. He didn't come into the Harvey House
anymore. I later saw him traipsing around Emporia in ragged
clothes. For a long while, I didn't realize he was the same man.*

*Before the closure of the Harvey Houses, when the railroad
connected towns and was the only reliable way to travel, I think
people were friendlier. The country lost something when the
railroad went; it seems a lot of history was left behind—the
pioneer history and feeling. On the train, people enjoyed meeting
people.*

*I remember going to visit my brother who was an engineer in
Needles. It was still a flourishing place in the 1930s. It was a big
division point with a huge depot that was always just loaded with
people. You could hardly walk through because of the people. It
was a hot spot and everyone loved it there. There was a lot of
connection between people on the trains.*

*In some ways, I think the depression years were the best days
for communication between people. Before, there was a group of
people with money, another group that was in between, and a
group with nothing at all. But during the depression everybody
was suddenly all the same.*

Gainesville, Texas, remained a busy freight depot even after the Harvey House closed in 1931, when the Santa Fe discontinued passenger trains over this section of the line. Joe Rison (see Chapter 5) remembers the changes brought in the 1930s:

Highways were being built out here and people were able to buy automobiles. There just weren't many people on the trains. Children still went down to the depot to watch the freight trains come in, but it was no longer the busiest place in town.

I remember in the late twenties and then in the depression, people would climb on the freight trains looking for work. I've seen as many as eighty people on one train going to the Kansas wheat fields. Even women with nursing babies. A man would take his entire family and everything he had, looking for work. Those people were following the crops. The official railroad policy was to get them off, but I didn't pay any attention to that. They were trying to make a living and they didn't bother anyone. If anyone asked me I would say I didn't see anybody.

There were a lot of hobos around the trains during the depression. The Santa Fe special agents would try to catch them. I remember one Purcell "bull" was after this one hobo. The thirty-six freight train was pulling out of Purcell and the hobo caught the boxcar and was trying to climb across the rods. He slipped and fell. The wheels cut off both of his legs at the knees. They called in a doctor and gave him some shots and did some other things but that was all. They put him on a stretcher in the baggage room where he waited for the southern freight train from Oklahoma City to take him to a hospital. I didn't sleep a wink that night thinking about him down there. The only thing he said was, "Did they get them both?" Someone told him, "Yea."

Gene Montgomery (see Chapter 6) in Albuquerque also watched hundreds of people riding the boxcars in search of work:

The early thirties were the worst—1932 and '33. Whole families would travel on top of the cars—grandparents, children, mothers with babies. They were coming out of the Dust Bowl looking for work in California. The railroad never said anything to them. Before the 1930s, the Santa Fe would have pulled them off. I remember the Santa Fe police saying to us, "Just leave them alone. It's a hard life for those people." This went on for all of the depression. For food, those people would often ask at the Harvey House. They would come to the back door. The local manager of a house would decide what to give them.

Bob O'Sullivan was traveling with his mother and sister by car from Denver to California in 1933. His mother started out with almost no money, just the promise from his father that money would be waiting at the Railway Express office in Albuquerque. But when the three reached Albuquerque in their Essex, packed to the roof with their belongings, the promised and greatly needed $25 was not waiting. Fifty-five years later in the *Chicago Tribune,* O'Sullivan recalled how the local Harvey House—the Alvarado— turned a dreadful experience into a pleasant memory:

It was hot and dusty and late afternoon as my sister and I waited for my mother to come out of the Albuquerque Railway Express office.

When she did, she was very upset. She stopped on the steps of the loading dock for a few seconds, wiped her eyes, came to the car and got in . . .

. . . When I asked if we could get something to eat, she didn't answer for a moment. Then she said, "Of course we can. We have to, don't we?"

She drove about two blocks along the railroad tracks to the Harvey House Restaurant and took us inside. It was a huge dining room, smelling of good things to eat and almost empty.

When a waitress came over to show us to a table, Mother took her a few feet away from my sister and me and spoke to her in a low voice. The waitress listened and then went to the kitchen. She came back with a man who was wearing a suit.

He and my mother talked for a few more minutes. He nodded and led us all to a table where he pulled out a chair and seated my mother. My sister and I sat on either side of her.

"What would you like?" the waitress asked.

"Perhaps sandwiches for the children," my mother said, "and I'd like a cup of coffee." The girl was starting to write it down when the man put his hand over her order book.

"Why don't you let me order for you?" he said. Then not waiting for an answer from my mother, he told the girl we would all start with hot soup and then we'd have the beef stew, mashed potatoes, bread and butter . . . and coffee for the lady. He asked my sister and me if we wanted milk or hot chocolate.

We both said, "Yes, sir."

"Milk and hot chocolate for the children and some of the cobbler all around. Does that sound all right? . . . and these people are the guests of Fred Harvey."

I saw my mother say, "Thank you," but I didn't hear her voice . . .

When the last of the cobbler was gone and we rose to leave, my mother pushed a couple of coins toward the waitress. The girl pushed them back with a smile.

"Oh, no, ma'am. You're Mr. Harvey's guests," she said and placed two bags in front of my mother.

"The manager said I was to wrap up what you didn't eat, so you could take it along."

. . . In the car my mother and my sister looked in the bags, which clearly contained a greater volume of food than we'd had for dinner.

"What's in them?" I asked.

"Loaves and fishes," she said. "Loaves and fishes."[1]

Joanne Stinelichner George (see Chapter 4) also remembers hungry people turning up at the depots and Harvey Houses in the 1930s:

Harvey people were always nice folks with good hearts. During the depression, there were lots of migrant workers on the trains. It was rough for those people. We all felt sorry for them and treated them kindly—most Harvey employees were thankful they had a job at all. Sometimes the workers would come to the back door and

the chefs and cooks would let them work for some food. It wasn't
really within the rules, but no one said anything about it. We just
did it.

Elizabeth Hazlewood (see Chapter 4) worked at the Canadian Harvey
House until it was closed down in 1939. The dining room closed first in
the mid-1930s, but the lunch counter remained open for train customers.
Fewer and fewer passenger trains were routed through Canadian and by
the late 1930s, dining cars made the stop at the Harvey House obsolete.
At the same time, the Santa Fe Railway moved its shops and ninety-six
Canadian employees and their families to Amarillo. What was left of the
Santa Fe in Canadian was destroyed by an explosion in the roundhouse,
a disaster that was followed by the collapse of the railroad bridge over the
Canadian River.

"It affected the people of Canadian tremendously," Elizabeth recalls of
the late 1930s. "But thankfully, this country had always had ranching;
ranching and wheat kept us alive."

Canadian's Harvey House kitchen facilities were pulled out and sent to
larger houses able to remain open after 1940—Albuquerque's Alvarado and
Las Vegas's Castañeda.

Eventually even the Amarillo Harvey House fell to the same fate as those
in Canadian, Emporia, Gainesville, and Waynoka. The presence of the Santa
Fe Railway shops and offices could not keep customer traffic at the Harvey
House at its previous level, and the house closed in 1940. The *Amarillo
Daily News* of January 30, 1940, announced the closure saying that the
twelve employees at the Harvey House would not lose their jobs but would
be transferred to positions at other Harvey Houses.

The Harvey system sought ways to keep their employees working as
houses closed. Joanne Stinelichner George had attained the level of a house
manager, but in the late 1930s and 1940s, was often sent out to work as
a relief manager or headwaitress. Even managers with years of seniority
were forced to take jobs in less desirable locations, often at a distance from
their families.

Katheryne Krause Ferguson (see Chapter 5) recalls that her husband,
Irwin Krause, was made a manager on the dining cars that ran from Los
Angeles to Chicago:

Shirley Temple in Las Vegas,
July 1938.
(Credit: Ruthanna Caster)

Front entrance of La Posada with Harvey touring cars, couriers and drivers waiting for passengers.
Winslow, Arizona 1930. (Credit: University of Arizona)

Harvey ice cream was sold track side throughout the Southwest in the 20's and 30's. Young Walter Reichenborn worked as an ice cream vendor at the Castañeda train platform, while his sister worked as a Harvey Girl, 1933.
(Credit: Margaret Reichenborn Craig)

"Master Suite" in La Posada.
(Credit: University of Arizona Special Collections)

He would be gone for eight days and was then home (in Chicago)
for two. Those were tough times. So many Harvey Houses closed
and managers were placed on trains. Irwin was in charge of
everything, including the waiters. There were no girls on the
trains, only Negro waiters. It was a very hard job for my husband
but he never complained. He had to stock the train and then
remain on board until it left. He couldn't come back home, even
if it was six hours before the train was due to depart. That was
the rule.

We lived in Chicago for three years while Irwin worked on the
dining cars. That schedule ended when he was sent to manage
the house in San Bernardino in 1935.

I remember how we could see the haze that was the Dust Bowl
from Chicago. That was in 1933. Later, when we returned to
Kansas and passed through Syracuse, the beautiful lawn at the
Sequoyah Harvey House was completely covered with sand. The
Sequoyah was closed. It broke my heart that they never uncovered
that lawn again.

Harvey architect Mary Colter built one last elegant Harvey House before
the depression. La Posada, Colter's favorite building, was built in 1929 in
Winslow, Arizona. It cost the Santa Fe one million dollars. At the time, the
railroad was optimistic about the future of its tourist clientele and passenger patronage, and the extravagance of La Posada was deemed worth its
great expense. Had the Santa Fe waited another year before reaching its
decision to build the grand hotel, it would probably never had been finished.

La Posada (the Resting Place) was Colter's rendition of the great *ranchos*
built by the wealthy Spanish *dons* who had lived in the Southwest in the
1700s and 1800s. Built on eight acres, La Posada sprawled by the tracks
with archways and great portals, a tile roof, smooth, pink plastered walls,
and wrought-iron grilles reminiscent of Spanish Mediterranean architecture popular in Florida and California. Inside were seventy guest rooms,
five suites, a lunchroom of Spanish tile that seated 120 people, a large
dining room and numerous corridors and lounges. To maintain the feeling
of a great ranch house, Colter combined rustic, even crude pieces of
furniture with imported, rare furnishings throughout the hotel. As in all of

her buildings, her touch was everywhere: in the choice of pillow coverings, in the Navajo rugs on the floor of each guest room, in the light fixtures in the corridors, even in the size and style of the gardens and orchards surrounding the hotel. La Posada was a work of art, inside and out, and the hand behind every stroke was Mary Colter:

> There were hand-hewn benches and chairs next to a
> two-hundred-year-old antique chest that had once hauled grain
> from Spain to the New World. Rare old Spanish plates and
> Chinese copper jars stood inside a primitive Mexican trastero
> (cupboard). Other treasures included blue-and-white Chinese
> Chippendale jars in the lobby and a fine old samovar in the
> dining room. One of the lampshades was made from a cardinal's
> umbrella.[2]

In spite of the changes and difficulties experienced by the Santa Fe and its customers during the depression, La Posada became a successful winter resort for wealthy Easterners, and an oasis in the hot Arizona summer for all travelers, by train and car, in the thirties and forties. After miles of parched mesas and prickly cactus the only view out the train window, climbing off the train in Winslow and walking up the shaded, lawn-surrounded path to the Harvey lunchroom was akin to finding sudden paradise. It was not rare that transcontinental passengers on the Santa Fe, upon discovering La Posada during a meal stop, changed their itineraries and spent a night or two in Winslow's Harvey House.

The Harvey family of employees at La Posada was like crews at all of the great hotels: a huge kitchen (La Posada had the most modern electric kitchen available in 1930) meant a large kitchen staff and twenty to thirty Harvey Girls. They worked split shifts in the lunch and dining rooms, serving at least three meal trains a day and a large patronage from the local community. They lived in the old Harvey House across the tracks from La Posada. In the 1930s, most of the Winslow Harvey Girls were sent in from the Kansas City office, but during World War II until La Posada closed in 1957, most were local women, the majority married with families.

Business was still good at the Harvey Houses in Las Vegas, Santa Fe, Albuquerque, and the Grand Canyon in the 1930s. Harvey Girls previously working in Kansas were sent out to these houses, and new women hired in Kansas City were sent directly to New Mexico, Arizona, and California.

Ruthanna Walz (see Chapter 6) worked at the Castañeda in 1937:

> *The Castañeda had about thirty-five Harvey Girls, many of whom were going to college part-time in Las Vegas. We worked however late the trains ran. Sometimes they were four or five hours late. We knew from the dispatcher; it was all written on a blackboard in the kitchen. Sometimes we could go to our rooms for a few hours, but usually we weren't free. You'd think with the dining cars on the trains, nobody would get off. But everybody did. It was cheaper to eat in the Harvey House than on the train. Besides, people wanted to get off the train for awhile.*
>
> *The baker at the Castañeda was a pilot. When he wasn't baking pies and donuts—the baked goods were out of this world!—he would be out in his own plane. I flew with him. It was the first time I was ever in a plane and it was an open cockpit!*

Ruthanna worked at the Castañeda for two years before leaving to get married. She returned to work briefly as a Harvey Girl at the Alvarado during World War II, when her husband was sent to boot camp.

Warren Caster, Ruthanna's future husband, was raised in Vaughn, New Mexico. "My dad was one of the few people in Vaughn who didn't work for the railroad," Warren recalls:

> *He was a schoolteacher. Vaughn had only ranching and the railroad in those days. The Harvey House was the social center of town. I remember going to the Harvey House when I was young and thinking how the Harvey Girls, dressed in black and white, looked like nuns.*
>
> *I was at the high school graduation with my father the night that Lindbergh and his pilots, who had been forced to land outside of Vaughn, came up to the Harvey House and spoke. It caused quite a stir for people out in a place like Vaughn in the 1920s.*

Warren went to Las Vegas to attend college. His brother was also in school in Las Vegas, and had worked for Harvey in Vaughn. Warren went with him when he went into the Castañeda looking for work. Warren's brother, because of his previous experience, was given a job right away. Warren was offered a part-time job washing dishes:

> *Jobs were very hard to come by. They ran a tight ship at Harvey's. There were a lot of rules for the employees. I didn't live in the dormitory—I didn't want all those rules.*
>
> *The hardest day I ever worked was Easter Sunday: I usually worked a ten hour day on weekends, with a few hours off between meals. But on Easter I worked straight through.*
>
> *I think I was finally promoted to night clerk because I broke so many dishes. When I was promoted, I saw how fast the trains came in and out. There was no dilly-dallying around. People got frantic in the house. After, there was a lull in activity, just cleaning up.*
>
> *The pay wasn't that good, but if I didn't want the job, there were ten guys out there waiting for the job who did. It was the same for the Harvey Girls in the 1930s.*

World War II initiated a brief but memorable revival of many Harvey Houses closed in the 1930s. Because Harvey served the railroad, and the railroads were the primary means of cross-country transportation for troops, Fred Harvey became the official "mess hall" for men riding the Santa Fe Railway. "That's what Fred Harvey did during the war," Katheryne Krause Ferguson remembers, "it served the military."

In 1943, more than one million meals were prepared each month in Fred Harvey Houses and dining cars.[3] The inundation of Harvey Houses by troop trains meant the weakening and eventual loss of the Harvey standard in many houses. Small Harvey Houses were expected to serve two thousand soldiers in a given day, with just as many box lunches prepared and served onto the trains themselves.[4] The Harvey system's six thousand wartime employees rose to the challenge of such numbers, even when their own ranks diminished as Harvey Girls and other Harvey employees went off to join the service. But the war left Harvey a fragmented system where the standards and quality of food and personnel fluctuated from house to house.

The loss of the "standard" was found in all areas of Harvey operation. Among the Harvey Girls, it began with the lessening, even dropping of contractual demands: the promise not to marry and the promise to stay with Harvey for six to nine months were omitted by managers looking for women to fill a uniform. Over-thirty, married, and divorced women were hired and many dating rules were ignored. Uniform detail changed—white hose was not even available in most places; laundry services were not as extensive and long-sleeved white blouses were so impossible to keep clean they were finally cut off to become short-sleeved.

The Harvey Girls changed quickly from a precision group of women at least outwardly mirroring one another, to a corps of waitresses that included women who under the old "standard" would not have measured up (educational background, marital status, physical poise) and would have been turned away at the Harvey employment offices in Kansas City and Chicago.

Katheryne Krause Ferguson remembers how the quality of people working in the Harvey Houses began to change:

> They took just about anybody who walked into their office in Kansas City. I remember when we were in Barstow they would send out ten girls from Kansas City and maybe two would stay. The others just wanted their way paid to California. They wouldn't even stay overnight. The real Harvey Girls were very fine, but they were before the war and they're the ones to talk about.
>
> Of course, there were outstanding ones during the war. I remember two older women who came from West Virginia just because they wanted to do something for the war effort. They were very high-class women. One of them had a brother who was president of a military institute back East. They were exceptional.
>
> But the overall quality of the Harvey Houses was beginning to slip. I remember seeing the first paper napkin on a table during the war. That was really something to me.

Retired Harvey Girls often returned to their posts in Harvey Houses needing experienced waitresses. But the young Harvey Girls of the 1940s worked within a system that was losing its precision and mystique; the classy, highly trained and regimented women of the 1920s and 1930s were no longer the norm in Harvey Houses. Harvey still offered young women honest work and decent pay, but the Second World War only prolonged the irreversible death of the Harvey organization and the Harvey Girls that had begun in the 1930s.

Joanne Stinelichner George was sent out to reopen houses in Texas and Kansas at the beginning of the war:

> We had to rehire many girls to meet the demand of the troop trains. I was sent all over the place, helping to organize small houses that had been closed down—Brownwood, Slaton, Emporia. There was a lot of business—two trains would come in instead of one. We would prepare five hundred box lunches at once for the trains, and then also be ready to serve trainloads of men in the dining and lunch rooms. It wasn't the depression that changed the Harvey Houses forever, it was the war.

Joanne was German-born and raised, and all of her family lived in Germany:

> I was able to return home to Germany six times in my years with Harvey. All of my family was there. It was sometimes very hard during the war to be German. Fortunately, I was treated well at the Harvey House. The local newspaper editor came down to the Bisonte in Hutchinson in 1941 and interviewed me. He wrote a nice article in the paper. They wanted information about Germany in those days. All the Harvey people were good to me. They didn't care that I was German.

Along with retired Harvey Girls, Harvey managers also hired the wives, mothers, and sisters of servicemen seeking a way to contribute to the war effort. In La Junta, Colorado, nineteen members of a local women's club joined up as reserve Harvey Girls, and in Winslow, Arizona, twenty-five local women, calling themselves Victory Girls, volunteered their services as waitresses whenever the manager needed them. Winslow, the largest troop stop on the Santa Fe, fed some thirty thousand service men and women in October of 1943. Albuquerque's Alvarado Hotel even used the volunteer services of some of its patriotic guests.[5]

In addition to Harvey Girls, Harvey Houses that were major troop train meal stops—Albuquerque, Winslow, Needles, and others—employed a separate staff of women waitresses called "troop-train girls." Troop-train girls served only the military. These women were hired locally and did not undergo the rigorous training of the Harvey Girls. They were not hired to serve the public and there was no time to learn the "Harvey way." They lived in quarters on the premises and were on call twenty-four hours of the day.

The war ended the Harvey system's scarcity of Indian and Hispanic Harvey Girls. In New Mexico and Arizona, local Harvey managers hired Hopi, Zuni, and Navajo Indian women in large numbers as fewer and fewer Harvey Girls were available out of the Kansas City and Chicago offices. During the war years, with the exception of the headwaitress and two other seasoned Harvey Girls, the entire staff of waitresses at Gallup's El Navajo Hotel were Navajos from a nearby Mission School.[6] By 1943, the Alvarado had a substantial crew of Spanish-American troop-train girls serving the military.[7]

Although the troop regiments were often segregated with all-white and all-black troop trains crossing the country's rail lines, the Harvey Houses were not informed as to an upcoming train's racial makeup. The message sent to the house manager simply indicated numbers and time of arrival. The Harvey House staff served all military personnel, regardless of race, the same menu at the same dining and table arrangements.

The large, elegant Harvey Houses underwent many changes during the war. El Tovar at the Grand Canyon became a rest stop for hundreds of soldiers on furlough from the desert Training Center in Arizona.[8] Needles, Barstow, Albuquerque, Winslow, and Las Vegas Harvey Houses became major troop meal stops, and were arranged to serve hundreds of men at one time. Porches, hallways, lounges, patios—any open space—were utilized in addition to dining and lunch rooms. All the family-style round tables were replaced with banquet tables, and local customers were banned from the dining areas when a military train came in. This caused many ill feelings between local residents and the Harvey Houses they so loved to patronize.

Katheryn Krause Ferguson remembers a letter to the editor of an Albuquerque newspaper complaining that "Fred Harvey once welcomed local people and now will hardly let them in. But Harvey welcomed them with open arms: they were just swamped with troops," she adds. Harvey's intention may have been to continue serving the non-military public, but limitations of space and personnel often made this an impossible wartime aspiration.

Fred Harvey began a vigorous wartime advertising campaign hoping to explain its difficult situation to patrons all over the country. Private Pringle became Harvey's in-house name for all servicemen. The needs of Private Pringle, Harvey advertisements explained, came first in Harvey Houses:

> *With the armed forces first on our list, we're trying hard to give real Fred Harvey service to everyone. But with food rationing so severe and trained personnel so scarce, there are times when we must ask civilian patrons to wait their turns. Sometimes we can't even serve them a meal.*
>
> *We're grateful for your good-humored acceptance of this temporary situation. When Private Pringle's big job is done we promise you again the Fred Harvey hospitality you have learned to expect.[9]*

Food preparation and choice, for so many years the pride of the Harvey company, had to be modified during the war. Many foods were no longer available, and the sheer numbers of troops to be served made most menus obsolete.

"The war was a new experience for everyone at Harvey's," Addie Park Bassett (see Chapter 4) recalls of her time at the Barstow Harvey House:

> *At first we tried to give all the boys our usual special Fred Harvey service. We about killed ourselves with over three hundred men to serve. Our good manager Mr. Krause would stay up all night trying to get information on the trains so we would have some idea of how many people we would have to feed the next day. But so many of the troop movements were secret and we would find out nothing until they rolled up to the front door. And almost everything was rationed. Well, it didn't take very long to discover we couldn't give our usual Fred Harvey service. A lot of things were changed. We removed all the beautiful linen table cloths,*

The mythical "Private Pringle" was Fred Harvey's representative of the thousands of men and women in uniform during World War II. This advertisement ran in Santa Fe Magazine in December of 1943, and asked the civilian traveling public to be patient and good-humored when the arrival of a troop train into a Harvey House meant service delays. (Credit: Courtesy Fred Harvey)

Harvey House coffee shop, Kansas City Union Station during World War II. (Credit: Santa Fe Railway)

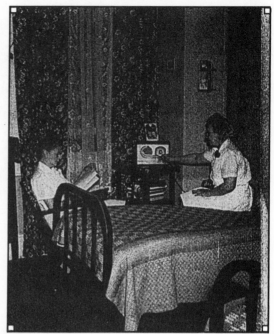

Veteran Harvey Girls like Effie V.
Aleshire and Hazel B. Roberts in
Barstow, were called back into
service during the war.
(Credit: Santa Fe Railway)

La Posada Harvey Girls, 1951, were a combination of local and out-of-state women, married and single, ranging in age from teenagers to the mid-forties. A local women's group made the aprons which were sold to the public as fast as they were finished. (Credit: Marie Knaak Zismann, third from left)

*moved out our eight-, four-, and two-seater tables, closed in the
front of the veranda, and put in banquet-type tables. That's how
we could seat 344 people at one time.*

*I remember one night we got off work and were told we were to
feed five hundred men the next day. Well, the next day came and
went and we served no less than 2,400 men!*

The Santa Fe was planning to close the Castañeda in Las Vegas, New
Mexico, but troop movements through this section of the railroad kept this
Harvey House open another eight years. Before the war, there were plenty
of Harvey Girls from whom to choose the Castañeda's crew, but as the war
progressed, management in Las Vegas, like that at the Alvarado in Albuquerque, La Posada in Winslow—all large houses—was always seeking
women to fill the large quota of Harvey Girls needed to serve the troops.

Margaret Reichenborn came to Las Vegas from Kansas in 1941. Her
grandparents were Kansas homesteaders, her mother's side German immigrants. Margaret's brother was already living and working at the Castañeda
and he suggested she try for a job as a Harvey Girl. Knowing nothing about
the Harvey system, Margaret applied for work at the Castañeda:

*I was accepted and worked the next two weeks without pay. The
first year I worked as a Harvey Girl, the system and service was
excellent. But then it began to change with the enormous number
of troop trains. They came in all day, even at three and four in
the morning. We would serve two to three hundred men at one
time and we could hardly serve passenger trains or local
customers. Most of our busboys were called in to the service, and
the management began hiring a lot of young boys and girls from
town to help with the busing and waitressing.*

*When I first got to the Castañeda, there were about eight to ten
Harvey Girls. When the troop trains started coming through, there
were about twenty-five Harvey Girls. They were mostly local girls.
They didn't have to meet the old contracts—no promise not to
marry, and they weren't strict about the rules. They were really
desperate. They took anybody.*

*It really changed the Harvey standard. During the war, we
couldn't even wear the same uniforms. We couldn't get white*

hose, then we couldn't get any hose at all. We had long-sleeved white shirts, and we had to keep those clean. But it got so difficult we finally cut off the sleeves to make it easier. Our laundry was done in Albuquerque, but only the skirts.

We often had a lot of very inexperienced waitresses working under very difficult circumstances. I became head waitress after a few years, and even though it was a hard time at the Harvey House, I enjoyed the work, the Harvey people and the railroaders immensely. We all did the best we could.

Evangeline Stine came in to Las Vegas in 1942 from Wagon Mound, New Mexico, where her father and mother were ranchers. She was seventeen and she found a job at the Harvey House:

When I arrived, there were Harvey Girls from all over, but many were local girls, also. Las Vegas was the only place for girls like me, from out in the ranch country, to find work or go to school.

We were worked very hard, six days a week, usually with part of Sunday off for church. I worked from six in the morning until 2 P.M., and then whenever a troop train came in. They used to wake us up at all hours—when you're young you don't mind that—we'd make hundreds of box lunches.

The men were always real friendly to the Harvey Girls. They were often very lonely and they asked for our names and addresses. Each of us received hundreds—literally hundreds—of letters. We couldn't even remember who the boy was who had written it. I had a milk carton full. One train came through with French troops on board. We couldn't understand them and they couldn't understand us. Still, they wrote us lots of letters, most of which we could never read.

Although they hired a lot of local girls, there were still many they turned away. Working as a Harvey Girl, even during the war, was a privilege. I felt lucky to have the job. I tried to get one friend a position, but they turned her away.

Many Harvey Houses during the war allowed local customers a seat in the lunch room during hours that the troop trains were not due in. Those that struggled to maintain "normal" service in the house found the atmosphere, even the type of customer, changing. The Kansas City Harvey House, once the favorite local social gathering spot, was in such a state of daily confusion and overcrowding that the personable, small-town feeling was completely lost. Where once the Harvey Girls had served twenty-five familiar people for breakfast, they were now serving between sixty and ninety harried, often rude, travelers. Long waiting-lines were common and the mood among train passengers and all Harvey patrons was often frantic and anxious.

Harvey Girl Molly Quinn watched one woman take not only another customer's seat at a table, but his food, too:

> We had a long line waiting at the door. One woman, refusing to get in line, stood eyeing the tables from her place near the cashier's counter. I had just served a man and his son orders of waffles, and they had partially eaten them, when the man decided to remove his overcoat. He walked over to the coat rack, and as he did, this woman dashed to his seat and began eating his waffles. I was so startled I couldn't think what to do. The man came back and told her she was eating his dinner. She didn't pay any attention, except to take a drink of the coffee.
>
> I went over then and very politely told her to leave, or at least go get in line. She looked up long enough to tell me that she was hungry and had to make a train. Then she turned back to the waffle. Before we could do anything about it she had finished. I ordered another meal for the poor man and then wrote a bill out for the waffle and coffee and gave it to the woman. She got up, smiled, took the bill and paid it. The man started anew to eat the last waffle. [10]

The Alvarado Hotel in Albuquerque became a major troop train stop with both the dining and lunchrooms arranged to seat several hundred men at one time. Tables were also set up outside on the patios and walkways, and box lunches were made by the hundreds in the kitchen for those trains that did not have time to stop for a sit-down meal.

Viola Hern Archibeque wanted to help the war effort and had come to Albuquerque in 1942 looking for work:

I was too short to enlist so I thought I could find something else to do in Albuquerque. I was raised in Shoemaker, New Mexico, a small country town. I was just sixteen when I came alone to Albuquerque. I had a place to stay temporarily, but there was no work. Things were very tight. I was sitting on the patio of the Alvarado waiting for a train home when I got to talking to this man who turned out to be a VIP of the hotel. I told him I was trying to do my part in the war but there was nothing available. He said I had a job at the Alvarado if I wanted it. I took it!

I had room, board, and thirty-five cents an hour as a troop-train girl. There was no set schedule. We never really knew when a train was coming in because it was all very secretive. The average day had a breakfast train at 4 A.M. of five hundred or so men. We had to serve them a standard meal on paper plates. Then there would be a lunch train, usually an evening train, with maybe a couple trains in between. Sometimes there were so many men we would even set up tables in the lounge. We worked twelve hours a day, easily.

We were on call at the hotel for all hours of the day and night. We had an hour to set up after they called us. We worked a seven-day week—I couldn't even get away long enough to get away to church!

The troop-train girls wore white uniforms with a white apron and little black ties. We had to do our own laundry, but the uniforms were provided. There were two full-time troop-train girls like me, and then a lot of other women who were part-time, usually going to school. They would come in at different times. When a train was due in, everything in the house was set up. The Harvey Girls would come in and help us. Sometimes the troop trains and the passenger trains would come at once; we would have to make box lunches in an assembly line. It was so busy even the manager would come and help, setting up, serving. Everything was very clean, but we couldn't do things like the Harvey Girls used to because of the troops. We had to use paper plates and napkins and learn to serve six tables of people off of one tray. It was very nerve-wracking.

There were still lots of famous people around the Alvarado. I remember seeing this very dignified man in uniform waiting on the platform outside the lunch room. People were walking by him and staring, but leaving him alone. I went out to see who it was—it was Gene Autry. He looked very pensive. I also served Humphrey Bogart and Lauren Bacall, and Alan Ladd and his wife stayed at the hotel. Frank Sinatra was there, too, making a movie.

Before the war, they weren't hiring a lot of Spanish and Indian women as Harvey Girls, but that changed. And there were married women with children working there also. My roommate at the hotel was a divorced woman and she was like my mother because I was so young. People looked out for each other in the Harvey House.

The second year I was at the Alvarado I helped the salad girl, who was not a Harvey Girl, deliver a baby upstairs in the girl's dormitory. We didn't even know she was pregnant! Somehow she had hidden it. I didn't know what to do but it happened very quickly and I had to stay with her. Someone ran downstairs and went for a doctor, but he was too late. After the birth, the baby was kept in the dorm for a week. No one said anything to the management. The girl was only a teenager and finally had to write her parents. About the time the manager found out, she was going home. We all took turns caring for that baby.

Gene Montgomery (see Chapter 6) still came to the Alvarado to eat his meals, but he remembers the priority was to feed the troops, not local customers or Santa Fe men:

Hundreds of troops were fed in a few minutes at the Alvarado. They were fed outside on the porch. The arrival of the troops was not publicized. In the telegraph office I'd get a message that might say, "Main 132, maybe 500." Just a two hour warning for the Harvey people. But Fred Harvey was ready for them.

Japanese prisoners of war were brought through Albuquerque, too. They were brought into the Alvarado with soldier police, and Fred Harvey fed everybody. There was often a lot of confusion.

During the war, the eighty-two miles of double track between Barstow and San Bernardino, California, carried twenty to thirty freight trains in every twenty-four hour period.[11] These Harvey Houses served hundreds of men and also their families who followed them to southern California.

"When the war started," Katheryne Krause Ferguson remembers, "people came out to California in crowds. All kinds of people came to see their boys before they were sent out." She continues:

> There were a lot of hysterics among these people. They were very upset. The troops would come in on special trains and unload in this great big room in Barstow. People would be waiting, trying to get food. They would all come in at once, and they would gather at the counter, yelling at the girls, "I want this! I want that!" Krause told the Harvey Girls to take orders only from people sitting at the counter. Let them finish, get up and then serve the next person. The girls were completely worn out by this situation, threatening to quit. It was very upsetting. Finally, the dining room was set aside only for the troops. Krause and the hotel clerks would take care of the tables, set them up, then when the troops came in, the Harvey Girls would go in and serve them. Everyone was worn out in Barstow. Finally, the whole place was closed to train passengers and local customers. Only railroadmen and the troops were served for the remainder of the war.

Irwin Krause is credited as the innovator of the first "round-the-clock" self-service cafeteria on the Santa Fe. During the war, the Barstow lunchroom was converted into a cafeteria where railroad employees could serve themselves food from hot plates and refrigerated boxes. This method worked very well, and Krause's system to serve the Santa Fe men was incorporated into other Harvey Houses facing the same surge of business during the early 1940s.

Katheryne remembers an early mishap in the cafeteria in Barstow:

> They had railroadmen build a counter at the back of the lunchroom, where they put little stoves to heat dishes, and containers of silverware, all kinds of things. Those shelves were piled with hot and cold food. People came in and served

themselves. It was only for railroadmen. Well, it wasn't too substantial—they had used old wood to build it. One night, something went wrong with one of the hot plates, a great big one, and they had to take it off fast. There were lots of other things on that shelf—pudding, heavy dishes in a big stack—but when the hot plate was removed the whole thing went over backwards. I thought it would never stop! Things were falling and crashing everywhere. There was a young boy pouring hot water into the coffee urn and he fainted and fell onto the floor.

During the 1940s, La Fonda accomodated the soon-to-be-famous scientists en route to "the hill," the secret city of Los Alamos, New Mexico. Los Alamos, located forty miles northwest of Santa Fe, was a community built practically overnight in 1943 to house the top-secret Manhattan Project of the United States Government. Remote and nearly inaccessible, the Los Alamos Laboratories under J. Robert Oppenheimer developed the first atomic weapons, most notably "Little Boy," dropped on Hiroshima on August 6, 1945, and "Fat Man," used on Nagasaki on August 8th. Niels Bohr, Enrico Fermi, Edward Teller, and many hundreds more scientists and technicians stepped off the Santa Fe train at Lamy, boarded a bus or special car, and after a brief stop in Santa Fe, headed up the hill to Los Alamos.

La Fonda was often the gathering place for visiting dignitaries connected to the work in the private, barbed-wire enclosed mountain town. Monte Chavez (see Chapter 6) remembers serving Oppenheimer and his guests. Although local residents like Monte were often aware that *something* was going on, it would be years before they really understood the seriousness of Los Alamos's raison d'être:

We served many large parties of "hill" people. Of course, no one knew who they were or what they were doing up there. It was very mysterious and secretive. We learned later how famous they really were.

La Fonda personnel made hundreds of box lunches each day and sent them down to Lamy where they were picked up by troop trains. Because La Fonda was off the main line, it never directly served the troops. However, there were often large groups of soldiers staying in Santa Fe, and Monte recalls at least one large fight that broke out in the main dining room between the Army and the Navy men:

> *Things were getting very tense so I went up to the band leader*
> *and told him to play the "Star Spangled Banner." All the*
> *previously arguing men stood at attention and within a few*
> *moments the military police and city police arrived and the*
> *incident ended.*

Harvey Girls hired in their late thirties and early forties became common during the war. Marie Knaak Zismann was thirty-nine years old, with children in college, when she began work as a Harvey Girl in Ashfork, Arizona in 1946. Marie's husband was a railroadman, and she knew the manager's wife in Winslow, but she did not accept offers for jobs at the Harvey House for many years because she wanted to remain home with her children. When Marie did begin work as a Harvey Girl, she lived at home, working a split shift around troop trains. Like other Harvey Girls living in Ashfork, Marie did not comply with any curfew rules, but she did follow Harvey rules about jewelry and dress. After a year of work at the Ashfork Harvey House, Marie went with her husband to Winslow where she worked as a Harvey Girl at La Posada for the next five years:

> *Harvey Girls in the late 1940s were paid fifty dollars a month*
> *plus tips at La Posada. We were given our meals while we*
> *worked. In Ashfork, we had our uniforms laundered, but not at*
> *La Posada.*
>
> *When I worked at the Ashfork Harvey House, it was very busy*
> *because of the war. We were feeding troop trains all day, and*
> *sometimes I'd get called in at four in the morning and get off late*
> *in the afternoon. We'd line up tables and feed three or four trains*
> *at one time. You'd be surprised how fast we could feed those*
> *troops!*
>
> *Most of the Harvey Girls were married, working like I was. In*
> *the summertime, we hired high school girls and there were special*
> *girls hired just to serve the trains.*
>
> *There were a lot of people using the trains in the 1940s.*

*Because Winslow was a division point, there were always a lot of
Santa Fe people changing there. We were all great friends. And I
loved the contact with people from all over the country I had at the
Winslow lunch counter!*

After World War II, automobile and plane travel were firmly established
in the West, and as passenger travel dwindled on the railroad, so did
customer loads at all Harvey Houses. Those houses that had been re-
opened were closed down again, and by 1948, even many of the large,
elegant houses—El Garces in Needles, El Vaquero in Dodge City, the
Castañeda in Las Vegas—were closed. After Harvey left these great hotels, their fate depended on the Santa Fe Railway, which owned them, and
on the interest among local residents which either protected them as
historic landmarks, or forgot about them and left them to decay beside the
tracks.

El Garces closed in 1948 after serving thousands of troops and people
heading for California during the war. The hotel could not retain enough
business to justify its operation after the war, and the great, sprawling
Harvey House was abandoned beside the Santa Fe tracks on the Mojave
Desert.

El Ortiz was closed in 1938. One eulogist claimed the hotel had once had
a clientele of "the great and near-great; salesman and statesman; financiers
and shoe clerks; artists, writers and musicians; Santa Fe 'high society,'
political and the 'Upper Palace Avenue' set," all of whom would mourn the
passing of the "littlest hotel in the littlest town."[12] Lamy was able to
maintain its Santa Fe depot with freight and passenger traffic, but El Ortiz
itself was torn down in 1943.

The Santa Fe moved its shops to Albuquerque from Las Vegas, New
Mexico, after the war, and closed the Castañeda in the summer of 1948.
Scheduled for demolition in the early 1960s, the Castañeda was "saved"
by a private sale to an oil distributor.[13]

Those houses not closed before 1950, with the exception of La Fonda
in Santa Fe, the Alvarado in Albuquerque, and the houses at the Grand
Canyon, struggled to continue operation although their clientele and importance decreased each year. The date of closure for Casa del Desierto in
Barstow is not certain, probably 1959. There was little or no use for the
hotel, but the restaurant portion of the structure remained open (but not

as a Harvey operation) for railroad employees until 1973. At that time, the Santa Fe Railway determined it had no use for the building and announced its pending demolition. The citizens of Barstow organized a "save the Harvey House" organization and after much press coverage and persistant community negotiation with the Santa Fe, the city of Barstow was made legal agent of the depot and Casa del Desierto.

El Navajo in Gallup, New Mexico, was not as fortunate as Casa del Desierto. The Harvey House closed in 1957, and was completely torn down the same year. Mary Colter's tribute to the American Indian became a parking lot.

La Posada was one of the last great hotels owned by the Santa Fe. Marie Knaak Zismann worked at La Posada until 1952, and witnessed its decline in the years before it closed in 1957:

> *When I was working at La Posada, even in the early 1950s, the standards were kept up. It was still a popular place for people to come in the winter—mostly easterners. It was one of the best hotels in those days. But later in the fifties, before it was closed, things were being cut back. Slowly it was losing the Harvey standard. When La Posada closed, people in Winslow felt very bad about it. It was one of the last beautiful buildings on the line.*

Viola Hern Archibeque also worked at La Posada before it closed:

> *Things were getting slower. Business was dwindling and the trains didn't stop there for any length of time, and never for the night. They just went on through. We started getting some people who were traveling through by car, but it wasn't the same.*

La Posada was closed down and put up for sale by the railroad in 1957. The Santa Fe never sold the building, and eventually used it for its own offices. But the sale of all of its interior treasures broke the heart of its very elderly designer, Mary Colter. Of La Posada's closing Colter said, "There is such a thing as living too long."[14] Colter died the following year.

Alvarado Harvey Girls moved into private homes and apartments in the late 1940s when a union was formed among hotel employees. Although the Alvarado remained open, and was very popular among local residents, train schedules in the 1950s and 1960s centered less and less around meal stops at the hotel.

Gene Montgomery remembers the changes of the fifties and sixties at the Alvarado:

> *After the war, people knew they could fly and cars were also used a lot more. The Santa Fe kept passenger trains on the line even after other railroads pulled them because they couldn't make money. The Santa Fe trains were still pretty full, but people were eating on the train—there weren't many Harvey Houses left on the line. And the dining cars were by Harvey and were beautiful—silver and linen, beautiful dishes. It was very classy.*
>
> *Things were changing, but the railroad was still a mighty nice way to travel. People were friendlier and it was easy to meet people when you were all on the train. I used to think people would come back to the trains, but the plane and car were too convenient in the end.*

Viola Hern Archibeque remembers that there was no parking for people who came to the Alvarado by automobile:

> *They had a bellboy who would park cars for people across the street. But the business was not like it had been during the war. You didn't even need a reservation to stay overnight.*

"Besides, it was difficult to reach the Alvarado," Gene Montgomery remembers:

> *Route 66 did not have easy access to the hotel. In the late sixties, the Alvarado still had big parties and local customers, but the Santa Fe decided they weren't making enough money and so they just went in and closed it. People were very upset about this, but there was not enough pressure on the railroad to stop them from tearing it down.*

The Alvarado closed in 1968, and was torn down in 1970. Many Harvey employees and railroad people went and watched the razing of the hotel. Opal Sells Hill (see Chapter 4) was there:

> *There were quite a lot of us old-timers watching. They had gutted the hotel and sold all of the fine furniture and art work. In the last days before it closed, local patrons were taking napkins, pieces of silverware, all sorts of things. People felt very badly about it being torn down.*
>
> *It was like watching our own home being destroyed. That's how Harvey Houses were to employees and railroad people . . . very special places.*

Even though La Fonda's prominence and reputation in the 1950s and 1960s did not change, train service to Santa Fe via Lamy lessened and most of La Fonda's guests were coming by automobile. More and more employees were hired locally, and in 1950, after a local union was formed, all Harvey personnel were required to move out of La Fonda.

"That really changed the feeling at the hotel," Monte Chavez says, "at least as far as the workers were concerned. The service and quality of La Fonda didn't change, but slowly the Harvey system was changing."

In 1969, the Santa Fe Railway sold La Fonda, but tourist business in Santa Fe was not dependent on the railroad and La Fonda continues to be a busy social and tourist center in the Southwest.

CONCLUSION

ALTHOUGH HARVEY HOUSES DISAPPEARED almost entirely along the Santa Fe
Railway after the Second World War, the Harvey business itself continued
on dining cars and in urban restaurants and hotels in California, New
Mexico, Arizona, and in Illinois. (AMFAC bought Fred Harvey, Inc., in
1968). But the era of the Harvey Girls, of Harvey Houses as a way of life
and a standard for food and passenger service along the Santa Fe, was over.
Harvey Girls became a group of women known only to those who had
traveled on the Santa Fe before the 1950s, or by those who were related
to a former Harvey Girl, Harvey employees, or Santa Fe railroadman.

Their own words reveal who they really were. They were not necessarily beautiful, adventurous, extraordinary women. They were most often
ordinary women who valued themselves and believed they had something
to offer. Harvey Girls were young women, still girls sometimes, who had
enough self-motivation to leave home and loved ones in pursuit of "some-

thing of their own," whether it was money, a chance to travel, a home away from mother and father, or even a husband.

> . . . *evidence accumulates that there were two Wests: a female and a male one. Now that we know this, we need to describe and delimit women's Western sphere, just as other historians have done for Eastern women.*[1]

The West of the Harvey Girls from the turn of the century until World War II was the West of railroad towns, the West of new communities, of travelers and tourists exploring a new region of America. It was a West that was civilized, organized, and regulated within the boundaries of the Harvey House, but was often rough, rustic, and unpredictable beyond its walls. Harvey Girls had the best of two worlds: the familiarity and security of the Harvey system, and the challenging unknowns of the West surrounding them.

What can we learn from their collected oral histories? Above all else, we learn that the Harvey Girls of the 1880s until the 1940s worked very, very hard. Many who later went on to become nurses or teachers or businesspersons found themselves well prepared. Other careers often seemed easy in comparison to work as a Harvey Girl. Their daily lives were centered around mundane tasks and routines, but those daily routines were infused with such a dignity and sense of purpose as to elevate the Harvey Girls, in their own minds as well as in the eyes of many travelers and nearly all railroadmen, to a professional standing worthy of respect and admiration. Their job, waiting tables, serving food, picking up after meals three times a day, was not glamorous. But those Harvey Girls who lived and worked in the resort hotels of the Southwest did live in a world far removed from the average lower-class, even middle-class, working woman. The poorest farm girl could become headwaitress of the finest Harvey hotel in New Mexico or Arizona, working alongside the best chefs of the world, serving and interacting with the world's most elite travelers. For these women, it was a glamorous life. It is no wonder so many women made waitressing for Harvey their profession, choosing a career as a Harvey Girl over marriage until they were well into their thirties and forties.

The Harvey Houses of the early twentieth century had virtually no competition. Fortunately for both railroad passengers and Harvey employees, Harvey was sincerely committed to quality business practices. His product "standard" reflected his unvarying demand in good food, clean accomodations, and efficient, impeccable service. The Harvey personnel "standard" reflected an equally exacting list of appearance and behavioral expectations. Strict and often limiting, the "standard" did, however, give Harvey employees a predictable environment that fostered a sense of belonging and professional accomplishment among men and women alike.

The Harvey system exhibited a paternalistic attitude towards its women employees, and it did limit its employment opportunities—at least with respect to the position of Harvey Girl—to white women who met its standard of appearance, character, and attitude. Today, such a obviously discriminatory and personally invasive "standard" would come under severe public criticism. But Harvey was not interested in changing the status of women or minorities. He was interested in changing the status of railroad passenger services.

Early Harvey Girls, before the turn of the century, were most often midwestern railroader's and farmer's daughters. They were women who needed work to support themselves or to help their families through financial difficulties. They were women who would work as Harvey Girls, but who would probably never have worked as conventional waitresses. Waitressing was what a Harvey Girl did, but it was not who a Harvey Girl was.

Later, Harvey Girls were often women interested in finding work that was also a form of higher education, a path to social and economic advancement. Harvey House work was extremely appealing to lower- and even middle-class women who desired to see more of the world than their native home towns. Harvey was an adventure they could afford, a job that provided more than an income. For women with limited means and finite family resources, Harvey was a ticket west to a new "family" of women and men living independently, together. This family of Harvey workers may have been the single most attractive aspect of the Harvey Houses. The pay was sufficient, and the Harvey business itself respected, but the promise of a community of people living within a structured social environment probably hastened the application of countless young women.

Their own words reveal the profound influence Harvey and the Santa Fe Railway exerted on their lives. Harvey Girls learned how to hold their own personally and professionally with demanding train passengers, rowdy cowboys, flirtatious railroaders, aloof celebrities, weary salesmen, suspicious society ladies, and stern Harvey superintendents. The world within the Harvey restaurant was not a cloister. Harvey Girls became women well educated in the needs, moods, affectations, and habits of people from all over the United States and even the world. Harvey Girls were among the most upwardly mobile women of the American West, crossing social boundaries in their daily routines, playing the role of mother and sister to travelers rich and poor, famous and infamous.

Harvey originally sought women expressly interested in making the Harvey House the sole focus of life for at least a year. But as the times changed, especially in the 1920s and early 1930s, the system expanded to accomodate women actively pursuing other careers. College women were welcomed and accomodated in Harvey Houses near college campuses. Evidently, the Harvey company was not prejudiced toward energetic women working their way through college and ultimately aspiring to lives and professions beyond the Harvey House.

The Harvey Girls were a highly valued asset to Harvey. This was reflected in Harvey's willingness in later years to allow flexibility in contracts and daily schedules to accomodate married Harvey Girls, college women, farmer's daughters, and schoolteachers. Even so, Harvey did not challenge contemporary views toward women in the work place: women managers were possible but rare; male employees enjoyed a wider range of job mobility within the Harvey system. A few Harvey Girls moved up into the higher ranks of the company after years of service, but most moves for women were lateral. Women had their place in the Harvey House: it was a relatively good one if it was as a Harvey Girl, less remarkable if it was as a maid or kitchen helper.

Within the male/female structure of the Harvey system, from the late 1800s until World War II, there was an atmosphere, both social and professional, of equality and fairness toward *all* individual employees. Among Harvey employees themselves there was mutual respect, the result of shared responsibilities and equal importance within the house. There were, of course, those at managerial levels, with the elevated status appropriate to their position. But Harvey employees were a family, and among them were generated warm relationships based on common experiences and shared goals.

Between the Harvey Girls themselves there was little discrimination concerning personal background or educational and economic opportunity. Once established in a house, the Harvey Girls viewed one another as equals, with the possible exception of the headwaitress, who was often a mother/authority figure to the rest of the girls. The Harvey Girls developed strong sisterly bonds; they helped one another through personal problems and professional difficulties. Personality, responsibility, and the ability to cooperate and to share the workload earned a woman a secure place in the Harvey Girls dorm. Social class and economic advantage were lost in the daily routines of the house and dormitory.

During the Second World War, Harvey Girls were, in the best and most exhausting sense of the phrase, part of the war effort. They were the front line of the home front. It is ironic that the single most important service the Harvey Houses ever offered—feeding thousands of men en route to war—was also the most overwhelming factor in the eventual disintegration of the system. Although the depression years had begun the decline of Harvey along the railroad, the war forced Harvey Houses into such extreme degrees of service and efficiency as to nearly erase the last vestiges of the Harvey standard.

The war gave the Harvey Girl era a natural ending. Instead of confronting and struggling with what would probably have been inevitable changes stemming from the social and ideological forces at work in the 1950s (La Fonda, the Alvarado, and other houses that remained open, did in fact contend with labor unions and a splintering of the Harvey "family" after 1945), the disappearance of the Harvey Girls is historically linked to the extremes of war, and to technological progress in the form of automobile and plane transportation. The Harvey Girls and the houses they served rose heroically to the demands of a country at war, and collapsed into the dust afterwards. For Harvey old-timers, this was an appropriate and worthy end.

NOTES

INTRODUCTION

1. E. D. Branch, quoted by Walter Rundell, Jr., in "Concept of the 'Frontier' and the West," *Arizona and the West: A Quarterly Journal of History* (Tucson: University of Arizona, Spring 1959), p. 22.
2. Nancy F. Cott and Elizabeth H. Pleck, *A Heritage of Her Own* (New York: Simon and Schuster, 1979), p. 9.
3. Julie Roy Jeffrey, *Frontier Women: The Trans-Mississippi West 1840–1880* (New York: Hill and Wang, 1979), p. 202.
4. June Sochen, *Herstory: Record of the American Woman's Past,* 2nd ed. (Palo Alto, California: Mayfield Publishing Company, 1982), p. 166.

CHAPTER ONE

1. Henry Inman, *The Old Santa Fe Trail* (Minneapolis: Ross & Haines, 1966), p. viii.
2. Ibid., p. 144.
3. Susan Shelby Magoffin, *Down the Santa Fe Trail and Into Mexico* (Santa Fe, New Mexico: William Gannon, 1975), pp. 79, 80.

CHAPTER TWO

1. James Marshall, *Santa Fe, The Railroad That Built An Empire* (New York: Random House, 1945), p. 44.
2. Keith L. Bryant, Jr., *History of the Atchison, Topeka and Santa Fe Railway* (New York: Macmillan Co., 1974), p. 21.
3. Marshall, p. 50.
4. Bryant, p. 29.
5. Marshall, p. 177
6. Bryant, p. 104.
7. The Editors of *Look* magazine, *The Santa Fe Trail* (New York: Random House, 1946), p. 103.
8. Bryant, p. 136.

CHAPTER 3

1. L. L. Waters, *Steel Trails to Santa Fe* (Lawrence, Kansas: University of Kansas Press, 1950), p. 261.

2. Lucius Beebe, "Purveyor to the West," *The American Heritage,* vol. 18, no. 2 (February 1967), p. 28.

3. Dee Brown, *Hear That Lonesome Whistle Blow* (New York: Holt, Rinehart and Winston, 1977), p. 142.

4. Keith L. Bryant, Jr., *History of the Atchison, Topeka and Santa Fe Railway* (New York: Macmillan Co., 1974), p. 107.

5. Brown, p. 144.

6. Brown, p. 142.

7. *The Kansas City Star* (1915), quoted in Beebe, p. 30.

8. John W. Ripley and Robert W. Richmond, eds., *The Santa Fe in Topeka* (Shawnee, Kansas: Shawnee County Historical Society, 1979), p. 10.

9. Ibid., p. 10.

10. Beebe, p. 14.

11. Elbert Hubbard, "Tribute to Fred Harvey," *The Leavenworth Times,* (n.d.—probably February, 1901).

12. Beebe, p. 99.

13. From unidentified SFRR speaker, "Ticket Agent Talks," December, 1920.

14. Joseph A. Noble, *From Cab to Caboose; Fifty Years of Railroading* (Norman: University of Oklahoma Press, 1964), p. 106.

15. *Dodge City Globe,* February 24, 1917.

16. Erna Fergusson, *Our Southwest* (New York: Alfred A. Knopf, 1940), p. 194.

17. Ibid., p. 195.

18. James David Henderson, *Meals by Fred Harvey: A Phenomenon of the American West* (Fort Worth: Texas Christian University Press, 1969), p. 20.

19. Lenore Dills, *Horny Toad Man* (El Paso, Texas: Boots and Saddle Press, 1966), p. 66.

20. *The Emporia Gazette,* May 3, 1903.

21. Whitefield Avery, "The Dining Room That Is 2,000 Miles Long," *Capper's Magazine,* September 1930.

22. *The Kansas City Journal,* August 26, 1917.

23. Dickson Hartwell, "Let's Eat With the Harvey Boys," *Collier's,* April 9, 1949.

CHAPTER 4

1. Sandra L. Myres, *Westering Women and the Frontier Experience* (Albuquerque: University of New Mexico Press, 1982), p. 1.

2. Christiane Fischer, *Let Them Speak for Themselves: Women in the American West, 1849–1900* (Hamden, Conn.: Archon Books, 1977), p. 13.

3. See Julie Roy Jeffrey's discussion of Frederick Jackson Turner's theories and their specific application to men in the frontier West in *Frontier Women: The Trans-Mississippi West 1840–1880* (New York: Hill and Wang, 1979), p. xii.

4. Julie Roy Jeffrey, p. 62.

5. Richard A. Bartlett, *The New Country: A Social History of the American Frontier 1776–1890* (New York: Oxford University Press, 1974), p. 345.

6. Western Writers of America, *The Women Who Made the West* (Garden City, New York: Doubleday, 1980), p. ix.

7. Jeffrey, p. 12.

8. *Boston Daily Evening Voice,* quoted in Alice Kessler-Harris, *Out to Work* (New York: Oxford University Press, 1982), p. 98.

9. *Boonville* (Missouri) *Observer,* August 12, 1847.

10. Myres, p. 261.

11. Ibid., p. 259.

12. Ibid., p. 260.

13. Ibid., pp. 266, 268.

14. Jeffrey, p. 21.

15. Kessler-Harris, p. 102.

16. "Harvey Tamed the West With Good Food and Pretty Girls," *The Topeka Capital,* December 9, 1951.

17. Kessler-Harris, p. 72.

18. Nancy F. Cott & Elizabeth H. Pleck, *A Heritage of Her Own* (New York: Simon and Schuster, 1979), p. 367.

19. William H. Chafe, *Women and Equality: Changing Patterns in American Culture* (New York: Oxford University Press, 1977), pp. 31, 35.

20. Ibid., p. 23.

21. Kessler-Harris, pp. 135, 136.

22. See Frances Donovan's book about her experiences as a waitress, *The Woman Who Waits* (Boston: Richard Badger, 1920).

23. Mary Lee Spence, "They Also Serve Who Wait," *The Western Historical Quarterly,* vol. 14, no. 1 (January 1983), p. 23; Spence's article offers a detailed study of waiters and waitresses of the West.

24. Ibid., p. 21.

25. Ibid.

26. All of these figures (excepting those collected by Spence) are based on national, not regional, averages. Source: U.S. Department of Commerce, *Historical Statistics of the United States, Colonial Times to 1970,* Bicentennial Edition (Washington, D.C.: Bureau of Statistics, 1975).

27. Some of the variations of the cup code developed over the years were: a cup turned upside down meant hot tea; a cup right side up in the saucer meant coffee; upside down and tilted against the saucer, iced tea; upside down and away from the saucer, milk. Another variation: if the handle on the cup was pointed towards six o'clock, coffee; handle at high noon, black tea; handle at three o'clock, green tea; handle at six o'clock, orange pekoe; if the cup was removed, it indicated an order for milk.

28. Erna Fergusson, *Our Southwest* (New York: Alfred A. Knopf, 1940), p. 198.

29. Benita Eisler, *The Lowell Offering* (Philadelphia and New York: J. B. Lippincott Company, 1977), p. 15.

30. See Thomas Dublin's *Women at Work: The Transformation of Work and Community in Lowell, Massachusetts, 1826–1860* (New York: Columbia University Press, 1979), for a complete study and analysis of the Lowell factory women.

31. Based on author's interviews, conversations, and correspondence, and library and archival materials.

32. Kessler-Harris, p. 137.

CHAPTER 5

1. Keith L. Bryant, Jr., *History of the Atchison, Topeka and Santa Fe Railway* (New York: Macmillan Co., 1974), p. 116.

2. Lenore Dils, *Horny Toad Man* (El Paso, Texas: Boots & Saddle Press, 1966), p. 164.

3. Nina Wilcox Putnam, "The Harvey Girls—Tamers of the Wild West," *The American Weekly,* August 15, 1948, p. 7.

4. William E. Curtis, *The Chicago Record,* May 9, 1899.

5. Will Rogers to Opal Sells Hill, personal scrapbook, 1924.

6. Putnam, p. 6.

7. Ibid.

8. S. E. Kiser, quoted in Bryant, p. 116.

9. "The Harvey Girls," Metro-Goldwyn-Mayer promotional material, Arizona State University Fred Harvey Special Collection, Tempe, Arizona.

10. Putnam, p. 7.

11. Carl Becker, "Kansas," in *The Heritage of Kansas,* ed. Everett Rich (Lawrence: University of Kansas Press, 1960), p. 344.

12. Ernie Pyle, *Home Country* (New York: William Sloane Associates, Inc., 1947), p. 291.

13. Florence Historical Society, "The First Harvey House," brochure, p. 3.

14. Ibid., p. 5.

15. Ibid., p. 6.

16. Harriet E. Cross to Ann Davis, February 17, 1972, Flint Hills Oral History Project, Emporia State University, Emporia, Kansas.

17. William E. Moran, *Santa Fe and the Chisholm Trail at Newton* (Topeka, Kansas: First Impressions, 1970), p. 16.

18. *Hutchinson News,* May 8, 1983.

19. Joseph Jefferson O'Neill, "Dodge City in Technicolor," *Santa Fe Magazine,* May 1939.

20. Charles Goodnight, quoted in Edwin C. McReynolds, *Oklahoma, A History of the Sooner State* (Norman: University of Oklahoma Press, 1954), p. 258.

21. Richard R. Dykstra, *The Cattle Towns* (New York: Knopf, 1968), p. 62.

22. Ibid., p. 100.

23. Joseph A. Noble, *From Cab to Caboose; Fifty Years of Railroading* (Norman: University of Oklahoma Press, 1964), pp. 103, 104.

24. Kay Hildebrand, " 'Harvey Girls' Long a Part of Kansas City Scene," *Kansas City Star,* February 17, 1946.

25. Letter from Myrtle Tyler to author.

26. Kay Hildebrand, " 'Harvey Girls' Long a Part of Kansas City Scene," *Kansas City Star,* February 17, 1946.

27. Hamilton County Historical Society, quoted in Dorothy Melland, "Last Call for Last of Kansas's Famed Harvey Houses," *Hutchinson News,* October 20, 1974.

28. *Syracuse Journal,* July 31, 1908, quoted in Dorothy Melland, op cit.

29. Syracuse Commercial Club, 1908, quoted in Dorothy Melland, op cit.

30. "Lamy, the Town the Railroad Built," *The Atom* (Los Alamos Scientific Laboratory), April 1966, p. 18.

31. Ibid., p. 19.

32. *Raton Reporter,* April 4, 1940.

33. Virginia L. Grattan, *Mary Colter, Builder Upon the Red Earth* (Flagstaff, Arizona: Northland Press, 1980), p. 25.

34. "Lamy," p. 19.

35. *Albuquerque Morning Journal,* July 29, 1911.

36. Dils, p. 13.

37. Ibid., p. 12.

38. Ibid., p. 149.

39. Ibid., p. 13.

40. Ibid., p. 14.

41. *Our Mineral Wealth,* June 21, 1901, quoted by Karin Boudy, "Mohave Footprints," *Kingman Miner,* February 2, 1979.

42. Corb Sarchet, "Toads in Coffee Cups Greeted Customers of Harvey House," *Wichita Morning Eagle,* May 7, 1953.

43. Only the most wealthy and notable persons traveled the TAT. Fares were high—coast to coast in 1929 cost more than three hundred dollars, but included all meals, both on the ground and in the air, stopover privileges, transportation to central business districts, thirty pounds of luggage and a 10 percent discount if a passenger was willing to make the return trip in less than three months. The Ford Trimotors were said to be the safest, most comfortable airplanes known to man, with a pilot, copilot, steward, and seating for eight passengers. Anne Morrow Lindbergh, accustomed to the two-seater, open-cockpit planes she learned to fly with her husband Charles, wrote home to her family about the luxuries of the TAT planes:

The ship is beautifully decorated inside, painted a cool gray-green with the most comfortable green leather-covered chairs, that are adjustable. Little green curtains and blue-shaded lights. There is a white uniformed attendant shouting in my ear that he will get anything I want. . . . There is a radio operator on board who looks as though he were playing a kazoo; he has a round metal box fastened to his mouth and he is talking *into it.*

[from Anne Morrow Lindbergh, *Hour of Gold, Hour of Lead* (New York & London: Harcourt Brace Jovanovich, 1973), p. 55.]
44. *Woods County Enterprise,* July 29, 1929.
45. Lindbergh, p. 52.
46. *Canadian Record,* August 25, 1910.
47. Ibid.
48. Ibid.
49. Will Rogers, *The Autobiography of Will Rogers* (1949; reprint, New York: Avon, 1975), p. 9.
50. Erna Fergusson, *Our Southwest* (New York: Alfred A. Knopf, 1940), p. 196.

CHAPTER 6

1. For further reading on the life and work of Mary Colter, see Virginia L. Grattan's *Mary Colter, Builder Upon the Red Earth* (Flagstaff, Arizona: Northland Press, 1980).
2. For further reading on the Indian Detours see Diane H. Thomas, *The Southwestern Indian Detours* (Phoenix: Hunter Publishing Co., 1978).
3. The last Montezuma built by the Santa Fe Railway cost $800,000. Built of stone and wood, this hotel had 172 rooms, a 77-room annex known as the Mountain House, a 60-by-100-foot casino, a bowling alley, a large bathhouse and twenty-room hospital, a stable, a power plant, an ice house, and a depot.
4. *Las Vegas Optic,* May 13, 1880.
5. *Las Vegas Optic,* June 13, 1881.
6. *Las Vegas Optic,* January 4, 1881.
7. *Las Vegas Optic,* October 1, 1881.
8. Byron Truman Mills, interviewed by James E. Bell, November 1949: "A Glimpse of Early Las Vegas," Historical Methods Seminar, New Mexico Highlands University.
9. Keith L. Bryant, Jr., *History of the Atchison, Topeka and Santa Fe Railway* (New York: Macmillan Co., 1974), p. 113.
10. *Las Vegas Daily Optic,* August 16, 1935.
11. *Las Vegas Daily Optic,* May 28, 1948.
12. Erna Fergusson, *Albuquerque* (Albuquerque: M. Armitage, 1947), p. 37.
13. Erna Fergusson, *Our Southwest* (New York: Alfred A. Knopf, 1940), p. 201.
14. Charles Amsden, quoted in Fergusson, *Our Southwest,* p. 201.

15. William Allen White, *The Emporia Gazette,* n.d., Arizona State University Fred Harvey Special Collection, Tempe, Arizona.

16. Grattan, p. 100.

17. Fred Harvey promotional brochure, 1940; Dorothy Woodward Collection, New Mexico State Records and Archives, Santa Fe, New Mexico.

18. Ernie Pyle, quoted in Fergusson, *Albuquerque,* p. 37.

19. Maurice Trimmer, "Ernie Pyle Called Albuquerque 'Home'," *New Mexico Magazine,* October 1960.

20. Germaine L. Ramounachou Moon, *Barstow Depots and Harvey Houses* (Barstow: Mojave River Valley Museum Association Publication, 1980), pp. 22, 23.

21. Fergusson, *Our Southwest,* p. 202.

22. El Tovar, "man on the shore," was named for Don Pedro de Tovar, one of Coronado's top men, but not the European who was the first to lay eyes on the Grand Canyon. Tovar was exploring what is now the Hopi reservation and heard tales about a huge canyon. He sent word back to Coronado, who sent Don Garcia Lopez de Cardeñas to the canyon. Cardeñas is credited with the discovery of the Grand Canyon.

23. John Willy, "Fred Harvey's Facilities and Service at the Grand Canyon," *The Santa Fe Magazine,* 1928, Arizona State University Fred Harvey Special Collection, Tempe, Arizona.

24. Sam Lowe, "El Tovar at 76," *Arizona Highways,* April 1981, p. 6.

25. Willy, p. 29.

26. T. M. Pearce, *New Mexico Place Names* (Albuquerque: The University of New Mexico Press, 1965), p. 62.

27. Grattan, p. 42.

28. Ibid., p. 44.

29. Fergusson, *Our Southwest,* p. 265.

30. Grattan, p. 50.

31. Ibid.

32. Peter Hertzog, *La Fonda: The Inn of Santa Fe* (Portales, New Mexico: Bishop Printing and Litho Co., 1962), p. 31.

33. Grattan, p. 52.

34. Hertzog, p. 32.

35. Ernie Pyle, *Home Country* (New York: William Sloane Associates, Inc., 1947), pp. 75, 76.

36. Grattan, p. 106.

CHAPTER 7

1. Bob O'Sullivan, "It's 55 years late, but thanks, Mr. Harvey, for the memory," *Chicago Tribune,* December 11, 1988.

2. Virginia L. Grattan, *Mary Colter, Builder Upon the Red Earth* (Flagstaff, Arizona: Northland Press, 1980), p. 60.

3. Jack Mullen, "America's Best-Fed Travelers," reprint of *The Santa Fe Magazine,* December, 1943, p. 3.

4. James David Henderson, *Meals by Fred Harvey: A Phenomenon of the American West* (Fort Worth: Texas Christian University Press, 1969), p. 36.

5. Mullen, p. 9.

6. Ibid.

7. Ibid., p. 30.

8. Ibid., p. 17.

9. Ibid., p. 27.

10. Kay Hildebrand, " 'Harvey Girls' Long a Part of Kansas City Scene," *Kansas City Star,* February 17, 1946.

11. Keith L. Bryant, Jr., *History of the Atchison, Topeka and Santa Fe Railway* (New York: Macmillan Co., 1974), p. 272.

12. "Lamy, the Town the Railroad Built," *The Atom* (Los Alamos Scientific Laboratory), April 1966, p. 19.

13. The brick Harvey House, once the center of New Town Las Vegas, was scheduled for demolition in 1963. A local oil distributor intervened and bought the hotel, converting the interior into apartments. In the 1980s, the Castañeda was featured in the film *Red Dawn.* Today, the Castañeda is not in use.

The Montezuma Hotel in Las Vegas has changed hands many times in the last eighty years: in 1913, the Santa Fe Railway sold the hotel and its 1,500 acres to the Las Vegas Y.M.C.A.. The Y sold it to the Bible Film Company. In 1921, it became a Baptist college, and from 1940 until 1972, the Montezuma was a seminary for the training of priests under the auspices of the Roman Catholic Church of Santa Fe. At one time or another, the property has been scouted for use as training quarters for major league baseball teams, a sanitarium for tuberculosis, and the location for several motion pictures. Today the Montezuma is the home for the North American branch of the World College, and is a campus for high school students from all over the world.

14. Grattan, p. 111.

CONCLUSION

1. Susan Armitage, "Western Women's History: A Review Essay," *Frontiers, a Journal of Women's Studies* (Fall 1980), p. 73.

SELECTED BIBLIOGRAPHY

Beck, Warren A. *New Mexico, A History of Four Centuries,* Norman: University of Oklahoma Press, 1962.

Bryant, Keith L. *History of the Atchison, Topeka and Santa Fe Railway,* New York: Macmillan Publishing Company, Inc., 1974.

Cott, Nancy F. and Pleck, Elizabeth H. *A Heritage of Her Own,* New York: Simon and Schuster, 1979.

Donovan, Frances. *The Woman Who Waits,* Boston: Richard Badger, 1920.

Dils, Lenore. *Horny Toad Man,* El Paso, Texas: Boots & Saddle Press, 1966.

Dublin, Thomas. *Women at Work: The Transformation of Work and Community in Lowell, Massachusetts, 1826–1860,* New York: Columbia University Press, 1979.

Dykstra, Richard R. *The Cattle Towns,* New York: Knopf, 1968.

Eisler, Benita. *The Lowell Offering, Writings by New England Mill Women,* Philadelphia and New York: J. B. Lippincott Company, 1977.

Fergusson, Erna. *Albuquerque,* Albuquerque: M. Armitage, 1947.

Fergusson, Erna. *Our Southwest,* New York: Knopf, 1940.

Grattan, Virginia. *Mary Colter, Builder Upon the Red Earth,* Flagstaff: Northland Press, 1980.

Gregg, Josiah. *Commerce of the Prairies,* Norman: University of Oklahoma Press, 1954.

Henderson, James David. *Meals by Fred Harvey; A Phenomenon of the American West,* Fort Worth: Texas Christian University Press, 1969.

Hertzog, Peter. *La Fonda: The Inn of Santa Fe,* Portales: Bishop Printing and Litho Co., 1962.

Horgan, Paul. *The Centuries of Santa Fe,* New York: E.P. Dutton & Company, Inc., 1956.

Inman, Henry. *The Old Santa Fe Trail,* Minneapolis: Ross & Haines, Inc., 1966.

Jeffrey, Julie Roy. *Frontier Women: The Trans-Mississippi West 1840–1880,* New York: Hill and Wang, 1979.

Kessler-Harris, Alice. *Out to Work,* New York: Oxford University Press, 1982.

Lindbergh, Anne Morrow. *Hour of Gold, Hour of Lead,* New York & London: Harcourt Brace Jovanovich, 1973.

Magoffin, Susan Shelby. *Down the Santa Fe Trail and Into Mexico,* Santa Fe: William Gannon, 1975.

Marshall, James. *Santa Fe, The Railroad That Built an Empire,* New York: Random House, 1945.

Matthaei, Julie A. *An Economic History of Women in America,* New York: Schocken Books, 1982.

McReynolds, Edwin C. *Oklahoma, A History of the Sooner State,* Norman: University of Oklahoma Press, 1954.

Myres, Sandra L. *Westering Women and the Frontier Experience,* Albuquerque: University of New Mexico Press, 1982.

Noble, Joseph A. *From Cab to Caboose; Fifty Years of Railroading,* Norman: University of Oklahoma Press, 1964.

Pike, Zebulon M. *The Expeditions of Zebulon M. Pike,* New York: F. P. Harper, 1895.

Pyle, Ernie. *Home Country,* New York: William Sloane Associates, Inc., 1947.

Rich, Everett, ed. *The Heritage of Kansas,* Lawrence: University of Kansas Press, 1960.

Rogers, Will. *The Autobiography of Will Rogers,* New York: Avon, 1975.

Stratton, Johanna. *Pioneer Women: Voices From the Kansas Frontier,* New York: Simon & Schuster, 1981.

Thomas, Diane H. *The Southwestern Indian Detours,* Phoenix: Hunter Publishing Co., 1978.

Waters, L. L. *Steel Trails to Santa Fe,* Lawrence: University of Kansas Press, 1950.

Western Writers of America. *The Women Who Made the West,* Garden City, New York: Doubleday, 1980.

APPENDIX A

NAME	BORN	HARVEY AFFILIATION	INTERVIEWED
Viola Hern Archibeque	1926, NM	Troop Train Girl, NM 1942	Albuquerque, NM Sept 1983
T. F. Ball		historian; re: Effie Jenks, Harvey Girl, NM, 1920s–1950s	personal correspondence
Maude Webster Bay		Harvey Girl, Waynoka, 1929	Waynoka, OK, June 1983
Wayne Bay	1907, OK	pantryman, Waynoka, 1929	Waynoka, OK, June 1983
Addie Park Bassett	1906, MO	Harvey Girl, NM, CA, 1927–1967	personal correspondence
John Preston Brady	1910 KS	busboy, Emporia, 1926	Topeka, KS, June 1983
Gary Brittain		grandmother & aunt: Harvey Girls, TX, NM, AZ	telephone interview, July 1983
Ruth Brittain		mother: Harvey Girl, TX	telephone interview, June 1983
Ruthanna Walz Caster	KS	Harvey Girl, NM, 1936–1939	Santa Fe, NM, June 1983
Warren Caster		dishwasher, clerk, cashier, Castañeda, 1937–1939	Santa Fe, NM, June 1983
Helen Chapman		Harvey Girl, Waynoka, 1926	Waynoka, OK, June 1983
Zadie Miller Chapman	1899, MO	Harvey Girl, Waynoka, 1920	Waynoka, OK, June 1983
Monte Chavez	1911, NM	bellboy, maître'd, La Fonda 1929–1988	Santa Fe, NM, Nov. 1983
Kamel Cohlmia	OK	busboy, Waynoka, 1935	Waynoka, OK, June 1983
Theo Champion Conner		Harvey House cashier, Slaton, TX, c. 1920; brother: Gilbert Champion, Harvey employee c. 1920–1930; sister-in-law Harvey Girl	personal correspondence

NAME	BORN	HARVEY AFFILIATION	INTERVIEWED
Margaret Reichenborn Craig	1924, KS	Harvey Girl, Castañeda 1941–1943	Las Vegas, NM, Oct. 1983
Margaret Becker Crist	1887, KS	Harvey Girl, Syracuse, 1906	personal correspondence
Mary Calloway Dillingham	1893, KS	Harvey Girl, OK, 1922–1924	Waynoka, OK, June 1983
Katheryn Krause Ferguson		husband: Irwin Krause, manager, OK, KS, TX, NM, AZ, CA, 1924–1947	Albuquerque, NM, March, August 1983
Gladys Porter Douglass Fitzgerald	1906, OK	Harvey Girl, OK, 1920–1927	personal correspondence
Charles Folk		SFRR enginner, 1940s	telephone interview, July 1983
John Frenden	1908, Germany	Chef, NM, AZ, CA, OH, 1927–1973	Albuquerque, NM, Sept. 1983
Pauline Anderson Frenden	OK	Harvey Girl, NM	Albuquerque, NM, Sept. 1983
Elizabeth Alice Garnas	1909, Yugoslavia	Harvey Girl, NM, 1926–1929	Canadian, TX, May 1983
Joanne Stinelichner Thompson George	1894, Germany	Harvey Girl, manager, KS, OK, TX, NM, CA, 1916–1948	Topeka, KS, June 1983
Helen Whitnell Gillespie	1897, IO	mother-in-law: Harvey Girl, NM, 1886	Springer, NM, Oct. 1983
Bernice Myers Glenn	NM	Harvey Girl, NM, 1932–1936	Clovis, NM, May 1983
Violet Bosetti Grundman	1916, KS	Harvey Girl, Alvarado, 1936–1941	Albuquerque, NM, Sept. 1983
Cecil Hamm	1901, OK	busboy, OK, TX, KS, 1917, chef, AZ, CA, 1928–1942	Waynoka, OK, June 1983
Galys Hamm	OK	Harvey Girl, TX, KS, 1926–1928	Waynoka, OK, June 1983
Warren Harrington		busboy, Canadian, TX, 1929–1932	Canadian, TX, May 1983
Elizabeth Hazlewood	1897	Harvey Girl, Canadian, TX, 1926–1939	Canadian, TX, May 1983
Opal Sells Hill	1900, OK	Harvey Girl, KS, TX, NM, AZ, OH, 1924–1969	Albuquerque, NM, Dec. 1981, March 1983

NAME	BORN	HARVEY AFFILIATION	INTERVIEWED
Bertha Spears Hill	1908, OK	Harvey Girl, NM, AZ, CA, 1932–1942	Albuquerque, NM, Sept. 1983
Helen Huffman		Harvey Girl, Kansas City, 1919	personal correspondence
Ellen Mae Hunt Jones	1901, KS	Harvey Girl, NM, CA, 1922–1926	Albuquerque, NM, Sept. 1983
Gerald Johnson		historian, Coyle, OK; re: Harvey Girls, NM, 1920s	personal correspondence
Mrs. T. R. Johnstone		sister: Janet Ferrier, Harvey Girl, NM, AZ, 1920s–1960s	personal correspondence
Dan Bruce Jones	1911, OK	night cook, busboy, storeroom man, OK, KS, TX, 1926–1928	Waynoka, OK, June 1983
Grace Jones	1913, KS	Harvey Girl, NM, 1929–1932	Topeka, KS, June 1983
Bernard M. Kane	1912, KS	ice cream wagon, KS, 1926 bellhop, NM, KS, 1927–1936	Topeka, KS, June 1983
Rachel Kelly	OK	Harvey Girl, Canadian, TX, 1927	Canadian, TX, May 1983
Johanna Klenke	1910, KS	Harvey Girl, KS, 1926–1930	Spearville, KS, June 1983
Hazel Williams McCullough La Duke	1904, KS	Harvey Girl, Dodge City, 1918–1919	Topeka, KS, June 1983
Olive Winter Loomis	1894, ARK	Harvey Girl, KS, AZ, IL, 1918–1940	Beloit, KS, June 1983
Hazel Lutz	1900, KS	Harvey Girl, Topeka, 1919	personal correspondence
Bertha Parker Maddux	1902, OK	Harvey Girl, NM, AZ, 1925–1926	Kingman, AZ, Oct. 1983
Una Gertrude Atchison Matthews	TX	Harvey Girl, Canadian, TX, 1925	Canadian, TX, May 1983
Ann R. McCormick	OK	Harvey Girl, OK, 1920s	personal correspondence
Bernice Black McLain	1907, NE	Harvey Girl, AZ, IL, 1926–1939	Kingman, AZ, Oct. 1983
May Etta Arnold McMichael	1908, KY	Harvey Girl, CA, AZ, 1929–1930	personal correspondence

NAME	BORN	HARVEY AFFILIATION	INTERVIEWED
Gene Montgomery	1899, OK	telegrapher, SFRR, NM, 1916-retirement	Albuquerque, NM, Sept. 1983
Margaret Moses		Indian Detours Courier, NM, 1920s	Santa Fe, NM, 1983
Virginia Bixby O'Donnell	1905, KS	Harvey Girl, KS, 1921	personal correspondence
Walter Reichenborn		newsstand manager, clerk, cashier, KS, NM, 1932–1941	Clovis, NM, May 1983
Joe R. Rison	1898	SFRR employee, TX, OK, 1916–1971	Gainesville, TX, April 1983
Lyle Rouse	1922, KS	father: SFRR employee, 1918–1961	Topeka, KS, June 1983
Della P. Sanchez		Troop Train Girl, AZ, NM, 1942	personal correspondence
Helen McCally Schell	1899	Harvey Girl, OK, TX, KS, NM, 1917–1933	Waynoka, OK, June 1983
Sis Schoene		mother: Elizabeth Hazlewood, Harvey Girl, Canadian, 1926–1939	Canadian, TX, May 1983
Helmut Schurig		father: Ernest Schurig, German-born Harvey chef TX, OK, CO, 1911–1940s	Gainesville, TX, April 1983
Cora M. Scott		Harvey Girl, Ashfork, AZ, 1919–1920	personal correspondence
Myrtle C. Short	1903, IL	Harvey Girl, Castañeda, 1920	personal correspondence
Charlotte Shorts	1898, KS	resident, Waynoka, OK	Waynoka, OK, June 1983
Jessie McCally Smith		Harvey Girl, AZ, OK, KS, CO IL, 1919–1934	Waynoka, OK, June 1983
Alice Stackhouse	1883, NY	Harvey Girl, NM, AZ, 1920s–1960s	Albuquerque, NM, Aug. 1983
Hazel Redenbough Felton Strickland	1906, KS	Harvey Girl, KS, NM, CA, 1920–1926	Topeka, KS, June 1983
Evangeline Stine Tapia	1926, NM	Harvey Girl, NM, CA, CO, 1942–1946	Albuquerque, NM, Oct 1983
Floyd A. Tucker	1908, TX	Harvey employee, TX, NM, CO, AZ, CA, 1920s–1933	Needles, CA, Oct. 1983

NAME	BORN	HARVEY AFFILIATION	INTERVIEWED
Myrtle E. Tyler		Harvey Girl, Kansas City, 1926–1948	personal correspondence
Mary Lou Lewis Urban	NM	Harvey Girl, OK, 1935–1937	Waynoka, OK, June 1983
Frances Watkins		Harvey Girl, NM, 1925	personal correspondence
Fern Pittman Taylor Whealy		Harvey Girl, Waynoka, 1930s	personal correspondence
Mrs. John Williams		mother & aunt: Harvey Girls, Ashfork, 1920s	personal correspondence
Mrs. Alvin Wilson		mother: Margaret Becker Crist, Harvey Girl, KS, 1906	personal correspondence
Frances Yarbrough	1905, TX	lifetime resident, Gainesville, TX	Gainesville, TX, April 1983
Marie Knaak Zismann	1907, KS	Harvey Girl, AZ, 1946–1952	Kingman, AZ, Oct. 1983

APPENDIX B

FRED HARVEY ESTABLISHMENTS

HARVEY LUNCH AND DINING ROOMS

YEAR EST.	LOCATION	YEAR CLOSED
1876	Topeka, Kansas	1940
1879	Lakin, Kansas	1880
1880	Coolidge, Kansas	?
1880	Emporia, Kansas	1937
1882	Raton, New Mexico	c. 1900
1883	Las Vegas, New Mexico	1899
1883	San Marcial, New Mexico	1929
1883	Rincon, New Mexico	1933
1883	Deming, New Mexico	1929
1883	Wellington, Kansas	?
1883	Arkansas City, Kansas	1933
1883	Wallace, New Mexico	?
1887	San Bernardino, California	?
c. 1887	Bagdad, California	?
1897	Galveston, Texas	1938
1899	Dearborn Station, Chicago	
1900	Mojave, California	1935
1900	Merced, California	1935
1900	Bakersfield, California	1948
1900	Los Angeles, California	1939

YEAR EST.	LOCATION	YEAR CLOSED
1901	Gainesville, Texas	1931
1901	Kingman, Arizona	1938
1903	Guthrie, Oklahoma	1930
1904	Carlsbad, New Mexico	?
1906	El Paso, Texas	1948
1907	Belen, New Mexico	1935
1910	Waynoka, Oklahoma	1937
1910	San Diego, California	1936
1910	Amarillo, Texas	1940
1910	Canadian, Texas	1939
1911	Houston, Texas	1948
1914	Kansas City Union Station	
1925	Chicago Union Station	
1930	Cleveland Union Station	
1933	Strauss Building	1938
1938	San Francisco Bus Terminal	?
1939	Hollywood Restaurant	?
1947	Painted Desert Inn	open
1948	Albuquerque Airport	open

Opening dates for the following lunch and dining rooms have not been accurately recorded:

	Brownwood, Texas	1938
	Chanute, Kansas	1931
	Cleburne, Texas	1931
	Colorado Springs, Colorado	1931
	Dallas, Texas	1923
	Fort Worth, Texas	1933

YEAR EST.	LOCATION	YEAR CLOSED
	Purcell, Oklahoma	1935
	Rosenberg, Texas	1923
	San Francisco, California Ferry Building	
	Silsbee, Texas	1923
	Slaton, Texas	?
	Somerville, Texas	1932
	Sweetwater, Texas	1933
	Temple, Texas	1933
	Wichita, Kansas	1935

HARVEY HOTELS

YEAR EST.	LOCATION	HOTEL, YEAR OPENED	CLOSED
1878	Florence, Kansas	Clifton, 1878	1900
1882	Las Vegas, New Mexico	Montezuma,	1903
1883	Newton, Kansas	Arcade, 1900	?
1883	Hutchinson, Kansas	Bisonte, c. 1901	1946
1883	La Junta, Colorado	El Otero, c. 1901	1948
1883	Lamy, New Mexico	El Ortiz, 1910	1938
1883	Albuquerque, New Mexico	Alvarado, 1902	1969
1887	Williams, Arizona	Fray Marcos, c. 1905	?
1887	Barstow, California	Casa del Desierto, 1910	1959
1887	Winslow, Arizona	La Posada, 1929	1957
1887	Needles, California	El Garces, c. 1901	1948
1899	Las Vegas, New Mexico	Castañeda, 1899	1948
1895	Ash Fork, Arizona	Escalante, c. 1905	?
1895	Trinidad, Colorado	Cardinas, ?	1933

234 · Appendix B

YEAR EST.	LOCATION	HOTEL, YEAR OPENED	CLOSED
1895	Seligman, Arizona	The Havasu, c. 1905	?
1895	Gallup, New Mexico	El Navajo, 1923	1957
1896	Dodge City, Kansas	El Vaquero, 1900	1948
c. 1900	Clovis, New Mexico	Gran Quivira	?
1905	Grand Canyon, Arizona	El Tovar, 1905	open
1905	Grand Canyon, Arizona	Bright Angel Lodge, 1934	open
1908	Syracuse, Kansas	Sequoyah	1936
c. 1910	Vaughn, New Mexico	Las Chavez	c. 1936
1929	Santa Fe, New Mexico	La Fonda	open

HARVEY NEWSSTANDS ON A. T. & S. F. RAILWAY

1900	Fresno, California		1923
1900	Stockton, California		1923
?	Ardmore, Oklahoma		?
?	Bartlesville, Oklahoma		?
?	Beaumont, Texas		?
?	Lawrence, Kansas		?
?	Oklahoma City, Oklahoma		?
?	Amory, Mississippi		?
?	Enid, Oklahoma		?
?	Henryetta, Oklahoma		?
?	Muskogee, Oklahoma		?

HARVEY NEWSSTANDS

Along the St. Louis and San Francisco ("Frisco") Line, part of the Santa Fe Railway until 1897.

OPENED 1896, CLOSED 1930:

Afton, Oklahoma

Birmingham, Alabama — also lunchroom

Cape Girardeau, Missouri

Fayetteville, Arkansas

Fort Scott, Kansas

Francis, Oklahoma — also lunchroom

Hugo, Oklahoma — also lunchroom

Joplin, Missouri

Madill, Oklahoma

Memphis, Tennessee

Monett, Missouri

Okmulgee, Oklahoma

Paris, Texas

Rogers, Arkansas

Sapulpa, Oklahoma

Snyder, Oklahoma

Springfield, Missouri

Tower Grove, Missouri

Tulsa, Oklahoma

APPENDIX C

MEZZANINE
TABLE D'HOTE LUNCHEON
75c

Selection   Friday September 30, 1927

Fried Flounder, Tomato Sauce
Potted Small Steak, Smothered Onions
Fresh Shrimps with Noodles au Gratin
Roast Home-made Veal Loaf, Mushroom Sauce
Mashed Potatoes   Cauliflower in Cream
Rolls or Bread and Butter

Coffee   Fresh Peach Pudding, Fruit Sauce
Tea   Milk   Raisin Pie   Ice Cream

Fred Harvey
UNION STATION
CHICAGO

SOUPS
Clam Chowder Manhattan 25
Consomme with Vermicelli 25
Cream of Tomatoes 25

RELISHES
Ripe Olives 15
Chow Chow 15

OTHER LUNCHES
No. 1—40c
Clam Chowder Manhattan
or Consomme with Vermicelli
Crabmeat Salad Sandwich, Mayonnaise

No. 2—65c
Fresh Vegetable Luncheon, Poached Egg
Bread and Butter

No. 3—65c
Chicken Croquettes, Cream Sauce
Bread and Butter   Candied Sweet Potatoes

SANDWICHES (Hot)
Roast Sugar Cured Ham, Candied Sweet Potatoes 45
Veal Loaf, Brown Gravy, Mashed Potatoes 45

SANDWICHES (Cold)
Sardine and Lettuce 35
Chicken Salad, Mayonnaise 45
Corned Beef, Ham or American Cheese 20

SALADS
Salmon and Celery, Mayonnaise 45
Lettuce and Tomatoes, French Dressing 30

DESSERTS
Fresh Peach Pudding, Fruit Sauce 20
Pies—Apple 15; Cherry, Gooseberry, Pumpkin
or Cocoanut Custard 20
Ice Cream—Vanilla 20; Chocolate 25
Raspberry Sundae 25   Chocolate Layer Cake 15
Honey Dew Melon 30   Casaba Melon 30
Blueberries and Cream 30
Sliced Peaches and Cream 30   Raspberries and Cream 35

BEVERAGES
Coffee (Cup) 10; Pot 20   Tea (Pot) 15   Postum (Cup) 10; Pot 20
Buttermilk 15   Milk, Certified 15   Cream, Glass 30

ANNOUNCING
Table d'Hote Dinner in Restaurant from Six to Eight p. m.
Two Dollars Per Person
In Lunch Room at One Dollar Per Person

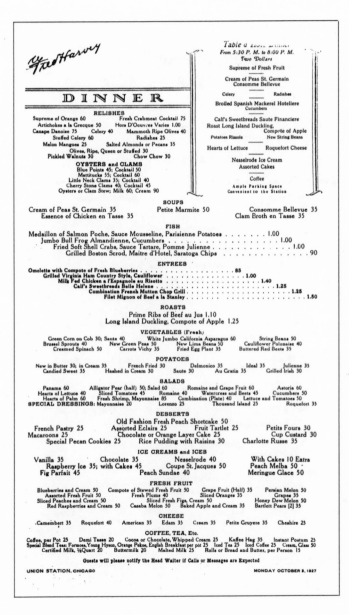

Fred Harvey

DINNER

RELISHES

Supreme of Orange 60   Fresh Crabmeat Cocktail 75
Artichokes a la Grecque 50   Hors D'Oeuvres Varies 1.00
Canape Danoise 75   Celery 40   Mammoth Ripe Olives 40
Stuffed Celery 60   Radishes 25
Melon Mangoes 25   Salted Almonds or Pecans 35
Olives, Ripe, Queen or Stuffed 30
Pickled Walnuts 30   Chow Chow 30

OYSTERS and CLAMS
Blue Points 45; Cocktail 50
Mattitucks 55; Cocktail 60
Little Neck Clams 35; Cocktail 40
Cherry Stone Clams 40; Cocktail 45
Oysters or Clam Stew; Milk 60; Cream 90

Table d'Hôte Dinner
From 5:30 P. M. to 8:00 P. M.
Two Dollars

Supreme of Fresh Fruit

Cream of Peas St. Germain
Consomme Bellevue

Celery ———— Radishes

Broiled Spanish Mackerel Hoteliere
Cucumbers

Calf's Sweetbreads Saute Financiere
Roast Long Island Duckling,
Compote of Apple
Potatoes Rissole   New String Beans

Hearts of Lettuce   Roquefort Cheese

Nesselrode Ice Cream
Assorted Cakes

Coffee

Ample Parking Space
Convenient to the Station

SOUPS

Cream of Peas St. Germain 35   Petite Marmite 50   Consomme Bellevue 35
Essence of Chicken en Tasse 35   Clam Broth en Tasse 35

FISH

Medaillon of Salmon Poche, Sauce Mousseline, Parisienne Potatoes 1.00
Jumbo Bull Frog Almandienne, Cucumbers 1.00
Fried Soft Shell Crabs, Sauce Tartare, Pomme Julienne 1.00
Grilled Boston Scrod, Maitre d'Hotel, Saratoga Chips 90

ENTREES

Omelette with Compote of Fresh Blueberries 85
Grilled Virginia Ham Country Style, Cauliflower 1.00
Milk Fed Chicken a l'Espagnole au Risotto 1.40
Calf's Sweetbreads Belle Helene 1.25
Combination French Mutton Chop Grill 1.25
Filet Mignon of Beef a la Stanley 1.50

ROASTS

Prime Ribs of Beef au Jus 1.10
Long Island Duckling, Compote of Apple 1.25

VEGETABLES (Fresh)

Green Corn on Cob 30; Saute 40   White Jumbo California Asparagus 60   String Beans 50
Brussel Sprouts 40   New Green Peas 50   New Lima Beans 50   Cauliflower Polonaise 40
Creamed Spinach 35   Carrots Vichy 35   Fried Egg Plant 35   Buttered Red Beets 35

POTATOES

New in Butter 30; in Cream 35   French Fried 30   Delmonico 35   Ideal 35   Julienne 35
Candied Sweet 35   Hashed in Cream 30   Saute 30   Au Gratin 35   Grilled Irish 30

SALADS

Panama 60   Alligator Pear (half) 50; Salad 60   Romaine and Grape Fruit 60   Astoria 60
Hearts of Lettuce 40   Sliced Tomatoes 45   Romaine 40   Watercress and Beets 45   Cucumbers 50
Hearts of Palm 60   Fresh Shrimp, Mayonnaise 85   Combination (Plate) 40   Lettuce and Tomatoes 50
SPECIAL DRESSINGS: Mayonnaise 20   Lorenzo 25   Thousand Island 25   Roquefort 35

DESSERTS

Old Fashion Fresh Peach Shortcake 50
French Pastry 25   Assorted Eclairs 25   Fruit Tartlet 25   Petits Fours 30
Macaroons 25   Chocolate or Orange Layer Cake 25   Cup Custard 30
Special Pecan Cookies 25   Rice Pudding with Raisins 30   Charlotte Russe 35

ICE CREAMS and ICES

Vanilla 35   Chocolate 35   Nesselrode 40   With Cakes 10 Extra
Raspberry Ice 35; with Cakes 45   Coupe St. Jacques 50   Peach Melba 50
Fig Parfait 45   Peach Sundae 40   Meringue Glace 50

FRESH FRUIT

Blueberries and Cream 50   Compote of Stewed Fresh Fruit 50   Grape Fruit (Half) 35   Persian Melon 50
Assorted Fresh Fruit 50   Fresh Plums 40   Sliced Oranges 35   Grapes 35
Sliced Peaches and Cream 50   Sliced Fresh Figs, Cream 50   Honey Dew Melon 50
Red Raspberries and Cream 50   Cassaba Melon 50   Baked Apple and Cream 35   Bartlett Pears [2] 35

CHEESE

Camembert 35   Roquefort 40   American 35   Edam 35   Cream 35   Petite Gruyere 35   Cheshire 25

COFFEE, TEA, Etc.

Coffee, per Pot 25   Demi Tasse 20   Cocoa or Chocolate, Whipped Cream 25   Kaffee Hag 35   Instant Postum 25
Special Blend Teas: Formosa, Young Hyson, Orange Pekoe, English Breakfast per pot 25   Iced Tea 25   Iced Coffee 25   Cream, Glass 50
Certified Milk, ½ Quart 20   Buttermilk 20   Malted Milk 25   Rolls or Bread and Butter, per Person 15

Guests will please notify the Head Waiter if Calls or Messages are Expected

UNION STATION, CHICAGO   MONDAY OCTOBER 3, 1927

Thanksgiving Day
1928

Dinner

Blue Point Cocktail

Cream of Chicken Reine Margot   Consomme Careme

Celery Hearts   Mixed Olives   Stuffed Mangoes

Lobster en cassolette, Dewey
Melba Toast

Filet Mignon, Nicoise
Braised Sweetbreads with Truffles, Perigord
Fresh Mushrooms Saute Aux Fine Herbes

Punch Maraschino

Roast Young Turkey, Chestnut Dressing, Cranberry Sauce
Roast Prime Ribs of Beef au Jus

Broccoli, Hollandaise   Baked Hubbard Squash
Sweet Potatoes, Florida   Mashed Potatoes

Salad Alexandra

Hot or Cold Mince Pie   Pumpkin Pie with Whipped Cream
English Plum Pudding, Hard or Spiced Sauce

Nesselrode Ice Cream
Fruit Cake

Roquefort Cheese
Toasted Water Crackers

Coffee   Tea   Milk   Cider

THE ALVARADO
Albuquerque, N. M.
November 29, 1928

JOHN H. WATSON,
Manager.

THE ALVARADO
by Fred Harvey

LUNCHEON

SOUPS
Clam Chowder, Coney Island 20   Chicken Broth, Vermicelli 20
Tomato Bouillon in Cup 20

RELISHES
Fruit Supreme 35   Celery Hearts 30   Radishes 15   Mangoes 20
Fresh Shrimp Cocktail 50   Oyster Cocktail 50   Canape Sardellen 50
Canape Caviar 50   Mixed Olives 20

FISH AND OYSTERS
Blue Points on Half Shell 45   Baked Oysters a l Ancienne 45
Oyster Stew 45   Cream Stew 60   Fried Selects 50   Pan Roast 50
COLD SLAW SERVED WITH ALL OYSTERS
Creamed Shrimp Newburg on Toast 75
Fried Filet of Sole, Tartar Sauce, Julienne Potatoes 50
Jumbo Frog Legs au Beurre Noir, Sliced Cucumbers 75
Broiled Live Baby Lobster (whole) Saratoga Chips 1.25
Steamed Alaska Cod, Drawn Butter, Boiled Potato 50
Baked Salmon, Portugaise, Parisian Potatoes 60

TODAY'S SUGGESTIONS
Frankfurters and Hot Potato Salad 45
Turkey Wings with Rice, Celery Sauce 45
Lamb Steak Saute, Vert Pre 70
Breast of Guinea Hen, Virginia 90
Club Steak with Smothered Onions........................90
Breaded Veal Cutlets with Fried Egg........................60
Chili Con Carne 25   Apple Fritters Glace 35
Omelette Financiere 50   Minced Ham, Scrambled Egg 50
Half Portion: Filet of Sole, Tartar Sauce........................35
HOT YOUNG NATIVE TURKEY SANDWICH, *Sage Dressing,*
Giblet Gravy, Cranberry Sauce, Mashed Potatoes........................60
HOT ROAST BEEF SANDWICH, GRAVY, MASHED POTATOES 40
ROAST PRIME RIBS OF BEEF AU JUS 75

VEGETABLES
Potatoes: Mashed or Steamed 15   In Cream 20   Baked Yams 20
Au Gratin 20   Lyonnaise 20   Hashed Browned 15   French Fried 15
Baked 20   Cauliflower 20   String Beans 20
Stewed Tomatoes 15   Fried Egg Plant 20   Brussel Sprouts 20
Baked Hubbard Squash 20   Artichoke 30   Peas in Cream 20
Bread and Butter Service 10

SPECIAL SANDWICHES
Cream Cheese and Apple Sauce 20   Loin of Pork 20   Chicken Salad 45
Vegetable Mayonnaise 20

COLD BUFFET
Cold Meats   **Salads**   **Cheese**
Roast Prime Ribs of Beef, Potato Salad 75
Head Cheese and Ox Tongue, Sliced Tomatoes 60
Virginia Ham and Sliced Chicken, Fruit Salad 1.00
Spiced or Bismarck Herring, Potato Salad 50
Artichoke Mayonnaise 35   Waldorf 35   Stuffed Devilled Egg, Russian 35
Avocado Salad 40   Camembert Cheese, Toasted Rye Bread 35
Special Salads—Plate Portions
Fruit 30   Cold Slaw 15   String Bean 15   Lettuce and Tomato 25

PASTRIES AND ICE CREAM
Pies: Apple 15   Vanilla Ice Cream 15   Frozen Eclair 30
Mince, hot or cold 15   Pineapple Ice Cream 20   Baked Apple 20
Pineapple 15   Lemon Sherbet 15   Orange Hearts 20
Raisin 15   Peach Sundae 20   Napoleon Slice 20
Cocoanut Cream 15   Date Parfait 30   Blanc Mange 20

COFFEE, TEA, MILK, ETC.
Coffee, per cup 10   Tea, per pot 15   Postum, per pot 15
Coffee, per pot 20   Iced Tea, glass 10   Cocoa, per pot 15
Milk, per bottle 10   Iced Tea, per pot 15   Lemonade 15
Ovaltine 15-25   Buttermilk 10   Malted Milk 25

FRIDAY, JANUARY 4th, 1929.   JOHN H. WATSON, Manager.

TEA SERVED IN LOUNGE 4 TO 5 P. M. DAILY
Not responsible for loss or exchange of wearing apparel or personal effects.
See other side for List of Mineral Waters.

Fred Harvey

DINNER

Souvenier Menu

HOUSTON MISSOURI PACIFIC GOLF ASSOCATION

DINNER FOR

FREEPORT COUNTRY CLUB GOLFERS

At FRED HARVEY'S

Sunday, August 30, 1936

———————————— 19th Hole ————————————

Chicken Soup, a la Penalty Stroke

Melon Supreme, au Lost Ball

Niblicks of Celery

Choice of

Water Hazard - Filet of Sea Trout, Grilled, Tartar Sauce

Birdie - Half Fried Spring Chicken, Country Gravy

Cow Pasture Pool - Broiled Filet Mignon, Mushroom Sauce

Out of Bounds - Buttered Summer Squash

On The Green - Green Garden Peas

Sand Trap - Head Lettuce, Thousand Island Dressing

Hole in One - Fresh Strawberry Parfait

Hanging on The Lip-Hot Rolls, Biscuits

Water Hole- Coffee, Tea, Milk or Buttermilk

The Houston Missouri Pacific Golf Assocation Hopes you Have Had
an Enjoyable Day. May We Expect You Again Soon

THE CASTANEDA HOTEL

LAS VEGAS, NEW MEXICO

SOUPS AND APPETIZERS

Soup, Cup 15, Bowl			.20
Ripe or Green Olives			.20
Orange Juice	.15	Celery	.20
Radishes	.10	Green Onions	.10

SALAD PLATES

Head Lettuce			.15
Sliced Tomatoes	.20	Potato Salad	.15
Combination	.20	Fruit Salad	.25
Chicken Salad	.45	Cottage Cheese	.20

Fresh Dressing Served with Above

SANDWICHES

Fried Egg	.15	Sliced Chicken	.40
Peanut Butter and Jelly	.20	Chicken Salad	.35

Pressed Ham Sandwich   .15

MISCELLANEOUS

Filets of Sole, Cole Slaw	.60
Jelly Omelette with Potatoes	.50

DESSERTS

Pudding	.15	Sherbet	.10
Ice Cream	.15	Fruit Jello	.15
Pie	.15	Prunes	.15

BEVERAGES

Coffee	.10	Cocoa, Cup	.15
Tea, Pot	.15	Postum	.10
Milk	.10	Buttermilk	.10

"We, in cooperation with the Famine Emergency Committee program for feeding the starving people of the world, are endeavoring to conserve on the use of oil and wheat.

We are required to offer the same portions as during April 4 to 10, 1943. However, the usual second roll, slice of bread, additional crackers, basket or plate of bread or rolls or extra helping of oil salad dressing will be served you only if you request it."

"All prices listed are ceiling prices or below. By Office of Price Administration regulations, our ceilings are based on our highest prices from April 4, 1943 to April 10, 1943. Records of these prices are available for your inspection.

Not Responsible for Loss or Exchange of Wearing Apparel or Other Personal Effects

Fred Harvey

LA FONDA
The Inn at the End of the Trail

DINNER

Suggestions

Please Order by Number

1. **Special Mexican Plate (Taco, Tamale, Enchilada, Salsa, and Fried Egg)** 1.30
2. **Shirred Eggs with Home-made Sausages, Baked Potato, and Cucumbers Vinaigrette** 1.60
3. **Broiled Salmon Steak with Lemon Butter, Whipped Potatoes, and Green Beans Fermier** 1.75
4. **Breaded Pork Tenderloin with Tomato Sauce, Long Branch Potatoes, Lettuce and Tomato Salad** 1.95
5. **Baked Spring Chicken with Giblet Gravy, Mashed Potatoes, and Corn on the Cob** 2.50
6. **French Fried Shrimps with Tartar Sauce, Julienne Potatoes, and Salad Princess** 2.75
7. **Roast Larded Loin of Beef, Mushroom Sauce, Special Baked Potato, and Mixed Green Salad** 3.00

FROM OUR CHARCOAL BROILER
Sirloin Steak for One 4.25, For Two 7.50
Tenderloin Steak 4.25   Club Steak 3.00
Minute Steak 3.25
Salisbury Steak 2.00   Lamb Chops (2) 3.50
Sugar Cured Ham Steak 2.65
Served with Baked Potato, Chef's Salad

LA FONDA SPECIALS
Santa Fe Omelette (Green Chili, Hot Rarebit, French Fried Potatoes, Green Salad) 1.50

Poached Eggs Benedict with Fruit Salad 1.50

Cup of Chilled Jellied Beef Bouillon with Corned Beef Spread Sandwich on Rye Bread 75

MEXICAN FOOD MENU ON REQUEST

Arrangements gladly made for special diet.—Suggestions or criticisms regarding our service will be appreciated. Not responsible for loss of wearing apparel or personal effects. There is a charge for meal service in rooms of 35c per person.

APPETIZERS
Chopped Chicken Livers 30   Prune Juice 30
La Fonda Canape 40
Fruit Cocktail 40   Tomato Juice 30
Shrimp Cocktail 75

SOUPS
Chicken Okra with Rice
(Cup) 30   (Bowl) 45
Consomme Royal (Cup) 30
Cream of Tomato (Cup) 30 (Bowl) 45
Onion Soup au Gratin (10 Minutes) 75
Jellied Consomme (Cup) 30

SALADS
(Dinner Portion)
Romaine and Grapefruit Salad 45
Chef's Salad 35   Mixed Green Salad 35
Lettuce and Tomato Salad 45
Harvey Girl Salad 35

SALAD ENTREES
La Fonda Special (Mixed Greens, Sliced Eggs, Julienne of Ham, Chicken and Cheese, French Dressing   1.25
Avocado and Grapefruit Salad, Thousand Island Dressing   1.50
Avocado and Shrimps Onate 1.75

CHEESE
Blue 35   Swiss 40   American 30
Philadelphia Cream 30   Cheddar 30

DESSERTS
Apple Pie 30   Melons in Season 45
Chocolate Eclair 25
Sundaes 35   Sherbet 25   Parfaits 40
Mint Chocolate Chip, Vanilla, Chocolate or Strawberry Ice Cream 25
Caramel Cup Custard 35   Pound Cake 25
Cream Cheese and Guava Jelly 40
Hot Pineapple Fritter with Brandy Sauce 35

BEVERAGES
Coffee, cup 20 pot 30
Ovaltine 25   Demi Tasse 15
Hot Chocolate, pot 25
Postum or Sanka, pot 25
Orange Pekoe, Ceylon, English Breakfast, Young Hyson or Oolong Tea, pot 25
Milk 20   Iced Tea, Glass 25
Iced Coffee, Glass 25

SANTA FE   JULY 11, 1954

Fred Harvey Coffee, Jellies and Preserves Available at Our News Stand

INDEX